Encore Hollywood

Encore Hollywood
Remaking French Cinema

Lucy Mazdon

 Publishing

First published in 2000 by the
British Film Institute
21 Stephen Street, London W1P 2LN

The British Film Institute is the UK national agency with responsibility for encouraging the
arts of film and television and conserving them in the national interest.

Set by W21 Ltd, Bristol.
Printed in Great Britain by St Edmundsbury Press, Bury St Edmunds

Cover designed by Barefoot
Cover image: *Nikita* (Luc Besson, 1990)

British Library Cataloguing-in-Pulication Data
A catalogue record for this book is available from the British Library
ISBN 0–85170–801–3 (pb)
ISBN 0–85170–800–5 (hb)

Contents

Acknowledgements

I would like to thank all friends, colleagues and family who have helped with the writing of this book. I thank Bill Marshall for his help in producing the PhD thesis upon which this book was based. My thanks also to Andrew Lockett and all staff at BFI publishing. Special thanks to JF for putting up with these remakes for so many years.

This book is dedicated with love to my father, Alan Mazdon (1932–1998)

1
Rethinking Remakes

On 23 September 1996, ITV screened *The Assassin*, John Badham's 1993 remake of Luc Besson's *Nikita* of 1990. In a review in *The Radio Times* of that week, ubiquitous British film critic, Barry Norman, discussed the film in the following terms, 'Another example of Hollywood's unfortunate tendency to remake fine Continental fare and turn it into sensationalist pap. [...] what was once witty if somewhat vacuous entertainment has become plain, one-dimensional thrills.' Upon close inspection, Norman's remarks seem somewhat confused. Although his condemnation of the remake is quite categorical, his assessment of *Nikita* smacks of indecision: 'fine Continental fare' suggests whole-hearted praise, yet Norman goes on to describe the film as 'somewhat vacuous entertainment' apparently negating his earlier enthusiasm.

To understand the discourses behind this confusion it is necessary to bear in mind that the film that forms the subject of Norman's critique is a Hollywood remake of a French cinematic work. As a result, his remarks must be inserted into a much wider body of (particularly French) criticism which condemns remakes, dismissing them as 'pap' purely because they *are* remakes and, by extension, ignoring the 'vacuity' of the French films upon which they are based, terming them 'fine Continental fare' simply because they are the source of a remake.

Norman's review tells us very little about the film to be screened and virtually nothing about its French source. Do they share the same narratives? To what genre conventions can they be seen to adhere? Who are the films' stars and how are they mobilised in each work? Evidently this silence is symptomatic of the review's status as media criticism which is rarely more than impressionistic. However, what it also reveals is the critic's antipathy to the very practice of remaking French films in Hollywood and an unproblematic valorisation of the source film (and European films in general) as inherently superior to the products of Hollywood.

The remake is an extremely prominent feature of contemporary Hollywood production. Since the beginning of the 1980s an increasing number of films have been transposed and transformed and yet it is very difficult to find any analysis of the process which avoids the type of assumptions visible in Norman's critique. The current prevalence of the remake must have significant implications for contemporary production while also revealing much about the material and aesthetic climate of 1980s Hollywood, yet these potentially fascinating areas of research are invariably ignored.

So a close analysis of the practice of remaking French films in Hollywood seems timely. However, to simply study the films while ignoring the critical condemnation and silence outlined above would seem to be a rather partial exercise. The act of remaking the films and the various ways in which they are received should be seen as related components of a wider process of cross-cultural interaction and exchange. The work which follows will set out to analyse the remakes of the 1980s and 1990s, to determine why they are produced and what they reveal about the cinematic and cultural contexts from which they emerge. Nevertheless, I would like to begin by attempting to describe the various discourses at work in the critical tendency to dismiss these films as 'pap'. This dismissal of the remake says much about the cultures which produce these films and the relationships between them. By problematising this partial and reductive account of what I believe to be a fascinating cinematic phenomenon, I hope to make explicit the need for study of the remake.

Since the earliest days of its cinematic production Hollywood has adapted, copied, plagiarised, and been inspired by other works. The terminology used to describe this phenomenon is dependent on the position of the critic but in short it is fair to say that Hollywood has constantly remade. This process can take various forms: the adaptation of a literary text, a 'true' story or a mythic theme, adaptation from another audiovisual medium, parody, cinematic sequels and series, and the reworking of earlier screenplays. Those films based on non-cinematic works can be termed adaptations (such as the Merchant-Ivory adaptations of E. M. Forster's novels) and certain texts are adapted more than once (consider the numerous cinematic versions of Victor Hugo's *Les Misérables*). Sequels and series are those films which continue a theme or a character introduced in an earlier cinematic work. Whereas there will tend to be some narrative continuity between sequels, series may have no connection beyond characters, locations or themes (compare the *Terminator* sequence and the *James Bond* series).

Remakes are specifically those films based on an earlier screenplay, for example sound remakes of silent films, 'auto-remakes' or those films made twice by the same director (*The Man who Knew too Much*, directed by Alfred Hitchcock in 1934 and 1956), Hollywood remakes of earlier Hollywood works (*Sabrina*, directed by Sydney Pollack in 1996, a remake of Billy Wilder's *Sabrina* of 1954), and Hollywood remakes of non-Hollywood cinema. Thus the remake can be seen to cross both spatial (national) and temporal (historical) boundaries. The practice of remaking foreign films has been a particularly prolific part of the Hollywood adaptation process and the large majority of the films chosen for remaking are French. Indeed, since 1930 Hollywood has remade over fifty French sound films, outstripping by a significant majority its remakes of the products of any other country, excepting of course those of the United States themselves.[1]

The term 'remake' can then be used to describe many forms of cinematic adaptation. While not wanting to deny the existence or indeed the significance of these various processes, the term will be used here to refer specifically to Hollywood remakes of French full-length cinematic works made during the sound era; in other words, those Hollywood films based upon earlier French screenplays and the films to which they gave rise. Although these remakes are part of the wider process of cinematic adaptation and, more specifically, part of a Hollywood process of remaking 'foreign' screenplays, focus on the French example is necessary by virtue of the sheer numbers involved. It is also vital to distinguish between the remakes of the silent period and those of the sound era; huge numbers of silent films were remade as the cinema industry converted to sound in the late 1920s. The practice took place in similar proportions in all national industries as these early films provided easily accessible material for the new medium. The process was not questioned and did not give rise to the same types of discourse surrounding later remakes and as such the two processes demand differentiation.

These various definitions of the 'remake' demonstrate the diversity of adaptation within the cinema; cinematic adaptations can be based upon other films, novels, plays, television programmes and comic strips. The process of adaptation, whose very frequency shows it to be of extreme significance, leads to cross-fertilisation, aesthetically as one art form borrows from another, temporally as works from another age are adapted, spatially as cultures adapt across national boundaries, and culturally as works shift between location in 'high' and 'popular' cultures. This cross-fertilisation can be of great value to the producer of the adapted work and indeed to the culture in which it is situated and its sense of national identity. The adaptation of a 'classic' work both brings a new audience to an integral product of the national culture and gives rise to a work immediately possessing a certain degree of cultural capital. This increases if the adaptor of the 'classic' work also has cultural status (for example, eminent film and theatre directors) helping the adaptation itself to become a 'classic'. These works, with their three-tiered cultural capital, play an important role in the formation of the national culture, particularly when the 'classic' works adapted are indigenous products.

An example of adaptation of an indigenous 'classic' work being used to invoke a national cultural identity can be found in Claude Berri's *Germinal* of 1993. This film's cultural capital was multifaceted; a well-established and much admired director, a script based upon Emile Zola's novel, and various French cinema stars including Gérard Depardieu. As a result the film provided the perfect vehicle for reassertion of a French cultural identity.[2] Its timely arrival as the French government 'defended' French culture against the onslaught of the GATT agreements led to extra copies being made and the launching of *Germinal* into a ratings battle against Steven Spielberg's highly successful *Jurassic Park* (1993). The extent to which films are marketed according to their source texts does seem to depend upon the status of the source, be it economic or cultural. The Merchant-Ivory adaptations of the novels of Forster are publicised as such, thus establishing a ready-made audience: the readers of Forster's novels and all those who enjoy this type of 'literary' cinema. Other films, whose source is unlikely to improve either their financial success or indeed their cultural status, will not be marketed as adaptations.

Despite, or perhaps because of, the prevalence of adaptation, writings on the subject tend to reveal a certain sense of anxiety. Adaptation is often seen to decentre the work, to threaten its identity and that of the author. The higher the cultural status of the work to be adapted, the greater these anxieties tend to be. As we have seen, this anxiety can be annulled when the adaptation itself takes on high cultural status, but if this is not the case the 'original' is seen to be threatened. Thomas Leitch betrays this anxiety in his discussion of remakes.[3] He claims that of all forms of adaptation only remakes compete directly with other products of the same aesthetic medium without economic or legal compensation. When the film remade is itself an adaptation, Leitch claims that the producers of the remake deny the cinematic work entirely, citing only the 'original' text as a source. Remakes compete with the films upon which they are based rather than creating new audiences for their source. He states that if a remake does invoke its source it is to entice spectators into the cinema, only to deny this relationship once the film begins, 'The true remake admires its original so much it wants to annihilate it.'[4]

It is this anxiety which lies at the very heart of the condemnation of the remake process described at the beginning of this chapter. Many forms of cinematic adaptation will depend upon their relationship to the source text and will be marketed accordingly; for example, audiences are likely to view *Terminator 2* in order to revisit the themes, characters and narrative seen in the first film of the series. This is not necessarily the case with remakes, which can use the source film as part of their identity but may equally be publicised as 'original' works. In other words, the very existence of the remake can be seen to threaten the identity of the film upon which it is based. We shall see that the association between source film and remake is rarely this simple. Nevertheless, it is this quasi-Oedipal relationship which is overwhelmingly posited by critics of the practice.

The remake has enjoyed varying degrees of success at the box-office. Leonard Nimoy's *Three Men and a Baby* of 1988 grossed $168 million at the American box-office and $250 million worldwide. Other films, for example John G. Avildsen's *Happy New Year* (1987) which made only $100,000 in the United States and Nora Ephron's *Mixed Nuts* of 1996 which went straight to video, were commercial disasters. A similar variety characterises the style, genre and indeed age of the films selected for remaking. It is however possible to discern a certain homogeneity when one examines the critical discourse surround-ing the practice of remaking. The large majority of work on remakes is journalistic and certainly in France its attitude is overwhelmingly negative.[5] Remakes rarely achieve criti-cal approbation; they are almost routinely described as inferior to the French 'original' and their commercialism is condemned. In 1938 this attitude was expressed unequivo-cally by P. A. Harlé in his discussion of *Algiers* (1938), John Cromwell's remake of Julien Duvivier's *Pépé le Moko* (1937). He points out the dangers of remakes for the French film industry, claiming that they are produced simply in order to make money and that in the process they prevent the success of the 'original' film, 'The sale of the rights to a French film can destroy its career overseas [...] the remake is dangerous.'[6] André Bazin later expressed similar sentiments. Like Harlé he perceived the remake process as utterly commercial, claiming that films were selected according to their reception at the box-office, 'When a film has been successful enough to retain some commercial value, nobody bothers to re-circulate the original, instead the film is remade.'[7] Bazin manifestly shares Harlé's opinion that remakes have a detrimental effect upon the films on which they are based.

More recently still the French director Luc Besson rearticulated these misgivings. His film *Nikita* of 1990 was remade by John Badham in 1993. Initially Besson intended to be involved in the remake process but he pulled out at the last minute expressing his dis-like of what he also perceived to be a purely financial procedure.[8] Perhaps not surprisingly Besson claimed that films are selected for remaking solely on the basis of their commercial success; American studios want new ideas without excessive financial risk, the rights to a successful French screenplay come cheaply by Hollywood's standards hence the popularity of remakes. Besson, not a disinterested observer, bemoaned the fact that Hollywood studios frequently purchase the distribution rights to French films in order to prevent their release in the United States before that of the remake effectively destroying their chance of success in the American market. Besson here echoes somewhat uncannily the comments of both Harlé and Bazin. Despite their very different positions within, and relationships to, the film industry (Harlé was editor of the trade magazine *La Cinématographie française*, Bazin was a highly influential film critic and Besson is a popular contemporary director) each condemns the remake process for its impact upon the career of the French source films.

There has been one attempt in France to produce a collection of serious comment on remakes; in 1989 *Cinémaction* published an edition entitled 'Le Remake et l'adaptation', edited by Michel Serceau and Daniel Protopopoff. However, despite some useful filmographies and interesting attempts at definition, the essays tend to re-express the type of negative critical response voiced by Harlé, Bazin and Besson. Once again remakes are condemned as a commercial practice. They are described as an act of violence against the films from which they develop and it is claimed that only very rarely is a remake not inferior to its 'original'.

These arguments are evidently highly simplistic. They enable a description of the practice of remaking as a one-way, vertical trajectory from the high art of the French 'original' to the popular commercialism of the American 'copy'. What is striking about these arguments is that they rest upon a whole set of binary oppositions; French high culture as opposed to American popular entertainment, the value and tradition of French art as opposed to debased Hollywood commercialism, and the authenticity of the French 'original' as opposed to the American 'copy'. Binary divides of this type render easy the task of the critic wishing to evaluate a particular text. In the words of Fredric Jameson, value itself, '... fatally programs every binary opposition into its good and bad, positive and negative, essential and inessential terms'.[9] It is clear that in order to attempt a more detailed study of the practice of remaking all these oppositions require close examination. They are bound up with notions of the national, of the distinction between high and mass culture and indeed what we understand a cinematic text to be. To claim that the production of a remake and the subsequent non-release of the French film in the United States will limit the career of the source film can not perhaps be gainsaid. To argue that the French 'originals' are by definition 'better' than their American 'copies' is far more problematic and reveals a host of assumptions about the relative merits of French and American cultural production and the relationships between the two.

The remake, as a process of exchange between France and the United States, is bound up with the cultural practices of these countries, particularly cinematic practices, both material and aesthetic. This system of exchange is in turn located within the social and political relations between the two nations. A one-way trajectory from a valuable French 'original' to a debased American 'copy' depends upon a straightforward understanding of what constitutes French and American cinema and a clear distinction between the two. However, even the most cursory glance at the list of films remade since the 1930s will prove the difficulty of establishing such distinctions and definitions. Many of the remakes may indeed be popular comedies but the films upon which they are based belong to the same genre and as such can perhaps make no more claim to artistic 'value' than their Hollywood counterparts.

It does then seem apparent that these accounts of the remake practice say much more about constructions of French and American cinema and culture and the relations between them than they do about the films themselves. The relations between the United

States and France have always been extremely complex. Different constructions of the other within each nation are bound up with politics, cultural and moral issues, and the debate about modernity. These perceptions cannot be neatly divided into political oppositions; at any one time, in either country, numerous positions can be discerned. Largely due to its political and economic strength, particularly since the Second World War, the United States has tended to serve as a foil against which France defines itself. Thus the ways in which the United States is perceived in France at a given moment can tell us a great deal about French self-perception. Although France does not serve as a model for the United States in the same way (although French cultural artefacts can be seen to fulfil this role at certain junctures), it is fair to say that American constructions of France are closely linked to the way in which this nation perceives its position and influence within a global economy.

In his work *Seducing the French: The Dilemma of Americanisation*, Richard Kuisel describes these relations since the Second World War as part of a wider narrative about modernity.[10] For post-war France, faced with the prospect of economic and industrial modernisation, the United States symbolised the results of this process. In order to fulfil its political and economic ambitions France had to modernise, yet there were anxieties about what this would mean for French national identity. As early as 1930 Georges Duhamel's highly successful work, *Scènes de la vie future*, had given voice to France's growing concerns about the implications of modernisation; the expansion of the machine, utilitarianism, vulgarity, industry and the concomitant disappearance of 'French' values such as humanity, idealism, and art. Duhamel made no explicit reference to the United States in his work, however his concerns fed directly into the ongoing debate about modernisation. This debate over modernisation, commonly equated with Americanisation and the preservation of French identity did not really abate even as France engaged in the modernisation of its material infrastructure. Even by the 1970s, debate between the 'modernists' and the 'protectionists' was still fierce and farmers' protests at globalisation in the late 1990s were bound up with the discourses of anti-Americanism. Although these debates were ostensibly about economic policies they were evidently coloured by fear of the loss of French traditional identity. This fear of modernisation is intrinsically bound up with the discourses surrounding the opposition between high and mass culture. French anxieties about Americanisation and the loss of a discrete national identity in the post-war period were fostered by the perception of the United States as the producer of a mass, undifferentiated culture. Not surprisingly Hollywood films were perceived as part of this debased mass production. Indeed, in many ways, the Hollywood studio system, where cultural artefacts were produced within a complex industrial structure, was seen to epitomise American 'art'. Against the mass culture of the United States, France posited the indigenous tradition of authentic, unique, 'high' culture.

Shifts in French society during the 1980s led to a questioning of identity and of the universal role of French civilisation. Perhaps in response to these uncertainties, early Socialist cultural policy placed a firm emphasis on national culture, its international role and its protection from external (read Anglo-Saxon) threat. These priorities were made apparent by Jack Lang's notorious speech in Mexico in July 1982 when he decried 'a certain invasion, a certain influx of images produced elsewhere ...' calling for '... a veritable cultural resistance. A veritable crusade against – let's give it its true name – this financial and cultural imperialism ... .'[11] Central to this cultural crusade were the audiovisual media, particularly television and cinema. France aimed to lead Europe in a cultural order which would provide a counterbalance to the economic might of the dominant culture industries. These aims are exemplified in Lang's proposal in June of the same year for an *espace audiovisuel européen* which would compete actively and aggressively with the products of the North American market.

Socialist cultural policy involved both a revivification of national culture and an affirmation of its international role, particularly through the audiovisual media. As Pascal Ory states, the Franco-centrism of the post-war years (notably apparent in De Gaulle's invocations of French grandeur) had, by the 1980s, given way to a cultural-centrism.[12] In other words, as political certainties faltered, culture became an increasingly important means of shoring up France's identity and its role in the world. Ory goes on to claim that cultural policy became central to national and international political debate. Thus, somewhat paradoxically, culture was seen as a vital tool for the affirmation of French identity while at the same time its enduring universality was undermined. The increased importance of culture in political discourse during the 1980s and the re-affirmation of the international role of French cultural production go some way to explain the negative critical reception of the remake process in France. The decline in anxieties over North America's political and economic threat may seem to suggest that a more positive reaction should have been dominant during this period. However, Socialist (and subsequently right-wing) cultural policy underlines an insistence upon the need both to protect and disseminate a French national culture; a new plurality within France must still be projected externally as intrinsically 'French'. Each of these acts can be seen to be curtailed by the Hollywood remake and so the discourses which surround and penetrate the practice emanate from and reinforce this particular political and discursive conjuncture.

Indeed, it is within the cultural field that France has frequently been most likely to display anxieties about America and an attendant nationalism. France has had some form of centralised cultural politics since the Renaissance. Its sense of cultural identity tends to be defined in opposition to the cultures of other nations, and America, as a dominant alternative model, has played a central role in this process of construction. It is possible to discern in France various attitudes towards culture, ranging from the Jacobin notion of a strong, centralised cultural policy to a liberal rejection of such a framework. During the 1980s a move towards liberalism and fragmentation can be perceived, yet the Jacobin tradition has always been strong in France, as is manifested by the role of the Minister of Culture and numerous state projects and sources of aid. The Americanisation of France was often perceived in terms of 'cultural imperialism'; this was especially true of Hollywood films whose success was seen to threaten the national industry. It is significant that the United States in turn have accused the French of cultural imperialism, largely due to the French insistence upon quotas and other forms of protection for the indigenous cinema industry. These attitudes have been shaped by the fact that both France and North America make claims to political and cultural universalism. Both countries want to impose a democratic and a cultural model (based upon their own 'founding' political moments, the Civil War and the French Revolution), exacerbating the fear of 'invasion' by the other. These discourses were to a certain extent subverted by the growth of multi-culturalism in France during the 1980s. However they did not disappear, and prior to this time they were extremely prevalent.

The Blum–Byrnes agreements of 1946 provide an interesting example of the interplay between these discourses. Typically, this set of agreements, signed in Washington on 28 May 1946 by James Byrnes, American Secretary of State, and Léon Blum, special envoy of the French government, have been invoked in France as an example of American cultural imperialism.[13] The agreements involved a whole set of economic measures nevertheless, within France the Blum–Byrnes agreements are almost systematically reduced to the measure which, it was claimed, very nearly brought about the end of the indigenous cinema industry. This is a gross simplification of a complex and diverse set of policies, but it is also a somewhat reductive assessment of the agreement pertaining to the cinema.[14] The crisis which hit the French film industry after the Second World War was, and frequently still is, blamed exclusively upon the Blum–Byrnes agreements. Internal factors, such as the damaged infrastructure and lack of investment of the war years, were and are consistently ignored. How to defend French cinema in the face of this onslaught became a debate about French national cultural identity and its preservation from the threat of American cultural imperialism. *L'Humanité* of 1 October 1947 decried the Blum–Byrnes agreements which it claimed were 'smothering' the intrinsic values of French cinema,

> Let's see less revolvers and machine guns between Madeleine and République! Broadway and Chicago can keep their streets of crime. Much good they do them and may they one day realise what a delinquent society they symbolise. Paris will happily do without them.

This type of discourse was not voiced by the Communist press alone, rather it emanated from across the political spectrum. On 19 December 1947, the *Comité de défense du cinéma français* (Committee for the Defence of French Cinema) was established by Jacques Becker and Marcel Carné. This organisation demanded the revision of the Blum–Byrnes agreements and on 4 January 1948 a march was held from the Opéra to the Madeleine. Many members of the profession took part, including stars such as Jean Marais and Simone Signoret. Their slogans denounced both the agreements and the United States and demanded increased protection for the national industry. As Jacques Portes points out, this passionate demonstration on the part of many of the most famous members of the French cinema industry played an important role in the continuing perception of the agreements as a supreme example of French refusal to remain silent when faced with the threat of American hegemony.

The demands expressed became increasingly simplistic, ignoring France's manifest need for the American product in order to fill the cinema screens its war-scarred production facilities were not able to satisfy. Finally, on 20 January 1948, the agreements were revised. The film import quota was reinstituted limiting dubbed imports from America to 120 films per year and increasing the screen quota for French films to five weeks out of every thirteen. The French government also established the *Fonds spécial d'aide temporaire*, a fund designed to offer financial support to the French industry. By

1950, the crisis had passed and French receipts once again represented over 50 per cent of the market. Certainly the revision of the agreements was instrumental in changing the fortunes of French production yet these changes were also due to the exhaustion of Hollywood's production of the war years, only released in France after the Liberation, and the ongoing modernisation of the French cinematic infrastructure.

The Blum–Byrnes agreements and the debates they provoked are a shaping moment in the creation of a 'national' cinema. They can also be seen to embody many of the central concerns of the dialogue between France and the United States. The United States' desire for free trade and easier access to French markets, and exasperation at perceived French recalcitrance were matched by a French desire to protect the national industry. The reduction within France of a complex set of issues into a vision of American cultural imperialism feeds directly into anxieties about how to maintain French identity in the face of modernisation and Americanisation, a dilemma at the very heart of French feelings about its powerful ally during the post-war period.

If anti-American sentiment in the domain of politics and economics had decreased by the 1980s, it continued to be voiced in the realm of culture. Indeed, perhaps somewhat paradoxically, accusations of American 'cultural imperialism' began to increase during this decade just as the United States' economic and political prestige declined, witness Lang's tirade in Mexico in July 1982. A significant mobilisation of these discourses took place around the opening of the 'Euro-Disney' theme park in the spring of 1992,[15] and most famously in the reactions to the negotiations of the Uruguay Round of the General Agreement on Tariffs and Trade (GATT) in 1993. The GATT was principally a means of extending a globalised economy based upon deregulation and free trade. However, attempts to deregulate the audiovisual market threw up deep divisions between European (specifically French) and North American conceptions of commerce and culture. American executives proposed that any trade agreement they entered into must provide equal opportunities for American intellectual services (including the audiovisual industry). They sought curbs on public funding for audiovisual production through European subsidies and objected to levies imposed on foreign films shown in France, claiming that this disadvantaged American production as almost 60 per cent of French box-office taxes (the *compte de soutien*) came from Hollywood films. Moreover, they argued that European quota systems inhibited equal access to markets and thus contravened the ethos of GATT.

The European reaction to these demands was not positive. The French government called for '*l'exception culturelle*', the exclusion of the audiovisual industries from the GATT agreement. They claimed that the loss of a form of protection for indigenous cinema and television industries would signal the end of European production and mean total dominance of the European markets by the United States. The audiovisual industry represents North America's second biggest export to the European Community; indeed in 1992 Europe imported $3.7 billion worth of American films, video and television programmes while exporting back audiovisual products worth only $300 million. European Community figures showed that in 1991 American production captured 81 per cent of Community cinema screenings and 54 per cent of all drama and comedies broadcast on television. The negotiations thus became a clash of ideologies, between a specifically French tradition of state cultural policy and aid for the audiovisual industries and an American rejection of any form of public regulation of culture and a total commitment to free trade.

The European position was largely due to French governmental pressure. Indeed, it is significant that in many European states, particularly Britain, the debate was perceived as being between the United States and France alone. French commentators in turn cited the British cinema industry, where lack of government protection meant that Hollywood products represented over 80 per cent of all screenings, as clear proof of the need for some form of protectionism. The outcome of the negotiations in the form of a decision to exclude the audiovisual industries from GATT, was hailed as a great victory by the French government. However, the incommensurable nature of French and American positions on the culture industry was emphasised by American reactions to this decision. Jack Valenti, head of the Motion Picture Association of America claimed,

> The real losers are the people of Europe. They will have much less choice [...] If you equate Europe's game shows and talk shows with Molière and Racine, then that's about culture. But the culture issue is a transparent cloak, and I want to disrobe Europe on this.[16]

The Wall Street Journal decried cultural exception, protesting that state protection led to cinematic production which did not correspond to public tastes, and claiming that it was a form of censorship equivalent to that practised during the Vichy regime.[17]

These reactions demonstrate only too well the rift which separates French and American conceptions of the audiovisual industries. For the United States negotiators, audiovisual production was no more than an industry and should be treated in the same way as any other form of material production. It was distinct from a European 'high' cultural heritage – 'Molière and Racine' – and thus did not demand protection in order to preserve specific cultural identities (their attitude was somewhat disingenuous as audiovisual production has long been used as an important means of propaganda by successive American governments). As an industry, film and television should be entirely deregulated and, following hegemonic American free-market ideologies, this would lead to diversity and consumer choice. Attitudes in France were quite different. There existed a wide consensus that deregulation of the audiovisual industries would lead to a standardisation led by Hollywood; protection of indigenous production in fact meant liberalism as it prevented uniformity and encouraged plurality, 'True liberals must be in favour of protectionism: without it we will end up with an American monopoly. If we increase commercial freedom in the image markets we will simultaneously reduce cultural diversity.'[18] Moreover, it was claimed that the United States' industries themselves exercised a form of protectionism as they refused to dub foreign cinematic imports, distributing them subtitled in a small circuit of art-house theatres effectively limiting their potential audience.

Above all attitudes were differentiated through a widespread insistence in France upon the cultural importance of audiovisual production and the necessity of abstracting this practice from other forms of industrial production. In line with state cultural policy, cultural production was proclaimed as being central to national identities; to forego protection of the film and television industries would mean an end to French 'difference' and an attendant American hegemony. Such claims emanated from politicians, journalists, intellectuals and members of the industry from across the political spectrum. In December 1993, Jacques Toubon, the incumbent Minister of Culture, declared to the Senate, '[...] we must have a more combatant international cultural policy against American aggression and the threat of cultural uniformity. [...] We will help to improve the promotion of the French culture industries overseas.'[19] Jack Lang hailed the outcome of the GATT negotiations as a 'victory for art and artists over the commercialisation of culture'.[20] In a speech delivered in Poland on 21 September, President Mitterrand declared support for *l'exception culturelle*, arguing that it involved '[...] the identity of our nations, the right of each people to have access to their own culture, the freedom to create and choose our own images'.

Political statements such as these were supported by those who worked in the audiovisual industry. Claude Berri likened European film-makers to 'redskins' thus situating the debate within a wider history of American 'imperialism' and the narrative framework of the very Hollywood production which threatened Europe.[21] Over 150 artists and intellectuals formed *Les États généraux de la culture* in defence of cultural exception. Certainly the threat posed by GATT was broadly figured in France as an American threat, an influx of debased mass culture, and thus reactions to it can be written into a history of French cultural anti-Americanism:

> Now that jeans and McDos have conquered the Old Continent, are series and superproductions made in the USA going to dominate our screens? While Uncle Sam seeks at all costs to obtain the liberalisation of audiovisual exchange, only France calls for cultural exception.[22]

However, GATT was not about trade with the United States alone. Rather it was about the advancement of a deregulated global economy. French invocations of cultural exception should be perceived as expressing an enduring resistance to the hegemony of American culture (Hollywood films are acceptable but there must be an indigenous alternative) and more general fears about France's national identity in the face of a globalised culture. 'The Old Continent' was not only endangered by an influx of American mass cultural artefacts but by a process which threatened to erode the very borders of that continent, subsuming it into an undifferentiated transnational mass, dominated by those able to wield economic power.

French reactions to the GATT negotiations echo and contextualise the discourses surrounding the remake process. Just as the deregulation of the audiovisual industries was claimed to threaten the preservation of French culture through an influx of American mass culture, so the remake was seen to undermine French cinema through the transformation of 'quality' French productions within the 'debased' context of Hollywood. In both sets of discourse, American audiovisual dominance was reduced to economic might. These similarities do seem to suggest that reactions to the remake process during the 1980s and 1990s are also not merely about 'Americanisation' but should be located within the wider concerns about French identity in the emerging global arena. Conceptions of globalisation in France tend to reduce it to 'Americanisation' or 'cultural imperialism'. This in turn is often described as the result of the growing impact of the mass media. So the remaking of a French film within the context of Hollywood is seen as an example of cultural imperialism while the adaptation of a French work within a 'high cultural' American context is seen as proof of the universality and the florescence of French culture.

'Cultural imperialism' itself is a highly problematic term. It posits a linear process from one (dominant) culture to another (dominated), ignoring the heterogeneity of individual cultural formations and the dialectical nature of struggles over power. Jack Lang's tirade against cultural imperialism in Mexico provides evidence of this first lacuna. Lang's speech did not receive popular support in France, indeed much of the French press condemned his jingoism and isolationism. Both the press and Lang claim to represent French public opinion and their disagreement suggests that this opinion is far from undifferentiated. The very concept of cultural imperialism rests upon a univocal national culture yet this is highly problematic. Indeed the very opposition between dominant and dominated which underwrites cultural imperialism is reproduced within the national context. To posit either the United States or France as dominant or dominated cultures begs various questions. North America may now be economically dominant but France has an enduring sense of its own cultural importance which undermines any attempt to see this nation as subservient to the United States. In reducing globalisation to cultural imperialism, French commentators ignore the complexity of this process as well as *local* processes of reception and mediation. Just as French films are remade in Hollywood, so American mass cultural artefacts are in some way 'remade' through consumption in France. Hollywood films are consumed in France within the framework of French exhibition and viewing practices and discourses about the cinema (film magazines, television shows and so on). Moreover, the products of global culture do not lead to uniformity as national audiences continue to consume the indigenous product.

It seems apparent that the negative discourses which surround and penetrate the remake process emanate from, and articulate, a specific conjuncture in which enduring French conceptions of identity and culture began to shift and falter. Rather than take on board these changes, many French critics and intellectuals became defensive of the 'national' identity, a defensiveness which was perpetuated in government cultural policy. The remake became an important focus of contention in this shoring up of French identity in the face of a globalisation exemplified by the products of Hollywood. It was perceived as clear proof of an attack upon all things French (an attack seen to be most prevalent in the realm of the audiovisual media and to be led by the United States) and so it was incumbent upon French critics to condemn the process. Rather than accept the remake as a form of healthy (and increasingly common) interaction, critics described it as a form of theft, a 'vampirisation' which, like the ongoing construction of the 'global village', threatened to suck the very life-blood of an intrinsically French cultural identity.

It is vital to stress the complexity of political, cultural and material relations between France and the United States. These feelings and perceptions can not be reduced to any single narrative but rather involve the interplay of discourses located within concerns about high and mass culture, modernity and tradition, progress, domination, and invasion and identity. As a new global economy led by the United States took shape after the war, the French nation engaged in a struggle to assert its own power as a political and cultural force, a struggle which can be seen to continue in the enduring disputes over the audiovisual media and the fear of a Hollywood produced homogeneity. This description of the political and cultural relations between France and the United States does begin to suggest the source of many of the anxieties displayed in contemporary French critique of the remake. Despite attempts to depict the practice as a recent phenomenon (and thus a new, and particularly dangerous, form of attack), these discourses are rooted in the very history which they set out to conceal (it is striking that even Carolyn Durham's recent study of the process fails to fully acknowledge or discuss the remake phenomenon prior to 1980). They say much about conceptions of French and American culture and the role of cinematic production in the establishment of a national identity, however they say barely anything about the actual films, who produces them, when, why and for whom. For this it is of course necessary to turn to the films themselves.

Between 1930 and 1950 nineteen films were remade in Hollywood while from 1950 to 1980 only six films underwent this process, one third of the number remade in previous years. Since 1980 over thirty French films have been reproduced in the United States. By examining the history of the practice, locating it within specific historic, material and aesthetic contexts, we can begin to answer some of these questions and begin to build up a picture of the remake that moves us well beyond the simplistic hostilities rehearsed by so many critics.

Until 1948 Hollywood was dominated by the studio system. Eight studios controlled this system: the vertically integrated 'Majors' (Paramount, Loews/MGM, 20th Century-Fox, Warner Bros. and RKO) and the three 'Minors' (Universal, Columbia and United Artists). Indeed the productions of the 'Big Five' represented about 50 per cent of the industry's annual output and about 75 per cent of class A features (those which received top billing in the best theatres). Of the nineteen remakes produced between 1930 and 1950, ten were produced and/or distributed by the Majors (20th Century-Fox, RKO, MGM and Paramount), seven by the three Minors and two by independent companies, thus the remake process was manifestly part of the dominant studio system. The *Motion Picture Herald* of 10 July 1948 gives a company-by-company breakdown of projected remakes, '... 20th Century-Fox has six on its schedule; MGM has four, Columbia, four; Warners, three; Paramount, two; RKO, two, and United Artists, Universal International, Selznick Releasing, Goldwyn Productions, Eagle Lion and Korda-Goldwyn, one each.'[23] The planned remakes were not all based upon French films yet these figures do show the important role of the remake in the production of the studio era.

The studio system was firmly established by 1930, adopting a structure that would change very little for the next twenty years. The infrastructure of this vast oligopoly concentrated access to money and distribution in the hands of producers and financiers. As Hollywood felt the effects of the Depression, producers attempted to restrict output. At the same time the studios sold some of their exhibition venues, creating a tension between the new exhibitors' desire for films with which to satisfy their audiences and the producers' wish to curb spending and production. This tension was manifested in a struggle between uniformity (or security) and novelty (with which to attract spectators). This negotiation led to the standardisation of plots into generic conventions which facilitated the development of variety within the familiar. Remakes also provided a solution to this tension; they were not entirely new and untested yet at the same time they permitted a reworking which enabled novelty.

Hollywood's genre conventions were consolidated throughout the 1930s and 1940s as the studio system became more firmly entrenched. Although independent producers grew in number during the 1940s, the Majors controlled distribution and exhibition, the key to control of the industry. This enabled the studios to define a dominant aesthetics, notably the aforementioned genre conventions. Other aesthetics, such as those developed in Europe, would be borrowed, appropriated or assimilated. The curbs on production brought about by the Depression were reduced as the economy improved. The growth of the double bill from 1931 meant a demand for increased production, not necessarily of great quality. This demand then diminished during the 1950s as the double bill was suppressed. This growth in production can be seen to explain the proliferation of remakes during the 1930s and 1940s; exhibitors demanded a vast number of films and the remake provided a ready source. Yet somewhat paradoxically, they can also be attributed to the reduction in production and the subsequent need to develop variation within the familiar. In both cases, the phenomenon is closely linked to the aesthetic and material practices at work in Hollywood at that time.

French cinematic structures of the 1930s and 1940s were very different from those established in Hollywood. The two major vertically integrated companies had collapsed, Pathé-Natan in 1936 and Gaumont in 1934. This resulted in great diversification in access to capital and distribution with about seventy independent producers each making one or two films a year. In economic terms this made the French industry extremely vulnerable, particularly to competition from Hollywood productions. However, in terms of aesthetics this situation enabled diversity and experimentation. The standardisation taking root in the American industry was not encountered in France. This diversity was reinforced by the fact that, in contrast to the Hollywood Production Code which favoured financiers and producers, French laws gave primacy to directors and secondary protection to other artistic workers. Directors were often able to work alone and were involved in many phases of production, avoiding the dictates of the producers and financiers experienced by directors at work in Hollywood. This diversity surely made France a fruitful hunting ground for American producers in search of novelty and originality which could then be remade and familiarised within the Hollywood system.

The financial implications of the remake process were evidently varied despite claims that it offered a 'safe bet' to the Hollywood studios, a less risky enterprise than the production of an original screenplay. According to the *American Film Institute Catalog*, RKO producer Pandro S. Berman bought the rights to *Michel Strogoff* from its producer, Joseph Ermolieff, for $75,000.[24] The production cost a 'modest' $400,000 yet failed to break even at the box-office. The same source claims that Fox purchased the rights to *Les Croix de bois* for $140,000 in 1932, a few years before RKO bought the rights to *Michel Strogoff* which was released in 1935 while MGM purchased the rights to *Pépé le Moko* for $38,000, a sum much closer to that paid by RKO. Having sold the rights to a film, the French distributors would usually be expected to sign a contract agreeing to release the film only outside the United States. Walter Wanger, who acquired the rights to *Pépé le Moko* from MGM, also purchased all prints of the film in order to prevent its release in the United States before that of the remake. However, he later considered the two films sufficiently different to merit the release of Duvivier's film in America, and in 1941, three years after the release of *Algiers*, *Pépé le Moko* was exhibited, an unusual decision according to the *New York Times* of 2 March 1941.[25] This suppression of the French film in favour of the remake is significant in that it has given rise to much comment since the 1980s by critics who describe it as a recent, and perfidious, practice (Carolyn Durham reiterates these claims in her work on the remake). These examples suggest instead that this was an accepted feature of the remake process during the 1930s and 1940s.

These figures demonstrate, albeit somewhat tentatively, the disparity in the sums paid for rights to French screenplays and the inability to guarantee the success of remakes at the American box-office. Nevertheless, although without more detailed statistical information it is impossible to draw firm conclusions, it does seem likely that despite figures such as these the remake was perceived as involving less risk than the production of an original screenplay. These films had already been tested on French audiences and thus had proved their potential popularity. In the words of Olin H. Clark, Eastern story editor for MGM in 1948, '... a picture which was a success ten, fifteen, or twenty-five years ago must have something fundamentally good about it, and thus is still a good screen story today.'[26] The films could also be viewed in a way that was impossible with a screenplay; producers could actually 'see' what they were buying. Both these factors would surely have been seen to offer a certain degree of security yet, as the career of *The Soldier and the Lady* reveals, in the unpredictable world of audience tastes no formula, however well tested, could guarantee success.

The vertical integration and horizontal co-operation of Hollywood during the 1930s and 1940s meant that French films were very unlikely to break into the American market. The control of distribution and exhibition by the five Majors created a domestic market almost entirely inaccessible to non-Hollywood products. This fact can be seen to underscore the remake process. French films were rarely distributed in the United States and even those exceptions to this norm would tend to receive an extremely limited release. French films could be remade and presented to American audiences as 'new' or 'original'; to an audience entirely unfamiliar with the French source there would be no concern over oppositions between 'original' and 'copy'. It is possible that some remakes were actively marketed as such, drawing on the French source as a means of attracting audiences. Nevertheless, the deliberate prevention of the release of the French source in the United States, at least before that of the remake, tends to suggest that the former scenario was more frequent.

This situation changed after 1948. In 1938 the American Justice Department launched a suit entitled 'The United States v. Paramount Pictures Inc. et al.'. The government accused the eight studios of monopolising the film industry and violating antitrust laws. The five Majors controlled exhibition and distribution as well as practising block booking and unfair pricing schemes in order to keep independent and non-Hollywood productions out of the first-run theatres. The three Minors did not own exhibition venues but they were accused of colluding with the Majors to prevent other films from penetrating the market. In 1948 the Supreme Court handed down a decision, declaring the eight studios guilty of monopolistic business practices. The Majors were obliged to divorce their theatre circuits from their production and distribution branches, splitting the existing companies into separate exhibition and production–distribution organisations. Unfair distribution practices were prohibited so that each film would be rented on an individual basis, regardless of other films or affiliation between exhibitors. Voting trusts were also established in order to prevent shareholders of the former integrated companies from taking control of both of the newly formed separate companies.

Despite the fact that the Majors and Minors continued to dominate distribution and thus to earn the majority of box-office receipts, the Paramount Decrees did have a significant impact on Hollywood. The divestiture of the theatre circuits meant that the Majors no longer had guaranteed exhibition venues for their products and consequently their output decreased. Studios and distribution chains were underused so the Majors provided finance, studio space and distribution for independent production and foreign films. For the first time in over a decade foreign films had equal access to the American market and by 1958 over 65 per cent of Hollywood's films were made by independent producers.

Because the five major studios no longer owned the first-run theatres the Production Code was seriously undermined. The Code of 1934 was in effect a self-censorship mechanism. The Motion Picture Association of America (MPAA) had obliged distributors to submit their films for approval by stating that no cinema belonging to the association would exhibit a film without this prior approval. However, many exhibition venues were now no longer part of the MPAA so enforcement of the Code became almost impossible. The Code was further weakened in 1952 when films were read into the First Amendment, assuring them the freedom of speech guaranteed to other art forms. This recognition of the status of film as art and an ensuing freedom was one of the factors leading to the development of an 'art' cinema in the United States throughout the 1950s and 1960s. The revisions to the Blum-Byrnes agreements in 1948 limited Hollywood's profit withdrawal from France to $3.6 million per year. This left about $10 million, part of which was spent on distribution rights to films that were then released in North America. Some of this money was also invested in French productions, leaving Hollywood producers with a vested interest in the success of the French product. Indeed, as Tino Balio points out, the domestic production shortage and declining audiences led to an urgent need to find products elsewhere, '... an executive of United Paramount Theatres told exhibitors that "it might be wise for [them] to consider ways and means of popularizing the foreign film" and "to establish an audience where there has been none before" (*Variety*, September 29, 1954).'[27] By the early 1960s the American art theatre circuit consisted of over 500 cinemas devoted almost exclusively to foreign films. At the same time, a domestic 'art' cinema continued to develop; for example, many directors were influenced by the work of the *nouvelle vague* in France. Changes in political culture as Cold War certainties came to an end and American identity was severely shaken by the events of the Vietnam conflict encouraged an interest in counter-cultural artefacts. Hollywood attempted to appeal to an expanding youth culture with such counter-cultural films. Both these influences can be seen to penetrate mainstream Hollywood production during the 1970s as well as encouraging experimentation and innovation on the part of independent producers.

These changes in Hollywood's industrial and aesthetic structures were accompanied by changes in the construction of audiences. During the 1930s and 1940s as cinema production was standardised into genre conventions and the development of the 'classical Hollywood narrative', so there was a tendency to perceive audiences as an undifferentiated mass. Most Hollywood products were designed for this homogeneous audience; the 'family' film, produced to appeal to all age groups, was a central part of Hollywood's output and such films frequently reaped vast profits at the box-office. As the industry underwent change after 1948 so the concept of audience began to alter. It was now believed that there existed several audiences in the United States; audiences for the growing 'art' cinema and a burgeoning 'youth' audience for example. Indeed by the late 1960s nearly 50 per cent of the American cinema audience was composed of sixteen- to twenty-four-year-olds. Studios began to produce large numbers of films aimed specifically at this audience, many of them dealing with the previously mentioned counter-cultural concerns. The advent of television also led to the differentiation of the Hollywood product in an attempt to woo audiences back into the cinema. These new products would exploit technology (CinemaScope and wide-screen pictures for example) not available on television. Many films, for example the youth films, would deal with subject matter deemed unsuitable for television transmission and as such these films would be directed towards specific audience groups. In 1968 the MPAA gave official recognition of the differentiation in audiences by setting up a Code and Rating Office which subsequently devised a complete rating system used to define a film's suitability for audiences of differing age groups. A Supreme Court decision of 1973 ruled that individual states could now reach different decisions on particular films, a further reinforcement of the growing differentiation within the industry.

It seems certain that these changes in the industry subsequent to 1948 were behind the decline in remakes during the 50s, 60s and 70s. The disappearance of the double bill during the early 1950s meant a diminished demand for production. The various changes and problems in the domestic market brought about by the Paramount Decrees and the development of television caused a significant decrease in the number of films produced by the Hollywood studios. This led to the opening up of the American market to independent and foreign productions thus encouraging a new diversification and the development of an 'art' cinema. This in turn led to the breaking up of audiences into various, diverse groups. Within this context the remake seemed less attractive as producers were no longer on the lookout for easily available sources. More importantly, French films could now find an audience in the United States and the former assimilation of different aesthetics into the hegemonic Hollywood system diminished as the industry diversified.

Beyond economic and material concerns lie issues bound up with the ideologies and the value systems of the film industry and indeed of the nation in which it is situated. Hollywood's remakes can be perceived as an implicit form of censorship in that they frequently incorporate and appropriate the products of another culture into the morals, values and standards of the receptor culture. Moreover, French films could, and probably did, fall foul of Hollywood's Production Code. Censorship laws in France during the period under discussion were not identical to those enforced in the United States; for example, they concerned themselves less with representations of sexuality than with political issues. The protection accorded to directors in France allowed them a degree of freedom not available in Hollywood where the Hays Code placed power in the hands of producers and financiers. The Code was very much part of the industry rather than being external to it and producers accepted its dictates as it enabled the production of the highly successful 'family' film. Edward Benson attributes the principal differences between *La Chienne* (Jean Renoir, 1931) and its remake of 1945, *Scarlet Street* (Fritz Lang), to differences in censorship codes, both implicit and explicit.[28] Indeed, *Scarlet Street* was initially banned by the Motion Picture Division of the State Education Department of New York, inviting speculation that by remaining close to its French source it had flouted the Production Code. Walter Wanger, producer of the film, agreed to cuts in order to achieve the lifting of this ban. The first script of *Algiers* (1938) submitted to the Hays Office was deemed unacceptable for the following reasons:

> ... because of the suggestion that the 'two leading female characters are both kept women'. [...] A memo from Production Code Administration Director, Joseph I. Breen to Wanger, dated 18 February 1938, requested changes pertaining to references to, 'sex appeal', Pépé's promiscuity and Pépé's suicide at the end to escape punishment. Other memos in the file indicate that Wanger and screenwriter John Howard Lawson were instructed to change the ending so that 'Slimane's men would shoot Pépé, rather than having him actually commit suicide'.[29]

Evidently both *Algiers* and *Pépé le Moko* transgressed numerous aspects of the Production Code; references to sexuality, depictions of 'loose' women, suicide and the law's failure to triumph. In order to achieve wide release in the United States, the producers of *Algiers* were obliged to modify their screenplay. When *Pépé le Moko* was eventually released in the American market it was publicised as the 'full', 'unexpurgated' version. The distributors played on its Frenchness, the fact that it was not subject to the Production Code and was thus likely to be somewhat more explicit than the products of Hollywood. Indeed, this has proved to be an enduring popular perception of French films in the Anglo-Saxon markets.

Two different forms of censorship were practised in Hollywood during the period under discussion: ideological censorship, which could be sexual, political or religious in nature, and aesthetic censorship. Either form could be explicit, as in the dictates of the Production Code, or implicit or unacknowledged, as in the case of aesthetic appropriation. Both forms can serve to explain the proliferation of remakes during the 1930s and 1940s. Aesthetic censorship was practised as French films were assimilated into the dominant Hollywood genres and styles; in many respects *Scarlet Street* bears more resemblance to *The Woman in the Window* (1944), an earlier film also directed by Fritz Lang and starring Joan Bennett, than it does to *La Chienne*. *The Road to Glory* (1936), Howard Hawks' remake of *Les Croix de bois* (1931), was a clear attempt to imitate and profit from the success of Lewis Milestone's *All Quiet on the Western Front* (1930). Explicit ideological and moral censorship was also carried out as the case of *Pépé le Moko* demonstrates. Many French productions failed to comply with the rulings of the Hays Code and, deemed unsuitable for the undiversified American audience, the most they could achieve was a very limited release. They were thus remade according to the values and dictates of the receptor industry and nation. American censorship of the cinematic product began to alter after 1948 when the Supreme Court invalidated every censorship criterion except that of obscenity, at the same time subjecting censorship boards to a set of strict requirements. It is significant that this ruling was handed down in 1948, the same year as the Paramount Decrees which also undermined the Hays Code. The relaxation of censorship, which surely played a part in the reduced interest in remakes on the part of the studios, can be seen to be located within the wider changes which took place throughout the industry after 1948.

Although criticism of the remake was voiced during the 1930s and 1940s (as P. A. Harlé's comments, cited earlier, reveal only too well), the practice was generally much better accepted than has been the case since the 1980s. As we have seen, it is significant that much of the apocalyptic debate of the 1980s, decrying the detrimental effects of the remake, makes no reference to these numerous early examples of the process, casting it as a *recent* manifestation of American cultural imperialism. This paradigm ignores both the history of the remake and the history of exchange and interpenetration between the two cinema industries. Prior to the development of sound cinema, 'national' cinemas as we understand them today did not exist. The absence of spoken dialogue meant that films could be transferred with ease from one country to another and the origins of a particular work were of little importance. Indeed, it was during the early years of sound cinema that French cinema had its major impact on American markets. The crossover between industries inherent to the days of silent production continued even as sound was developed. By 1929 many producers had decided that the only way in which to continue to penetrate valuable foreign markets was to shoot multi-lingual versions of each film. MGM imported actors and directors to make Spanish, German and French versions of its films while Paramount produced multi-lingual films in its Joinville studio near Paris. By 1931 soundtrack mixing technology had been improved and original sound effects could be added to new voices. In 1932 dubbing and subtitling were introduced and the expensive process of shooting multiple versions was gradually abandoned. Nevertheless, between 1929 and 1932 this process was a common feature of the cinematic landscape. Hollywood companies would shoot films in European languages and French producers would produce English language versions of their work. The fact that this practice coincided with the development of 'national' cinemas meant that it did not escape criticism, criticism which shares many of the negative attitudes voiced about the remake process and about the impact of American cinema in general (Hollywood's penetration of the French market and the subsequent production of an undifferentiated mass culture geared towards the standards and tastes of the American public). At the same time this practice and the concerns it engendered situate the remake within a wider process of transfer and exchange between Hollywood and France. The remake can to a certain extent be perceived as a continuation of multi-lingual production, an acceptable part of the development of cinema rather than a shocking example of American pilfering.

Another manifestation of this process of exchange was the employment of *émigré* personnel in Hollywood. This phenomenon is frequently depicted as an exodus caused by Hitler's rise to power in Germany. However, many European directors and actors emigrated to the United States long before the Nazi threat, attracted by the advanced facilities available. Although obliged to work within the conventions of Hollywood, many directors used styles developed in Europe to expand and enhance the dominant

aesthetics. Of the twenty-three remakes produced between 1930 and 1960, eight had
European directors; they included Anatole Litvak (*The Woman I Love*, 1937 and *The
Long Night*, 1947), Julien Duvivier (*Lydia*, 1941), Fritz Lang (*Scarlet Street*, 1945 and
Human Desire, 1954) and Otto Preminger (*The Thirteenth Letter*, 1951). Fifteen films,
over half those made between 1930 and 1980 had some *émigré* personnel, be they actors,
producers or scriptwriters. Many of these people were either of French origin or had
come to Hollywood via a period spent working in France. Such figures include Julien
Duvivier and Anatole Litvak as well as Charles Boyer, Maurice Chevalier, Jean-Pierre
Aumont and Adolphe Menjou. This system of exchange complicates the perception of
the remake as a straightforward American product. Both Anatole Litvak and Julien
Duvivier remade their own films in Hollywood so problematising attempts to describe
these works as 'American'. The input of European personnel undermines binary oppositions between French and Hollywood cinemas, a process which is continued in the
1980s by French financing of American remakes. At the same time, this exchange can be
seen to reinforce the acceptance of remakes and their proliferation during the 1930s and
1940s; rather than seeing Hollywood as stealing French products, French cinematic personnel can be seen to have penetrated Hollywood with their art.

One of the central concerns of the criticism of remakes emanating from the 1980s
and 1990s is the perceived distinction between French cinema's status as 'art' and Hollywood's production of mass cultural artefacts. As we have seen, cinema was not read
into the First Amendment until 1952 and until this time it was not perceived in the
United States as having the same status as other art forms. As a result the incorporation
of scenes from *Les Croix de bois* (1931) into *The Road to Glory* (1936) was unlikely to be
seen as problematic; indeed, 651 feet of footage from the French film was also incorporated into *The World Moves On* (Fox, 1934). The film did not yet have an original
status that could be threatened, a fact borne out by the multi-lingual versions of the early
1930s and the numerous remakes of silent films. The development of 'art' cinemas and
'national' cinemas as the century progressed, both in the United States and in Europe,
led to the polarisation between the products of Hollywood and France. It is significant
that until *Scarlet Street* in 1945, the longest time gap between a French film and its
remake was five years. The remaking of older 'classic' films only began to develop from
the late 1940s and can thus be seen to coincide with the growth of 'art' cinema. As this
opposition became firmly established so remakes became a cause for disquiet; French
films had a status which must be protected. The fact that this opposition was yet to take
hold during the 1930s and 1940s helps to explain the far wider acceptance of the process
at this time.

Like their counterparts of the 30s and 40s, many critics, both in France and the United
States, attributed the growing popularity of the remake after 1980 to a dearth of original screenplays. For example *France-Soir* in March 1993, criticised those Hollywood
directors 'who happily steal our films and make their own version' due to 'a script shortage'.[30] In November 1990, *Ciné Finances* claimed, 'Moreover this new wave [of remakes]
can be seen as proof – and also a cause – of the poverty of cinematic creation in the
United States.'[31] An executive of the TF1 production company (co-producers of various
remake 'sources' including *La Totale* and *Mon Père ce héros*, both 1991), claimed that this
practice would become more and more common as Hollywood studios were increas-

ingly in need of new material. Indeed the adaptation and reworking of 'non-original' material seemed to have become a staple of Hollywood production by the early 1980s. Of 116 films produced in 1982, nine were remakes (of both French films and others), eleven were sequels and series, and thirty-nine were some form of adaptation; of the 128 films produced in the following year, the figures stood at seven remakes, sixteen sequels and series, and thirty-seven adaptations.[32]

This account of the practice reinforces dominant discourses about the remake which stress the aesthetic superiority of the French product (French cinema as 'high culture') and which reduce the process to a purely commercial venture, an attempt by Hollywood to reduce risk and ensure profit, 'They want new ideas, certainly, but at the same time ideas which have proved their value. A contradiction in terms? Not necessarily. This is how America has become a specialist in sequels, series and, of course, remakes.'[33] There is some truth in statements such as these; in 1984, Barbara Boyle, then Orion's Senior Vice-President of Production, admitted that the cost of producing and releasing a film inevitably led to attempts to reduce risk and so encouraged the increased security offered by the already tested remake:

> The industry seems to run in cycles, and we are in a cycle of sequels, prequels and remakes because so much emphasis is placed on our marketing people many of whom are now heads of studios. With the cost of releasing a picture equalling the cost of the negative, you'd better start listening to your marketing people. ...[34]

Nevertheless, as analysis of the process prior to 1980 demonstrates, it is vital to deconstruct French critical discourses which ascribe the financial implications of the remake to the intrinsic quality of French cinema, abstracting the practice from the specific industrial and aesthetic structures in which it is located. Like their predecessors of the 30s and 40s, the remakes of the last twenty years suggest an attempt to reduce risk in Hollywood, a turning to French production as a source of material and a wider process of transnational interaction and cross-fertilisation. The economic and political climate of the 1980s in the United States, and the moves towards deregulation and the free market, saw the reinstatement of vertical integration in Hollywood. Conglomerates holding production and distribution companies began to reacquire theatre chains: for example, by 1991, MCA owned both Cineplex Odeon and Universal Studios. Moreover, the studios followed dominant trends by integrating with other firms to form vast concerns frequently involving foreign investment. This process had begun in the 1970s as the industry began to prosper, however it grew at an unprecedented rate during the 1980s. In 1981 United Artists was sold to MGM, then in 1982 Columbia Pictures was purchased by the Coca-Cola Company. Foreign investment grew from 1985 when Rupert Murdoch's News Corporation acquired 20th Century-Fox. Pathé Communications purchased MGM in 1990 and in 1992 Crédit Lyonnais foreclosed on loans to MGM and took over the company. The majority of this incursion of overseas capital came from Japan: Sony bought Columbia in 1989 and Matsushita took over Universal in 1991. In 1989 the American companies Time Inc. and Warner merged to become Time Warner, then the world's largest media company, holding significant interests in newspaper and magazine publishing, cable television and the music industry, as well as owning the Warner Bros. Studio.

The establishment of these companies meant that cinematic production in Hollywood was once again dominated by the small group of Majors who controlled domestic and international distribution. The lack of a mass-production studio system meant that, unlike the previous period of vertical integration, the 1930s and 1940s, production of the 1980s and 1990s tended to be initiated by independent producers. However, this production should not be seen as external to the large conglomerates as it could only achieve wide exhibition if it were distributed by the major companies. In 1994 five distribution companies – Buena Vista (Disney), Warner Bros. (Time Warner), Universal (Matsushita), Fox (Murdoch) and Paramount (Viacom) – achieved 69.6 per cent of the domestic box-office. Moreover, film-makers were dependent upon the Majors for financing and studio facilities: the studio production of the early years of Hollywood may have ended but the industry was, to all intents and purposes, vertically integrated.

The concentration of the industry in the hands of a small group of multinational conglomerates led to a reduction in the number of films produced and a concomitant increase in budgets. This tendency has been seen to date back to the success of *Jaws* in 1975.[35] The commercial success of this film demonstrated the value of saturation booking and extensive advertising which placed great importance on a film's performance at the box-office during its first few weeks of release. Consequently, the industry began to concentrate on fewer films involving vastly increased budgets. The Majors realised that over-production would harm all the dominant companies so no more than 150 films were released each year. Average budgets increased from $8.5 million dollars in 1980, to $18 million by the end of the decade, and $27 million in 1991. A large proportion of these budgets was devoted to intensive marketing; indeed between 1980 and 1995, average film marketing costs tripled, totalling $15 million or more. Major Hollywood productions frequently had to gross well over $100 million dollars in order to become profitable and thus not surprisingly, many films lost money at the box-office.

These changes in strategy led to the increasing importance of the 'blockbuster'. Perhaps somewhat paradoxically, expensive failures (notably Michael Cimino's *Heaven's Gate* in 1980 which cost $36 million and resulted in the sale of its production company, United Artists) demonstrated the necessity of increasing film budgets in order to ensure maximum distribution and marketing. However, risk was minimised by allocating this money to 'safe' projects. The blockbuster is characterised by innovations in technology (so increasing differentiation from smaller-scale independent and foreign productions), the presence of stars, expensive production values, and an emphasis on plot over character. Indeed the majority of blockbusters are action films with minimal narrative complexity. Such aesthetic choices are necessitated by the films' situation in a 'diversified, globalized, synergized market-place'.[36] In other words, major Hollywood productions, like the industry from which they emerge, can no longer be reduced to 'cinema' alone. Instead they are diverse cultural commodities which will be disseminated through various forms of media and merchandising: the book of the film, the soundtrack album, computer games, T-shirts and so on. In order to enable this diversification of the cinematic product, blockbusters tend towards open-ended, intertextual narratives which can be easily reformulated in other media.

Increasing film budgets meant an attendant decrease in the willingness of the Majors to take risks. This in turn led to the industry's growing reliance upon the aforementioned blockbusters as well as sequels, series, reissues and remakes. This latter group of films reduced risk as they involved formats (narratives or characters) that had already proved successful either in the contemporary domestic market (sequels and series), an earlier domestic market (reissues and remakes of Hollywood films), or an overseas market (remakes of foreign productions). The remake practice can not then be reduced to proof of the superior quality of French cinematic work and a corresponding lack of original material in Hollywood. Rather it can be seen to emerge from the changes in industrial and aesthetic structures experienced by Hollywood throughout the 1980s and 1990s. Indeed, comparisons can be drawn with the earlier period of florescence for the remake. In both cases vertical integration and domination by the major studios led to a stream-lining of the Hollywood product (the established genres of the 30s and 40s and the big-budget pictures of the 80s and 90s) and a concomitant desire to achieve innovation without risk, hence the popularity of the remake.

This is not to deny the success of the French films chosen for remaking; indeed much of their appeal for producers seeking low-risk ideas lies in their success at the French box-office. However, it should again be stressed that French films do not represent a rich source for Hollywood over and above other European production thanks to some intrinsic quality they may possess. Rather Hollywood continues to remake French films in far greater numbers than it remakes say Italian, Spanish or German films due to the fact that the French cinematic industry is significantly more healthy than those of its European neighbours (British films obviously represent a slightly different case as they can be distributed in the United States without dubbing or subtitling). The relative strength of the French industry is largely due to a continuing system of state support. The cinema was a crucial component of the cultural policy developments of the 1980s described earlier. Public funding via the *compte de soutien* comes from various sources, all handled by the *Centre national de la cinématographie* under the auspices of the Cul-ture Ministry. These include the *taxe spéciale additionnelle* which is levied on exhibitors and then channelled back into the industry, direct government contributions, a tax on pre-recorded videocassettes and, most significantly, a tax on television which now con-stitutes over half of the *compte de soutien*. Another important source of funding is the SOFICAs, tax shelters established by the Socialists in 1981 in order to encourage invest-ment in the industry. The *compte de soutien* provides two forms of aid: the *soutien automatique*, a compulsory levy on box-office receipts which is then invested in subse-quent production, and the *avance sur recettes* which is given to first-time cinematic works.

These systems of state aid, coupled with private investment and EU subsidies, mean that the French cinematic industry maintains production and distribution levels not experienced in other European nations. Evidently this helps to explain the frequency of Hollywood remakes of *French* cinematic works. Moreover, public investment does encourage diversity not apparent in the American industry. Indeed cinematic diversity was central to the early Socialist cultural project, witness their attempts to break down the distinctions between high art and popular culture by removing discrimination in terms of access to funding, and the establishment of an agency for the development of regional cinema in 1982. Such diversity encourages innovation and experiment and thus 'original' material able to appeal to Hollywood producers in search of new ideas.

Nevertheless, it would be wrong to over-emphasise the plurality of French cinematic production. Like Hollywood, the French industry is increasingly concentrated on big-budget productions, frequently heritage films, designed to reinforce cinematic prestige and to appeal to both domestic and foreign markets (and of course to combat the success of Hollywood productions). Both *Germinal* (1993) and *Le Hussard sur le toit* (1995) broke French cinematic budget records. The French films dominant at the box-office tend to be these 'super-productions' and popular comedies, and indeed the latter are frequently the films chosen for remaking. Moreover, despite government attempts to increase independent access to the domestic market, exhibition is still dominated by three groups, Gaumont, Pathé and UGC. These groups operate one-fifth of the country's screens but sell nearly half of the tickets. Each has signed an agreement to preserve free competition and to give independent exhibitors access to films, however their control of the market does suggest a certain homogeneity more akin to the American model than the frequently proclaimed 'diversity' and 'originality' of French cinema might suggest.

Nevertheless, unlike the action-based narratives of the Hollywood blockbuster, a significant number of French cinematic works, both comedies and *intimiste* dramas, are centred upon well-drawn characters and strong narratives. French producers lack the finances necessary for the technical innovation of Hollywood, hence the absence of an indigenous action genre. This is a distinction apparent in *True Lies* (1994) where the character and narrative-led comedy *La Totale* (1991), becomes a comic action adventure.

The continuation of this type of film-making in France does then provide a source of narratives which can be reworked within the aesthetic and industrial context of Hollywood. This perhaps begs the question as to why these films are not themselves distributed in the United States. This fact is partly explained by the tendency to subtitle foreign films. Distributors claim that the American public is too cinematically 'sophisticated' to accept dubbed works, hence films are subtitled and shown on a reduced circuit of art-house cinemas. Moreover, the changes in the American cinematic industry described earlier have reduced the space that began to be carved out for non-Hollywood production during the 1960s and early 1970s. Thomas Schatz perceives contemporary Hollywood as comprising three different classes of film: the blockbuster, the mainstream star vehicle with sleeper-hit potential, and the low-cost independent feature targeted for a specific market with little chance of achieving more than cult status.[37] Schatz's third category can be extended to include foreign productions; small companies, such as Miramax and New Line Cinema, finance and distribute overseas production, marketing it for small, niche markets. The distribution of French films in the United States is not then entirely absent but it is limited by industrial structures and the dominance of the major distributors. The remake however tends to fall into Schatz's second category, the 'sleeper' hit, which consists of medium-budget films, extensively marketed if they show any signs of early success at the box-office. French cinematic production is much more likely to reach a wide American audience via the remake than in its initial form.

The final factor influencing the proliferation of the remake process is the increasing globalisation of the cinema industries and their interaction and cross-fertilisation with other media. As previously stated, the media conglomerates of Hollywood frequently involve foreign investment; Japanese producers of hardware such as Sony and Matsushita perceived the advantage of investing in the software (films) for their products (televisions and video recorders). Indeed French companies such as Crédit Lyonnais also invested, suggesting the need to move away from the oppositions between French and American cinemas so central to the remake debate: if Hollywood is controlled by multinational conglomerates can we continue to perceive it unproblematically as an American industry? Moreover, French production companies are frequently involved in the financing of the American remakes so readily condemned by many French critics; for example Canal Plus co-produced *Sommersby* and Film par Film, D. D. Productions and Cité Films co-financed *My Father the Hero*. Indeed, there exists an active promotion in France of the remake process. A government sponsored agency, Unifrance Film, was set up for the express purpose of encouraging the international distribution of French cinematic works. However, it has also become closely involved in remake deals. Josette Bonte, Unifrance's West Coast Director claims that 'there is at least one contact here in our office per day regarding a remake.'[38] French citizen Victor Drai moved to Hollywood in order to develop the sale of remake rights, focusing particularly upon successful French comedies such as *Le Grand Blond avec une chaussure noire* of 1972. The annual Sarasota French Film Festival is another market for remakes and French distribution and production companies are becoming increasingly proactive in the sale of rights to Hollywood, 'Gaumont has set up an entire department dedicated to translating its back catalogue for Hollywood majors eagerly scouring the Left Bank for the next *Sommersby*.'[39]

What critics of the remake process tend to ignore are the advantages of the process for the French cinematic industry. The three French co-producers of *My Father the Hero* shared takings earned in French-speaking countries (apart from Quebec), acquiring 40 per cent of box-office receipts, 20 per cent of video sales and 50 per cent of televisual rights as well as 45 per cent of worldwide distribution profits after recuperation by Buena Vista/Touchstone of production and marketing costs. The sale of rights for a remake is frequently superior to the money the film could have made through distribution in the United States and this revenue will subsequently enable further French film production. There is an enduring tradition of exchange between French cinema and Hollywood both in terms of aesthetics and industrial practices. Indeed, like all film companies exhibiting in France, Hollywood must pay the tax automatically levied on all cinema ticket receipts and which is then reinvested in the French film industry. Thus descriptions of Hollywood and of the remake as sources of endangerment fail to acknowledge their status as important sources of revenue for French cinematic production.

This depiction of the remake as a process of exchange and interaction can be illustrated by the production and reception of *The Birdcage*, Mike Nichols' 1996 remake of Edouard Molinaro's *La Cage aux folles* of 1978. Nichols' film was produced by MGM-UA, a Hollywood studio whose enduring significance does not need to be underlined. However, as previously stated, MGM-UA was, at that point in time, owned by the French bank, Crédit Lyonnais, a fact which immediately complicates attempts to define the remake as straightforwardly 'American'. Moreover, the immense box-office success of Nichols' film (it earned $80 million in under four weeks when released in the United States proving to be Hollywood's biggest earner of that year so far) reversed the failing fortunes of MGM-UA subsequently enabling Crédit Lyonnais to put their acquisition on the market. The losses incurred by the studio had pushed the state-owned bank into technical bankruptcy, forcing the French government to support it through public subsidies worth more than $4 billion. In other words, the success of this particular Hollywood remake can be seen to have had important financial repercussions both within the United States and France. The French government was able to divest itself of a possession whose retention was neither politically nor financially advisable while the future of a 'great' Hollywood studio was, at least for the time being, secured.

It does then seem apparent that both the discourses surrounding the remake, and the proliferation of the practice itself during the 1980s and 1990s, arise from, and reinforce, a specific socio-historical, cultural and industrial conjuncture. An awareness of this dialectical relationship undermines the reductive negativity of much of this discourse, stressing the complexity of the process and its mobilisation at this time. Rather than reducing the remake to evidence of American cultural imperialism it is vital to perceive it as a far from isolated manifestation of the interaction and cross-fertilisation of the emergent global economy and indeed of the dissemination of the filmic product through the various audiovisual media. Moreover, critics of the practice should take into account both its own specific history and the endurance of exchange between France and the United States and indeed between French cinema and Hollywood. Critical hostility to the remake seems somewhat surprising given the existence of this ancestry.

The rhetoric around remakes is manifestly bound up with wider issues of production and reproduction, of authenticity and identity. It is then imperative to posit a new approach to the remake, an approach which avoids the sterile binaries and reductive value judgments described at the beginning of this chapter, allowing for the complexities of this particular form of rewriting and of the relations between source and target text. It is necessary to consider Franco-American political and cultural relations as well as the dynamics of exchange and influence between Hollywood and the French cinema industry and these relationships must be perceived in terms of change and mobility rather than being fixed in a particular relationship of dominance. The specific socio-cultural context of both source and target texts must also be analysed via a description of the material, historical and political conditions which surround and penetrate the moment of production and subsequent moment(s) of reception. Such description involves a study of 'national' contexts: what is the particular construction of the 'nation', how is the cinematic text located within this context, and moreover, in what ways is it mobilised to invoke or interrogate constructions of the nation or of national culture? Above all this approach to the remake involves close textual study of the cinematic work and the actual process of transposition. In what ways are the signifying structures of the source text replaced by target culture signifying structures? An analysis of these layers of meaning and the ways in which they alter as they move between the source and target cultures enables revelation of the filmic text's particular relationship to ideological formations. How are the values and the belief systems of the source text reinscribed within the target culture? How does the production and reproduction of both films work upon these systems?

This approach permits a study of the remake which avoids the sterile certainties of much critique of the process and its insistence upon the immanent superiority of the source text. Rather the plurality and the contigency of meaning and of textual possibilities should be constantly invoked; both source and remake must be seen as the site for multiple interpretations which can only ever be momentarily fixed in a particular reception situated in a specific temporal, spatial and social context. Rather than a search for origins (the linear causality of the relationship between the 'original' and the 'copy') a study of this kind involves a description of exchange and difference; the unbroken vertical axis which leads from the 'original' text to the remake as 'copy' is replaced by the circles of intertextuality and hybridity. Like Lawrence Venuti's advocation of a 'foreignizing' translation method which would resist fluent strategies through translations which reveal the plurality, the difference, the very 'otherness' of the source text,[40] this approach will show the remake to be a site of difference (of the numerous codes and discourses of which it is composed) rather than a site of the same (a straightforward copy). Such a study permits an understanding of why films are remade, why they tend to be so badly received by the critical establishment (despite possible commercial success), as well as the formal and ideological work which takes place in the actual process of transposition and in ensuing moments of consumption. It is to a study of this kind that we shall turn in the following chapters.

Notes

1. See List of Remakes, p. 152.
2. It should be noted that the film was mobilised rather differently by the French Left and the French Right. Indeed Mitterrand caused some controversy by stressing the film's articulation of a 'traditional' working-class culture and his hopes for the rejuvenation of the Northern mining communities it portrayed while enjoying a lavish meal on a train journey to these same locations for the film's launch.
3. Thomas Leitch, 'Twice-Told Tales: The Rhetoric of the Remake', *Literature and Film Quarterly* vol. 18 no. 3, 1990, pp. 138–49.
4. Ibid., p. 145.
5. There are numerous examples of this type of journalistic comment. The following is not an exhaustive list but does provide a useful cross-section: P. A. Harlé, *Cinématographie française* no. 1038, 23 September 1938, p. 11. *International Herald Tribune*, 11 November 1978. *La Revue du cinéma* no. 420, October 1986. *Ciné Finances* no. 17, 5 November 1990, p. 1. *The Economist*, 27 February 1993. *France-Soir*, 24 March 1993. *Studio* (French version) no. 73, May 1993, pp. 110–13. *Empire* no. 49, July 1993. As Carolyn A. Durham points out in a recent and very welcome addition to the analysis of remakes, this critical hostility is also voiced by a majority of American film commentators (*Double Takes: Culture and Gender in French Films and Their American Remakes* (Hanover: University of New England Press, 1998)).
6. P. A. Harlé, *Cinématographie française* no. 1038, 23 September 1938, p. 11. All translations, unless otherwise stated, are the author's own.
7. André Bazin, 'A propos des reprises', *Cahiers du cinéma* no. 5, pp. 52–6, cited in Daniel

Protopopoff and Michel Serceau (eds), 'Le remake et l'adaptation', *Cinémaction* no. 53, October 1989.

8. Luc Besson, *L'Histoire de Nikita* (Paris: Éditions Bordas et Fils, 1992).

9. Fredric Jameson, 'Reification and Utopia in Mass Culture', in *Signatures of the Visible* (London: Routledge, 1992), p. 16. For a more detailed discussion of notions of originality and authenticity see Lucy Mazdon, 'Rewriting and Remakes: Questions of Originality and Authenticity', in G. T. Harris (ed.), *On Translating French Literature and Film* (Amsterdam: Rodopi, 1996), pp. 47–63.

10. Richard Kuisel, *Seducing the French: The Dilemma of Americanisation* (Berkeley: University of California Press, 1993).

11. *Conférence mondiale des ministres de la culture*, organised by Unesco, Mexico, July 1982. His invocation of cultural imperialism did not meet with great popular support in France; indeed it has always been a paradox of French condemnations of American culture that they tend to contradict the tastes of the wider public.

12. Pascal Ory, *L'Aventure culturelle française* (Paris: Flammarion, 1989), p. 9. See also David Looseley, *The Politics of Fun: Cultural Policy and Debate in Contemporary France* (Oxford: Berg, 1995) for a comprehensive account of socialist cultural policy in the 1980s.

13. René Naegelen, 'Compte rendu in-extenso des débats sur les accords Blum–Byrnes (Séance du 1er août 1946)', *Le Film français* no. 88, 9 August 1946, p. 5.

14. Jacqes Portes, 'Les Origines de la légende noire des accords Blum–Byrnes sur le cinéma', *Revue d'histoire moderne et contemporaine* vol. 33, April–June 1986, pp. 314–29.

15. See Carolyn Durham's discussion of EuroDisney in Durham, 1998.

16. *Financial Times*, 15 December 1993, p. 6.

17. *Wall Street Journal*, 21 October 1993, p. 11.

18. Laurent Joffrin, 'Cinéma, télévision: les raisons de dire non au GATT', *Le Nouvel Observateur*, 28 October 1993, p. 76.

19. Cited in *Le Quotidien de Paris*, 12 December 1993.

20. Cited in Roger Cohen, 'A Realignment Made Reluctantly', *New York Times*, 15 December 1993.

21. Cited in Kurt Jacobsen, 'Trading Places at the Box Office', *Guardian*, 19 October 1993, p. 5.

22. Jacques Buob, *L'Express*, 7 October 1993, p. 70.

23. *Motion Picture Herald* vol. 172 no. 2, 10 July 1948, p. 13.

24. Alan Gevinson and Patricia King Hanson, *American Film Institute Catalog, Feature Films 1931–1940* (Berkeley: University of California Press, 1993).

25. Gene Brown and Harry M. Geduld, *The New York Times Encyclopedia of Film 1941–46* (New York: Times Books, 1984).

26. *Motion Picture Herald*, 10 July 1948, p. 13.

27. Tino Balio, *The American Film Industry* (Wisconsin: University of Wisconsin Press, 1976), p. 399.

28. Edward Benson, 'Decor and Decorum, from *La Chienne* to *Scarlet Street*: Franco-U.S. Trade in Film During the Thirties', *Film and History* vol. 12 no. 3, September 1982, pp. 57–65.

29. Gevinson and King Hanson, *American Film Institute Catalog*.

30. *France-Soir*, 24 March 1993.

31. 'Boom des "remakes" aux États-Unis', *Ciné Finances*, no. 17, 5 November 1990, p. 1.

32. K. Jaehne, 'Once is Not Enough', *Stills*, April–May 1984, p. 11.

33. *Studio* no. 73, May 1993, pp. 110–13.

34. Cited in *Hollywood Reporter* vol. 282 no. 10, 31 May 1984.

35. Thomas Schatz, 'The New Hollywood', in Jim Collins, Ava Preacher Collins and Hilary Radner (eds), *Film Theory Goes to the Movies* (London: Routledge, 1993), pp. 8–36.

36. Schatz, 'The New Hollywood', p. 30.

37. Schatz, 'The New Hollywood', p. 35.

38. Cited in Marc Mancini, 'French Film Remakes', *Contemporary French Civilization* vol. 13 no. 1, Winter/Spring 1989, pp. 32–46.

39. *Empire* no. 49, July 1993, pp. 68–72.

40. Lawrence Venuti, *The Translator's Invisibility* (London: Routledge, 1995).

2
The Remake in History

A brief glance at the remakes of the 1930s and 1940s reveals the presence of a number of extremely well-known films and film-makers. 'Classic' French films such as *La Chienne* (Renoir, 1931) and *Le Jour se lève* (Marcel Carné, 1939) were reproduced in Hollywood and important directors such as Howard Hawks, Fritz Lang and Douglas Sirk used the remake as a means of making their mark upon the American film industry. Perhaps one of the best known of these films is Julien Duvivier's *Pépé le Moko*. The film was released in France on 28 January 1937 and was both a critical and box-office success. Its re-release in Britain in 1998 coupled with Ginette Vincendeau's fascinating monograph bear witness to the enduring appeal of the film and its ability to transcend both historical and spatial boundaries.[1]

This straddling of spatial and temporal boundaries is most clearly demonstrated by the various remakes of Duvivier's film. *Pépé le Moko* was remade twice in Hollywood, as *Algiers* in 1938 and *Casbah* in 1948, and once in Italy as the spoof *Totò le Mokó* in 1949. As Vincendeau points out, echoes of the film can also be perceived in a range of other audiovisual texts, from Michael Curtiz' *Casablanca* of 1943 to Warner Bros.' *Pepe le Pew* cartoon series of 1945.[2] Duvivier's film was itself an adaptation of a novel written by 'Détective Ashelbé' (a pseudonym for Henri La Barthe) published in 1931, and references to the film can also be discerned in a number of other written texts, notably Jacques Ferrandez' striking *bandes dessinées, Les Carnets d'Orient*.

There are a number of possible reasons for the various reproductions of, and references to, *Pépé le Moko*. It typifies many of the best features of French film-making of a period often described as a key moment in the history of French cinema. Strong narrative structure and Henri Jeanson's innovative use of dialogue, a striking blend of French and 'Arab' music in Vincent Scotto and Mohamed Yguerbouchen's score, a remarkable *mise en scène* and of course the presence of that seminal star, Jean Gabin, combine to produce a multifaceted, endlessly fascinating film. However, the story of a notorious criminal, imprisoned in the Casbah in Algiers, who, through his love for a beautiful woman, finds both happiness and ultimately death is certainly not specific to French culture. Indeed, it echoes the themes of many Hollywood films of the period and at first sight the two American remakes may seem to be little more than straightforward 'translations' of their French predecessor.

Algiers was directed by John Cromwell in 1938 and, like its French source, proved a great success at the box-office. MGM had entered into negotiations with the producers of *Pépé le Moko* and acquired the Hollywood remake rights for 1,000,000 francs (then about $38,000). Duvivier and Mireille Balin (who played Gaby in the French version) were signed by MGM and went to Hollywood. Gabin refused to go, apparently attributing his decision to a favourite French wine which 'didn't travel well'.[3] In the end, neither Duvivier nor Balin participated in the remake and MGM, deciding that the story was 'too hot' for the Hays office censors to pass, sold the remake rights to Walter Wanger. Along with the rights Wanger purchased all prints of the film in order to prevent its release in the United States (much to the disgust of P. A. Harlé). As we saw in Chapter 1, the first script of *Algiers* submitted to the Hays office was deemed unacceptable and the PCA requested a number of changes. As we know, Duvivier's film was subsequently released in the United States and was circulated as the 'unexpurgated version' of *Algiers* so drawing upon a notion of French cinema as *risqué* and sexually explicit and problematising the source film's identity as 'original'.

It is true that in many ways *Algiers* can be seen as little more than a copy of Duvivier's film. Apart from the changed ending the narrative structure is almost identical, dialogue (although of course translated) is very similar, documentary shots from Duvivier's montage of the Casbah are incorporated in the remake's equivalent sequence, much of the musical score is re-used and characters' costumes and even physiques are striking in their resemblance to their French counterparts. *Casbah*, directed by John Berry, moves further from its apparent source. Indeed, the opening credits claim that the film is based upon Ashelbé's thriller and not on Duvivier's film at all. This is evidently somewhat disingenuous as the decision to remake the film a second time must surely be attributed to the success of the preceding versions and not to a little known French novel. Nevertheless, significant changes are made. *Casbah* is a musical and Pépé is played by Tony Martin, a popular crooner known for his roles as the romantic lead in a number of light Hollywood films of the 30s, 40s and 50s. This shift in genre and star produces a lighter, more romantic film. The score alters significantly, drawing upon typically Hollywood musical themes well suited to Martin's persona and vocal range. Like *Algiers*, the film transforms the original conclusion as Slimane's men shoot a fleeing Pépé. However, despite these changes *Casbah* retains much of the French source, including a very similar narrative and certain key scenes.

What these similarities and differences begin to suggest is the impossibility of seeing any of these films as either straightforward copies or original works or indeed of attributing either one a clear generic or national identity. *Pépé le Moko* may be the primary source film for this particular process of reproduction but it draws itself upon a range of other texts. As Vincendeau remarks, many contemporary critics saw Duvivier's film as an imitation of Hollywood gangster movies and it is indubitably inspired by Howard Hawk's *Scarface* (1932).[4] The film's 'exotic' North African setting echoes Josef von Sternberg's *Morocco* of 1930. The remakes in turn draw upon both these films and others. The presence of Peter Lorre in the role of Slimane in *Casbah*, combined with the film's conclusion in an airport, recalls *Casablanca* (1943). This circular process of reproduction and citation is extended as the films are themselves referenced in other texts. Graham Greene was a great fan of Duvivier's film and elements of Pépé can surely be discerned in the character of Pinky in *Brighton Rock*. Neither *Pépé le Moko*, *Algiers* or *Casbah* can be seen as wholly 'original' or as a simple copy. Different elements are combined and recombined to produce hybrid texts, gangster movies remade in the French context, French thrillers reproduced in Hollywood (as we shall see in chapter 6, this genre lies at the very heart of Franco-American cinematic relations). A number of key themes re-emerge in *Pépé le Moko* and its two Hollywood remakes and a closer examination of these themes enables a deeper understanding of why this film was reproduced and in what circumstances.Without wanting to reduce the plural meanings of these extremely rich texts I will focus here on two concerns: representations of race and space and constructions of gender (including the mobilisation of the films' stars). Each of these (closely interrelated) discourses can be seen to lie at the heart of the various versions of *Pépé le Moko*.

The different titles of the three films are rather surprising. The shift from the eponymous hero to the film's specific geographical situation to the Casbah seems to suggest that location becomes more important in the later films. The transformation of *Algiers* into *Casbah* does reveal much about these films' treatment of space. The specificities of the earlier film become a more generalised 'exoticism' in Berry's version. However, to argue that space and place are less significant in Duvivier's film is highly misleading, if not to say erroneous. The title changes are perhaps more to do with an unwillingness on the part of American producers to give their films foreign sounding names (Pépé le Moko) and a need to underline a location far less resonant among American cinema audiences than among their French counterparts.

The centrality of both Algiers and the Casbah are made explicit in the opening sequence of *Pépé le Moko*. The film begins with a map of the Casbah and then the camera moves back to reveal an office in the police headquarters in Algiers. This room is encoded as both French and not French. The police discuss Pépé and their attempts to capture him thus establishing a rule of law emanating from Paris. However, it quickly becomes apparent that laws which function in Paris serve little purpose here. The policeman based in Algiers reminds his Parisian colleagues that 'they are not in Paris now' and any attempt to enter the Casbah and arrest Pépé is likely to prove abortive. This 'otherness' is reinforced by the décor of the office (venetian blinds, palm trees outside the windows) and the sweating policemen who use their hats as fans. The policeman goes on to describe the Casbah and we then see a 'documentary' montage which via a series of location shots and rapid editing reveals this 'teeming', 'uncivilised', 'unknowable' space. A three-way relationship is established between Paris (France), Algiers and the Casbah. The police headquarters depict Algiers as a thoroughly colonised space, firmly subjugated to French civilisation. The Casbah on the other hand remains outside this process, a non-colonised and thus alien space. The montage sequence is accompanied by Inspector Meunier's authoritative voice-over yet his knowledge is limited to an acknowledgment of the uncontrollable, labyrinthine nature of the Casbah.

This relationship can be seen to reconstruct French colonial experience of the period. Algiers was perhaps the most westernised French colonial city and was considered by many to be an extension of France (an enduring notion echoed in Mitterrand's famous claim during the colony's struggle for independence that 'Algeria is France'). It is worth noting that the location scenes of *Pépé le Moko* were shot in Algiers, Toulon, Marseilles and Sète so suggesting an equation of these French Mediterranean cities with their North African neighbour. The film extends this construction of Algiers as intrinsically 'French' in its depiction of life outside the Casbah: the luxury hotel, the sleek ship and the clothes of Gaby and her friends connote a thoroughly non-colonial space. Nevertheless, it is the Casbah which dominates the film spatially and visually, both as the home (or prison) of Pépé and because it is the setting for the vast majority of the film's action. It contrasts markedly with the Frenchified, colonised exterior. The darkness, confusion and sheer otherness of this place are constantly emphasised in both the *mise en scène* and the dialogue (narrow streets, overhanging buildings, women of all shapes and sizes including 'mountains of fat which none dare assail'). Apart from the documentary footage included in the opening montage sequence, scenes in the Casbah were shot in the Joinville studios near Paris. This is revealing as it suggests the imaginary nature of this space. It is not 'real' but is reconstructed for the purposes of the fiction. It is the 'imaginary other' in the France/Algeria nexus, the dark, non-colonised space which both threatens (powerlessness, racial miscegenation) and offers illicit pleasures (sexual freedom and escape from the rule of law).[5]

This particular construction of location is firmly positioned within the film's moment of production and initial exhibition and it is perhaps not unfair to suggest that contemporary French audiences would draw upon their own knowledge of the colonial experience (gleaned in part through the Colonial Exhibition of 1931 and numerous other 'colonial' films of the period) in their reading of *Pépé le Moko*.[6] However, such specificities would be less accessible to an American audience unfamiliar with this colony and its relationship with France. Although the opening sequence of *Algiers* is almost identical to its French predecessor (including much of the documentary footage previously incorporated by Duvivier), it interestingly includes textual description of the Casbah shown over a shot of the harbour in Algiers. This is partly typical of Hollywood's tendency to render narrative details more explicit (and the film includes a number of examples of this process) but it is also an attempt to reinforce the attributes of a location far less familiar to an American audience. The Casbah depicted in Cromwell's film is rather less threatening than that shown in Duvivier's film. Although the introduction describes it as a 'melting pot for all the sins of the earth', it is less oppressive than the Casbah of *Pépé le Moko*. As Vincendeau points out, as Pépé and Slimane wander through the streets, the décor recedes into the background, giving more prominence to the actors and increasing the sense of space.[7] This can partly be explained by the film's generally lighter tone, revealed in the use of high-key lighting and the relatively uncomplicated romantic persona of Boyer in the role of Pépé. However, it also undermines the shift suggested by the film's title; rather than emphasising geographical location, the film's spatial setting takes second place to the characters/actors. This in turn implies a need to rewrite the specificities of the source film. Although *Algiers* does set up similar oppositions between Paris, Algiers and the Casbah (in line with its status as a more or less faithful 'translation'), it subtly shifts the emphasis away from this relationship and the connotations it bears for a French audience so making the film more accessible to its new American public.

This process is far more explicit in *Casbah*. The opening titles cover a panning shot across a city which we can assume to be Algiers. The music is essentially Western and melodramatic and includes elements of the film's principal set pieces. The titles conclude with a long shot of the entrance to the Casbah. We see Omar and a group of tourists arrive in the foreground. As they approach the Casbah he explains the origins of its name ('an old Arab word meaning fortress') and then as the film cuts to a medium close-up on the group, he advises them to stick together, warning them that it would not be wise to get lost in the streets of the Casbah. The group then enters the Casbah and Omar points out a 'typical Moorish café', recounting a local proverb about the effects of drink. In the foreground we see two men in Arab dress smoking long pipes and drinking: in other words, the racial others who are shown to be so unknowable in the earlier films here become little more than exhibits for tourists. This reconstruction of the Casbah as a tourist destination says much about the film's treatment of location and the colonial situation. The specificities of Duvivier's Algiers are recast as a generic exoticised space. Yes we are in the Casbah but this Casbah could be anywhere; it represents an exotic 'other' familiar from a variety of similar constructions (including the cinematic) and the particularities which marked the French film are absent.

This sense of the Casbah as 'theme park' is extended throughout the film. The darkness and the dangers which dominate *Pépé le Moko* are here reduced to the familiar worries of a group of tourists. Meetings between Pépé and Gaby largely occur at Odette's bar where their declarations are accompanied by the 'exotic' performance of Katherine Dunham's black dancers. These transformations are partly an attempt to make the film more accessible to an American audience. The process which began in *Algiers* is continued here as the colonial references so central to Duvivier's film are effaced in favour of a Hollywood 'orientalism' far more reminiscent of *Casablanca* than of French Algiers. They are also both cause and effect of the film's shift in genre and register. This tourist Casbah provides a far more suitable setting for the film's gentler, more sentimental

Pépé le Moko (Tony Martin) and Gaby (Marta Toren) admire the local attractions in *Casbah*.

approach to the narrative and the emphasis on the musical numbers sung by the suave, unthreatening Tony Martin.

The tripartite relationship established in *Pépé le Moko* between Paris, Algiers and the Casbah extends beyond the film's allusions to the colonial situation and is indeed central to the construction of the character of Pépé, his place in the Casbah and his relationships with Gaby, Inès (Line Noro) and Slimane (Lucas Gridoux). Pépé is safe within the Casbah: we first see him at Grand Père's (Saturnin Fabre) and witness his escape over the rooftops inaccessible to the police. However, he is of course also a prisoner. In a scene which takes place *chez* Inès after his initial meeting with Gaby, Pépé looks out over the rooftops which have enabled his escape towards the distant sea. He tells Inès of his desire to leave and refuses to take her with him, claiming that she would be no more than a 'portable Casbah'. The scene ends violently as she taunts him with the impossibility of his departure and his despised imprisonment is mirrored in his barely contained aggression. His love for Gaby is much more than sexual or romantic desire for a beautiful woman. The striking opposition between the dark, shadowy lighting of the gypsy-like Inès and the extremely bright lighting of the elegant Gaby makes explicit this construction of each woman as representative of a particular place and life-style. Just as Inès is the Casbah and so both comforts and yet disgusts Pépé, so Gaby is Paris, his past and his desired future.

This is emphasised in the scene where Gaby and Pépé, having discovered that they are both from Paris, exchange Parisian place names. As Gaby moves from the Champs-Elysées and progresses to the Opéra and the Boulevard des Capucines, Pépé leaves the rue Saint-Martin to travel via Gare du Nord, Barbès and La Chapelle. The pair meet on Place Blanche. Gaby's consumerist and upmarket trajectory arrives at the same destination as his working-class itinerary. This choice of destination is significant as it combines both the working-class and criminal elements of Pépé's imaginings and the bourgeois entertainment and consumption (epitomised by the Moulin Rouge which stands on Place Blanche) recalled by Gaby.[8]

The significance of their respective trajectories becomes more apparent when we compare them with their equivalents in the two remakes. In *Algiers* the two characters intone identical destinations and yet it is almost certain that for the majority of the American audience these places would have almost no cultural resonance. They would represent a homogeneous Paris and little else. In *Casbah* the itineraries are far shorter, covering only Montmartre and the Latin Quarter, both popular tourist destinations and as such familiar to non-French audiences. The recollection of Paris which both separates and unites Pépé and Gaby in Duvivier's film speaks volumes about their class identities and aspirations. As Vincendeau demonstrates, class lies at the heart of this film as it is embodied in the essentially working-class persona of Gabin and as it provides a means of identification (for working-class audiences) or titillating erotic appeal (for the bourgeoisie).[9]

Gaby represents Paris and thus freedom for Pépé but it is a very specific Paris, shot through with the discourses of popular culture and aspiration. The initial meeting between the characters is shown via a pattern of shot/counter-shot as Pépé is fascinated both by her jewels and her face and close-ups of her pearl necklace are matched by a close-up of her teeth. Both characters are given a similar number of close-ups and are equally brightly lit (unusual treatment for male stars but typical of much representation of Gabin in this period). The scene establishes complicity between them and their desires; Gaby has what Pépé wants, not because he is a jewel thief (he doesn't steal her jewels) but because like him she has aspired to something beyond her origins and to a degree, has fulfilled those aspirations.

These references to social class which anchor the film so firmly in its moment of production and yet, I would argue, simultaneously contribute to its lasting appeal do of course become problematic in the American context. Although the references to Paris remain unchanged in Cromwell's film, they unquestionably lose their cultural baggage through transposition to Hollywood. Just as Algiers and the Casbah are rewritten as a rather more general 'exotic' location, so this litany of Parisian haunts becomes nothing more than a means of constructing a totalised Paris as imaginary object of desire. The necessary elision of class specificities (which was surely continued during the film's reception) is echoed in the equation of 'oriental otherness' with the film's construction of 'Frenchness'. In other words, to an American audience it is very likely that the exoticism of the Casbah would seem no less strange than the heavy accents and foreign names of the film's leading characters. Charles Boyer in the role of Pépé contrasts markedly with Gabin in the earlier film and yet to American audiences it is probable that he simply provided a version of Frenchness which continued the film's exploration of exoticism and alienation.

In *Casbah* Paris is reduced to tourism (and thus to a Paris constructed entirely by and for non-French spectators) and class disappears entirely.[10] This in turn is in keeping with

Pépé le Moko (Charles Boyer) and Gaby (Hedy Lamarr) in *Algiers*.

the film's move away from the dark complexities of *Pépé le Moko* to a far lighter tone. Duvivier's Pépé may love Gaby but his love for her is as much about his own struggle for identity as it is about conventional romance. Berry's Pépé is a far less complex figure: his love for Gaby straightforwardly mirrors a host of other romantic Hollywood narratives and the problematics of class and identity disappear.

Bound up with these themes of alienation, class and romance are the films' respective constructions of gender. Evidently the relationship between Pépé and Gaby is to a degree predicated on the typical gender oppositions of the romantic narrative. However, closer analysis, particularly of the films' representations of masculinity, reveals a rather more complex set of negotiations taking place. Ginette Vincendeau has convincingly demonstrated the sexual ambivalence that lies at the heart of the Gabin persona.[11] The previously described scene in which Pépé first meets Gaby provides a clear example of the tendency to film Gabin in a manner which mirrors representation of his female co-stars. Frequent close-ups and bright lighting mean that Gabin is as visually important as Balin. He is frequently shown to be the object of the gaze (he is aware of his own desirability claiming 'j'ai du sex appeal'), and focus on his clothes and different parts of his body (notably in his descent from the Casbah towards the end of the film) fetishises him in a way more commonly associated with female stars. His relationship with Gaby and their shared desires and aspirations set them up as equals rather than opposites thus undermining straightforward gender oppositions. She is ultimately the catalyst for his descent to death but she is not the cause. Rather she mirrors the instabilities and ambivalence which lie at the heart of his own identity and which in the end lead him to his doom. Women are coded as dangerous in the film, indeed the Casbah itself is negatively gendered as female, but this danger is not absent from Pépé's own identity.

This doubling of gender is explored and extended in the relationship between Pépé and Slimane. Both characters are outsiders and prisoners, exiled and doubled by their liminal place within the colony. Pépé has a central position within the Casbah (he is 'le caïd des caïds') but this very position exiles him from his past and his future. Slimane works for the colonial authorities and as such can not truly belong to the world of the Casbah (indeed it is Pépé who defends his right to be there). However, when among his fellow police officers, he is marked as 'other'. We first see him silently entering the police headquarters as the Inspector discusses the capture of Pépé with his Parisian counterpart. His surreptitious entrance bears racist connotations of slyness and duplicity, he is called 'lazy' (another Arab stereotype), and his costume, which mixes a western suit and an 'Arab' fez, reinforces the doubling of his identity and his inability to fully affiliate with either colonised or coloniser.

This ambivalence is furthered in the homo-erotic nature of the relationship between Pépé and Slimane. In many ways Slimane is portrayed as the woman to Pépé's man: Gridoux is smaller than Gabin and tends to look up to him, Pépé compliments him on his 'permed' hair and 'mascara'. However, the relationship can equally be seen as Slimane's slow wooing of Pépé. His evident pleasure in the chase, his determination to draw out the process in marked contrast to the clumsy advances of his colleagues, suggest an erotic courtship which is reinforced by the visual representation of Gabin and the tendency to make him the object of Slimane's gaze. It is striking that it is Slimane who engineers the initial meetings between Pépé and Gaby and continues to manipulate their relationship

Pépé le Moko (Jean Gabin) and Slimane (Lucas Gridoux) gaze at Gaby (Mireille Balin) in *Pépé le Moko.*

for his own ends. Certainly Pépé can himself be seen to be coded as a pimp, notably via his costume and his relationship with Inès. However, here it is Slimane who becomes the pimp and Pépé his beloved, yet ultimately victimised, prostitute.

This combination of racial and gender ambivalence emerges from both the complex masculinity of the Gabin persona and from the film's particular construction of its colonial setting. As the film is remade so these doublings and ambiguities are gradually effaced. Although a similar closeness is established between Slimane (Joseph Calleia) and Pépé in *Algiers*, Boyer's persona is constructed around a rather more straightforward masculinity than that of Gabin and thus the homo-erotic element of that pairing is reduced. The pet names employed by the two men in Duvivier's film ('little lamb' and so on) are absent from this remake and Boyer is less likely to be the object of Slimane's gaze. Perhaps somewhat paradoxically, the very fact that these two characters share a heavy foreign accent (in contrast to the American accents of the majority of the film's actors) undermines the sexual coupling suggested in the source film. The lighter tone of the film and the elision of the colonial complexities reduce suggestions of their alienation and the ambivalence which engenders an erotic pairing. Instead their shared 'otherness' makes them complicit with one another as friends, a relationship which is reinforced in the film's final scenes when Slimane agrees not to put the handcuffs on Pépé, claiming 'I can't refuse an old friend.'

Gender representations in *Casbah* are essentially confined to the relatively straightforward binaries of the mainstream romantic narrative. Tony Martin is cast as an unproblematic romantic hero. Like Boyer, he is far kinder to Inez (Yvonne De Carlo) than his counterpart in the French film thus negating connotations of violence and prostitution. Moreover, in Berry's film Inez runs her own tobacco shop so acquiring an agency which reduces her status as kept woman and/or victim. The initial meeting between Pépé and Gaby (Marta Toren) also involves a shot/counter-shot structure between the two characters, however in contrast to the earlier films there are no close-ups on Gaby's jewels. As such she is not identified with, or reduced to, these possessions (and hence to Pépé's dreams and aspirations) but is instead presented as a more conventional object of romantic desire, a gesture in keeping with the film's overall narrative thrust. The character of Slimane is played by Peter Lorre in a manner which explicitly recalls his role in *Casablanca*. Clearly he is 'othered' in a manner similar to his predecessors. However, his earlier role in Curtiz' film, while reinforcing this process (he plays an outsider in both and he is not, of course, American), also undermines it. He is already familiar to American audiences who are used to seeing him in this type of role in a film reminiscent of *Casbah* and thus the 'otherness' so central to Gridoux's character is reduced. Slimane's position within the Algerian police force is also less ambivalent. In contrast to Gridoux and Calleia, we first see Slimane sitting in the police headquarters; he does not make the sly entrance of his predecessors and although he is silent, his presence makes him part of the proceedings from the outset. Nevertheless, his position is far from secure. He tells Louvain that he has just come from the Casbah (so distancing himself from his colleagues) and his alternative methods lead his superior to demote him to sergeant. However, Slimane is later reinstated when the abortive attempt to arrest Pépé proves the futility of traditional policing. Unlike his two predecessors, Berry's Slimane achieves a degree of recognition and acknowledgment of his place within the colonial authorities.

It is not Slimane who introduces Gaby to Pépé and so although he does control the relationship to a certain degree the connotations of pimping are again downplayed. The homo-erotic elements of the Slimane/Pépé pairing are also reduced, largely due to the uncomplicated matinée idol persona of Martin. The sense of pleasure in the chase is evident but it is figured more in terms of competition than courtship as is evidenced at the end of the film when the dying Pépé states 'You win Slimane' and he replies 'You knew I would.' Nevertheless, it would be unfair to claim that this intimacy has been entirely removed. Indeed, the ending is perhaps rather ambiguous as the talk of winning takes place as Pépé dies in his arms and Slimane lights him a cigarette, a gesture redolent of post-coital repose.

The differences between these three films are not of course limited to these negotiations of race, space and gender. Other transformations reveal the pressures of the Production Code: the endings change in the remakes, Gaby's 'sugar daddy' becomes her fiancé and Pépé himself becomes a gentler, less criminally ambiguous character. Narrative details are made much more explicit in the later films (a gesture typical of Hollywood production). As Pépé leaves the Casbah in Duvivier's film a number of close-ups on various parts of his body are superimposed over images of the sea and thus his potential freedom. In *Algiers* a similar montage includes images of the Champs-Elysées so emphasising these shots as representations of Pépé's hopes and aspirations. Similarly, at the end of both films we see Gaby on the deck of the departing ship gazing out over the Casbah. In the French film we are left to construe that the Casbah represents Pépé and the love she has lost. In *Algiers* this is made explicit as the point-of-view shot over the city cuts to an image of Pépé walking through the streets of the Casbah.

The role of the gangster in each film, which as we shall see in Chapter 6 connects them both to one another and to a broader French and American cinematic tradition, is also transformed through the remake process. Despite the aforementioned similarities with films such as *Scarface*, *Pépé le Moko* is very definitely a French gangster movie: criminality and violence are present in the film but are only very rarely foregrounded, for example in the killing of Régis (Fernand Charpin). The identity as gangster becomes as much a means of exploring identity and masculinity as a pretext for action. The relationship between Pépé and his fellow criminals is figured through the tropes of family and paternity, notably in the relationship with Pierrot (Gilbert-Gil), and thus is positioned in a tradition of similar negotiations in the French *policier* and other cinematic genres.[12] In *Casbah* Pépé's gang is far less prominent. An early scene shows them dealing with George the Fence who owes Pépé 8,000 francs. Any hint of violence is diluted by Pépé's smooth tone and humorous remarks. The scene ends amicably as he lifts George's wig so revealing his true identity, and the 'fence' leaves, happily promising to pay him his money. This suggestion that even his adversaries can not resist Pépé's charms is part of the reconstruction of the character as a relatively straightforward romantic hero. The reduced presence of his gang continues this process and reinforces the film's focus on the Pépé/Gaby narrative.

The reasons for the frequent reproduction of *Pépé le Moko* are manifest. It is certainly not an unproblematic film. Its racism, which becomes particularly apparent seen through the prism of post-colonial studies, is reproduced (albeit in different ways) in the American context and these discourses undeniably deserve the type of deconstruction carried out by Janice Morgan and a number of other critics. Nevertheless, the richness of the film, its articulation of a number of concerns, its strong narrative and fascinating *mise en scène* combine to produce a text which is highly translatable, open to rearticulation within new contexts because of its very ambiguities and complexities. *Algiers* and *Casbah* are not simple copies of Duvivier's film. Instead they rewrite and reproduce *Pépé le Moko* according to the aesthetic, cultural and moral norms of Hollywood. They are prime examples of the reasons for, and the reality of, remaking in the 1930s and 1940s.

We have already explored the reasons for the disappearance of the remake in Hollywood after 1950. Although the tendency to attribute the rise and fall of the practice to the number of 'good' scripts available in France and Hollywood has been more or less discounted, it is striking that the only remake of the 1970s should be based upon Henri-Georges Clouzot's critically and commercially acclaimed *Le Salaire de la Peur*. Clouzot's film was released in 1953 and starred Yves Montand and Charles Vanel. Its remake, *The Sorcerer*, was directed by William Friedkin, released in 1977, and starred Roy Scheider. Even the most cursory examination of the films demonstrates that they provide an interesting case study. *Le Salaire de la peur* (like *Pépé le Moko*) has become a 'classic' of French cinema thus positioning the pair of films in the art/popular culture duopoly central to much discussion of remakes. Moreover, as we have seen the two films emerge from moments of change both in terms of the global economy and America's position within that structure, and, perhaps more interestingly for the present argument, in terms of the cinema industry.

This discussion will of necessity be based upon the version of *The Sorcerer* released in Britain. Friedkin's film was neither a critical nor a commercial success in the United States and as a result the producers demanded that the film should be cut by approximately one hour for its release in Britain. The film's title was also changed to *Wages of Fear*. Despite these rather drastic modifications the film had no more success in this country and it was restored to its full length for release in France. This uncut version is not available in Britain hence the focus here on the shorter version of the film. It should be stressed that this is not the version distributed in either the United States or France so any conclusions as to the reception of the film in these countries are necessarily rather tentative. Nevertheless, this process is significant in itself. We are dealing with two remakes here: that of Friedkin and that of his producers. This reveals to what extent the film is a product of the Hollywood cinema industry and demonstrates the power of producers and financiers and the pressure they can bring to bear if a film does not prove successful at the box-office. The change in title seems to be an attempt to make a more explicit reference to Clouzot's film (and hence to acknowledge the film's status as a remake) and thus to attract a wider audience made up of those who generally choose to view Hollywood productions along with a smaller group, perhaps less likely to view a Hollywood film but familiar with the French source (which had proved extremely successful at the British box-office) and interested in comparing the two works. A similar process can be seen at work as the film was released in France as *Le Convoi de la peur*, a title which both recalls the source and yet differentiates the films. Both the American and the British titles will be used in this discussion to distinguish between the two versions of the film.

Friedkin himself did not acknowledge his film as a remake of *Le Salaire de la peur*. Instead he claimed to have based his work directly upon the novel of the same title by Georges Arnaud, also the source of Clouzot's film:

> The only thing I wanted from the original *Wages of Fear* was the premise. Four men sitting on a load of dynamite which I thought was a marvellous premise that could be updated, and I thought people would want to see such a film. [...] But I love the film, and I don't think of it as a re-make at all and I don't really compare it to Clouzot's film which I also happen to love.[13]

Indeed just as *Casbah* cites Ashelbé's thriller as its source, the film's opening credits describe the work as being based upon Arnaud's novel. There are various possible explanations for this denial. The director and producers may have cited the novel as a source in order to bypass copyright laws. In his account of the making of *Heaven's Gate* (Michael Cimino, 1980), Stephen Bach refers to the production of a musical based upon the successful French film *La Cage aux folles* (1978). Although the producers of the musical would have become familiar with this source through the film, and indeed the success of the film would have been perceived as a key factor in the potential success of the musical, Bach points out that producer Allan Carr had bought the English language rights to the French play upon which the film was based and his subsequent Broadway hit was

claimed to be based upon this play rather than the film 'for legal reasons'.[14] It seems that
the bypassing of a cinematic work in favour of its primary source was a means of avoiding legal complications in the United States. Nevertheless, the film's final credits dedicate
the work to Henri-Georges Clouzot so stressing Friedkin's debt to Clouzot's film. The
American director claims to be interested in the 'premise' of both novel and film yet it
is surely likely that he (and John Berry before him) would have become familiar with
this premise through the 'classic' film with which he admits to being familiar rather than
through a little known and long since out-of-print novel.

Friedkin's denial of his work's identity as a remake smacks of what Harold Bloom
termed 'the anxiety of influence', an Oedipal struggle to overthrow the 'original' and to
adopt this status for the reproduction. It also reveals the director's attempts to define his
film as the work of an individual auteur, to differentiate it from 'mass' production and
mark it as something other, a unique 'work of art'. Indeed Friedkin stressed the location
of the film within the artistic trajectory of his previous work thus attempting to posit
an individual cinematic 'œuvre':

> ... [*The Exorcist* (1973), *The Brinks Job* (1978), and *The Sorcerer*] are
> claustrophobic films and I think claustrophobia is an important element in the
> films I've made. And irrational fear – the fear of the unknown, what might
> happen; and generally something terrible does happen. A group of people in a
> tense situation, each deeply obsessed by something – that I guess is what I've been
> drawn to as a filmmaker. The characters that interest me are obsessed by one
> thing or another, be it religious fervour, the pursuit of a criminal, money, fame,
> recognition, freedom.[15]

Friedkin's anxiety was perhaps reinforced by the differing critical and commercial
trajectories of the two films. *Le Salaire de la peur* was both a critical and a box-office success. In 1953 it won the *Grand prix* at the Cannes film festival and Charles Vanel was
designated best male actor of the year for his role in the film. It took first place in a public referendum at the third Berlin festival also in 1953, and in 1954 the British Academy
of Film judged it the best film of the year. As well as gaining prizes and highly positive
reviews, Clouzot's film attracted large audiences in France and other European countries. In 1953 it was one of the most successful films released in France, gaining 497,209
entries in Paris alone and significantly outstripping the success of the current Hollywood Technicolor 'superproduction', *Quo Vadis*, which achieved 335,940 entries. In
contrast *The Sorcerer* achieved neither critical nor box-office success, hence the cuts and
title change described above. Friedkin's film was variously described as being too long,
excessive and simplistic, yet the subsequent cuts did little to change either critical or
public opinion. Indeed many critics vilified the film as a pale imitation of Clouzot's
work, 'As is the case with all remakes – there seems to be not a single exception to contradict the rule – it is merely a pale ghost of its former self, perhaps partially because it
has received an all-out Hollywood production.'[16] The films are perceived to be of very
different cultural status. Despite his denial of the influence of *Le Salaire de la peur*, Friedkin's film tended to be assessed by critics as a remake and was thus subject to the
oppositions and negativity typical of this discourse.

However, despite the critical positioning of *The Sorcerer* within these oppositions, the commercial trajectories of the two films can be seen to undermine the binaries constructed around French 'art' cinema and Hollywood 'mass' production. The highly successful box-office figures of *Le Salaire de la peur* prohibit straightforward perceptions of the work as an 'art' film despite its current cultural status. It was a popular work attracting a wide European audience (although this identity would of course have been complicated by the film's reception in the United States where the very fact that it was 'foreign' and subtitled would have meant that it was perceived as an art film). *The Sorcerer* (and *Wages of Fear*) did not attract large audiences thus problematising attempts to view the film as a Hollywood 'blockbuster' despite the large budget invested in the production of the work.

It is significant that many French critics saw Clouzot's film as being more akin to Hollywood production, particularly action films, than to the literary cinema dominant in France at that time. In 1964, as *Le Salaire de la peur* was re-released in France, a critic in *Les Lettres françaises* claimed that Clouzot's film owed very little to the traditions of French cinema and a great deal to the conventions of Hollywood:

> For twenty or twenty-five years, from the beginnings of sound to 1955, Hollywood has nurtured a genre in which well described social content (made fashionable by Roosevelt's New Deal) has served as a backdrop for classic story-telling. [...] So in 1953 Clouzot was mining an extremely fertile source. [...] *Le Salaire de la peur* has many 'American' qualities: essentially physical situations, well drawn characters, a highly efficient script in which nothing is left to chance.[17]

As his invoking of the discourses of auteurism suggests, Friedkin did not perceive his film as a 'typical' Hollywood production, describing it instead as 'the most expensive art film ever made'. Just like *Pépé le Moko* and its remakes, neither film can be located unproblematically within the oppositions established between French and Hollywood cinemas. This undermines any attempt to define a straightforward trajectory between the two films.

The deconstruction of the typical oppositions established between French 'art' and Hollywood 'mass production' is reinforced by the specific material practices within which each film is located. *Le Salaire de la peur* was a French–Italian co-production. As France was the majority partner the film is described as French yet evidently the Italian input problematises any attempt to see it solely as part of a uniquely French tradition. The film's wide success in Europe was bound up with its status as co-production and the multi-lingual aspects of its dialogue; characters speak in Italian, English, German and Spanish as well as in the dominant language, French. As a result the film could be viewed in these countries as a product that was not exclusively 'foreign' and it was able to overcome the pitfalls encountered by more specifically 'national' products, rejected because of their entirely 'foreign' identity and dialogue. As a co-production *Le Salaire de la peur* is part of a post-war attempt to construct a European cinema and a European audience as a means of retaliating against the threat of Hollywood. Co-productions enabled big budget production while spreading the risks involved across various national industries. The project was central to European production of the 50s and

Clouzot's film should be perceived as part of this process, as an attempt to appeal to a pan-European audience, rather than as a specifically French product.

The status of *Wages of Fear* as a Hollywood production is also somewhat more complicated than it may at first appear. As we have seen, the recession experienced in Hollywood during the 60s was followed by the emergence of two main cinematic tendencies which revived the industry and led to an expansion in production during the 80s. The phenomenal box-office success of a number of relatively modestly budgeted films led the industry to focus on the 'blockbuster'. At the same time a counter-tendency could be perceived in a group of directors who tried to create a new cinema which incorporated the techniques of art cinema within the conventions of mainstream production. As discussed in Chapter 1, this borrowing from the production of art cinema can be linked to the development of plural cinemas and audiences in the United States since the 50s and the wooing of diverse groups through the production of 'different' cinemas during the 70s. It is significant that Friedkin is often described as a central figure in this 'new' Hollywood yet he also directed one of the aforementioned 'blockbusters', *The French Connection* (1971).

Certainly *Wages of Fear* does seem to be situated at the cusp of these two currents. Friedkin himself saw the work as an 'art'(or auteur) film yet it is an unusual hybrid of the conventional Hollywood action movie (witness the depiction of the riot scenes for which he uses rapid editing, travelling shots and close-ups, his camera entering the crowd to stress the movement and the urgency of the situation thus creating a sharp contrast with Clouzot's brief aerial shot of the troubles) and art cinema techniques (the lack of closure and the non-heroic, ambivalent character construction for example). It seems apparent that neither *Wages of Fear* nor *Le Salaire de la peur* can be attributed unproblematically the status of 'art' or 'popular' production or indeed a straightforward national identity. Both films seem to have shifting identities, largely due to the specific material contexts from which they emerge and the ways in which they were received.

This instability in terms of 'art' and the 'popular' is revealed by the films very different depictions of character and relationships. Homosocial bonding, the exploration of heterosexual masculine relationships, is a theme central to Clouzot's film with particular focus upon the relationship between Mario (Montand) and Jo (Vanel). The initial meeting between these characters depicts the gaze of Jo as he watches Mario who moves slowly around him, clearly aware that he is being watched. This display and the gaze to which it gives rise suggest an attraction between the two men, rooted in shared nationality and mutual nostalgia. Clouzot extends this homo-erotic relationship throughout the film. Mario and Jo are seen to be constantly together, a couple reinforced by Mario's rejection of Linda (Vera Clouzot). Mario has been living with Luigi (Folco Lulli), who is feminised by his acceptance of the household tasks. Indeed the first time we encounter Luigi he is preparing a meal for Mario. However, Mario enters the home and claims to have met a 'real man'. Jo eventually usurps Luigi, taking his trousers and Mario's friendship.

The feminisation of Luigi and the close relationship between Mario and Jo suggest a 'threesome', with Luigi as the wronged wife and Jo as the 'other woman'. Nevertheless, Jo's masculinity is stressed in the film's early scenes; for example he dominates Luigi in a struggle in the bar. This stressing of gender becomes embodied in the transport of

Tense moments as Scanlon (Roy Scheider) and Nilo (Francisco Rabal) cross the bridge in
The Sorcerer.

nitro-glycerine. Through this journey true male identities can be fully achieved or
indeed lost entirely. Clouzot demonstrates the shifting power dynamic between Mario
and Jo: as Jo shows fear so he loses Mario's respect and thus his dominance. As the journey progresses Mario makes frequent reference to the feminisation of Jo, calling him 'a
girl' and 'a chick'. This culminates after the explosion of the boulder when Mario spurns
Jo, re-establishing his relationship with Luigi. Yet none of the characters succeeds in this
struggle for a full male identity. Luigi and Bimba (Peter Van Eyck) perish as their lorry
explodes; Jo lies dying, his head on Mario's shoulder, his power and masculinity finally
forfeited. Even Mario fails in this endeavour as his excessive behaviour, evidence of a
refusal to assume the responsibilities of the patriarch, leads him to his death.

Clouzot's clearly delineated characters and his depiction of homosocial relations suggest parallels between *Le Salaire de la peur* and films of the 1930s, notably *Pépé le Moko*
and Duvivier's earlier film *La Belle équipe* (1936) as well as the 'classical' Hollywood productions of the 1930s and 1940s. The implicit exploration of homo-erotic desire recalls
the relationship between Pépé and Slimane in *Pépé le Moko* while the bonding of the
two male characters through nostalgia for a shared but irretrievable past echoes the
union between Pépé and Gaby. This rearticulation of similar narrative concerns is fascinating as it does begin to suggest a common thread linking these French films which
in so many ways appear to eschew clear-cut identities. Friedkin's characterisation is
rather different. In *Wages of Fear* relationships between the protagonists are never developed (this may of course be exacerbated by the cuts in the film). Each man is shown to
have an individual history and in many ways this reinforces the isolation of the characters. It is significant that a single protagonist, Scanlon (Scheider), is at the centre of

Friedkin's film in contrast to the relationship which forms the heart of Clouzot's work. There are no important women characters in *Wages of Fear*, thus in many ways the film can be seen to be a 'man's' film. Yet somewhat paradoxically this 'man's' film does not show any bonding between the male characters. The sense of isolation is reinforced by the film's lack of dialogue. The men rarely speak and thus we learn little about them and their relationships.

The difference between the two films' treatment of character development is exemplified by the 'washboard' sequence. Clouzot uses this event to demonstrate Jo's growing fear and the shifting power dynamics in his relation with Mario. Even as the lorry crosses the uneven terrain we hear the two men speak and thus learn of their changing relationship. In contrast, Friedkin's depiction of this sequence is pure action. We see that Nilo (Francisco Rabal) is afraid as Scanlon puts his foot on the accelerator yet any dialogue between them is inaudible and their relationship remains unexplained and undeveloped. Indeed Scanlon is shown to be in control from the start of the journey, there is no sense of shifting dynamics in this film. As Nilo crosses the pool of water during the journey Scanlon remarks upon his 'nice legs'. Yet this feminisation of the character seems somewhat incongruous as we know so little about him and his relationship with Scanlon. There is a sense of a certain bonding between Nilo and Scanlon as the former lies dying towards the end of the journey. Scanlon talks to him in an attempt to keep him alive, asking him what he will do with the money from the oil company. Nilo replies 'get laid', an answer which provokes the laughter of the two men and a sense of closeness. Yet this moment forms a strong contrast with the death of Jo in *Le Salaire de la peur*. Nilo makes an individualistic affirmation of desire for another (a woman) while Mario and Jo share a mutual nostalgia and desire for the Paris they once knew.

Once again these features of Friedkin's film can be explained by its location on the cusp of two aesthetic tendencies in Hollywood. The lack of character development and the absence of fully formed relationships can be seen to locate the film in a tradition of action cinema in which characterisation and individual psychology give way to physical feats and special effects. However, by choosing not to develop fully drawn characters Friedkin prevents the audience from identifying with the protagonists thus differentiating his film from the 'classical' Hollywood narrative.

Clouzot's film, released in 1953, emerges from the events and discourses of the Cold War and the film works upon the anti-American ideologies prevalent in France at this time. Indeed, the film was censored when first released in the United States in order to remove references to the oil company which were deemed anti-American. Clouzot depicts a nameless South American country which is shown to be a place of poverty and despair both for the indigenous peoples and for the European *émigrés*. The only work available is at the American-run oil company and this work is shown to be highly exploitative and dangerous. When discussing the need for drivers to transport the supply of nitro-glycerine, an American worker suggests that the Union would never agree to such a risk. O'Brien, the head of the company's plant at Las Piedras, dismisses such concerns, pointing out that none of the workers are unionised. O'Brien is a key figure in this depiction of the oil company. His relationship with Jo suggests an ambiguous past, reinforcing an image of the company as being beyond the law, in control of the fate of its workers because of its financial power and thus able to set its own terms. The dangers of *Le Salaire de la peur* emanate from the oil company itself. The explosion at the oil well which kills many indigenous workers and provokes the hazardous lorry journey is not caused by any external factor. The only winner in Clouzot's narrative is the oil company, as the fire is extinguished and the well continues to pump out oil. The film depicts capitalism and wage labour as a source of danger. By locating these dangers within an American-run oil company Clouzot also seems to be suggesting the dangers of American imperialism.

As we have discussed, the early 1950s also saw the expansion of a new global economy led by the United States. Clouzot sets his narrative in a colonial location inhabited by Blacks, Indians and displaced Europeans. The poverty and the squalor of the location demonstrate that this country is firmly on the periphery of the new world order, exploited by capitalist America yet unable to fully participate in the developing global economy: its role is both active (it provides the oil) and passive (the oil wells are managed by an external body). This globalisation is suggested by the different nationalities of the *émigrés*; French, Italian, German, Dutch, Spanish and British, all have come to this location, to the edge, in order to escape. The four protagonists can be seen as liminal (and so once again recall the main characters of *Pépé le Moko*), poised on the threshold between this periphery and the emergent capitalist order. Their remaining in this periphery means death and this process is symbolised visually by the gradual blackening of Mario and Jo in the pool of oil. They are shown to be impotent, all their

Jo (Charles Vanel) and Mario (Yves Montand) in the pool of oil in *Le Salaire de la peur*.

endeavours lead to absorption or death and Clouzot here seems to suggest the futility of individual struggles within the new world order. The director does not offer us a 'happy' ending, neither Mario, Jo nor Luigi achieve their wish to return to their native country. It would seem that this is not a possible solution for Clouzot; to return would mean to enter the American dominated, capitalist order and thus an acceptance of impotence and mediocrity.

The Sorcerer/Wages of Fear emerges from a period of political uncertainties as the hegemonic discourses of the Cold War came to an end. From the mid-1960s diverse groups within the United States began to question America's role in the global economy. The protracted débâcle in Vietnam undermined America's international dominance and led to deep divisions within American society which were not healed by the eventual withdrawal of American forces in 1973. These political upheavals spawned the development of various counter-cultural groups in North America which gradually began to influence the mainstream media. Political debate was now positioned around diverse issues rather than fixed upon the Communism/Capitalism polarity of the Cold War. It is not insignificant that the powerful American Right of the 1990s attributed the 'ills' of contemporary American culture to the growth of counter-cultural identities during this period. These uncertainties and divisions can be seen to be played out in Friedkin's film as it seems to work upon ideology in a rather ambivalent manner.

The film apparently offers a critique of big business. As in Clouzot's film the American-run oil company is shown to be exploitative, employing workers on a casual basis and offering no security or protection. The manager of the plant states in an early scene that he will employ any man from anywhere, 'no questions asked'. The opening scenes of the film show an aerial tracking shot as a helicopter flies over the South American forest. The helicopter arrives at the oil well which is positioned in the middle of this lush greenery, its industrial structures forming a stark contrast with the surrounding landscape. This image suggests an ecological condemnation of the oil company's implantation, a theme which is reinforced by the depiction of the pipeline as it encroaches upon virgin forest, endangering the lives of the indigenous workers involved in its construction. However Friedkin's film also gives a somewhat stereotypical portrait of the unnamed South American country in which the narrative is situated. The police are shown to be corrupt, walls are covered with pictures of a military leader, and the people are shown to be volatile, reacting extremely violently to news of the explosion. This portrait coincides with much North American imagery of South America, frequently perceived as a place 'below' from which emerge the dark and the uncontrollable. In contrast to *Le Salaire de la peur*, the explosion in *Wages of Fear* is caused by terrorists thus danger does not come from the American oil company but from the violent political circumstances of the country in which it is situated.

However, even this interpretation of the film's treatment of contemporary ideology is far from straightforward. The 'corrupt' police officers are seen to drink Coca-Cola, the great American beverage, and an outdated publicity poster in the bar depicting a blonde woman drinking Coca-Cola is an object of fascination to Scanlon, leading him to memories of his past. It is possible to interpret these images as an exposure of the United States' influence in certain Latin American countries. What is clear about *Wages of Fear* is the impossibility of attributing to it any clear-cut political position. Just as *Le Salaire de la peur* works upon the hegemonic discourses of the Cold War so Friedkin's film, emerging as it does from a time of uncertainty, seems to shift between various political and ideological positions.

It is perhaps rather surprising to consider the similarities between the various remake processes described in this chapter. They occur at very different moments and while the earlier remakes are part of a common tendency to reproduce French cinema, Friedkin's film emerges at the end of an extremely barren period for the remake. Nevertheless, in each case we find films which do not fall easily into national or generic categories, we see implicit and explicit forms of censorship as the films move between cultures with differing political and moral dictates. Above all we see the transformation of narrative concerns (gender, race, sexuality and so on) whose very reoccurrence in each film suggests their enduring interest and appeal in both cultures. The release of *The Sorcerer* in 1977 signals the remake boom of the 1980s. At the same time it refers back to a popular film of the 1950s which in turn recalls productions of the 1930s, themselves the source of various remakes. What we are then beginning to see is the intertextuality of all cinema, the ongoing, omnipresent nature of filmic reproduction which in the case of the remake, reaches its apogee in the 80s and 90s.

Notes

1. Ginette Vincendeau, *Pépé le Moko* (London: BFI, 1998).

2. Ibid., p. 7.

3. Gene Brown and Harry M. Geduld (eds), *The New York Times Encyclopedia of Film, 1941–46* (New York: Times Books, 1984).

4. Vincendeau, *Pépé le Moko*, p. 31.

5. For further discussion of colonialism in the film see Janice Morgan, 'In the Labyrinth: Masculine Subjectivity, Expatriation and Colonialism in *Pépé le Moko*', in Matthew Bernstein and Gaylyn Studlar (eds), *Visions of the East, Orientalism in Film* (London: I. B. Tauris Publishers, 1997), pp. 253–68.

6. Vincendeau, *Pépé le Moko*, p. 55.

7. Ibid., p. 67.

8. Although the Moulin Rouge is not actually mentioned, its location would of course be familiar to many French spectators. It is striking that a reference to the same *Place Blanche* in Tania's (Fréhel) song (which extends this theme of nostalgia for Paris) is translated in the subtitles as 'Moulin Rouge' suggesting another means of rendering more accessible the film's cultural specificities (the music-hall is of course well-known worldwide and can even be seen to represent a particular notion of 'France' or *belle époque* Paris).

9. Vincendeau, *Pépé le Moko*, p. 64.

10. The range of accents employed in *Casbah* is quite surprising (Pépé's sidekick Max even has a pseudo-cockney accent) and says much about the film's generalised construction of the foreign.

11. See Claude Gauteur and Ginette Vincendeau, *Anatomie d'un mythe: Jean Gabin* (Paris: Éditions Nathan Université, 1993).

12. This exploration of paternity is indeed a key theme in a number of the remakes of the 80s and 90s.

13. William Friedkin, 'Tense Situations – William Friedkin in an Interview with Ralph Applebaum', *Films and Filming* vol. 25, no. 6, March 1979, pp. 12–21.

14. Stephen Bach, *Dreams and Disasters in the Making of* Heaven's Gate (London: Faber and Faber, 1986), p. 204.

15. Friedkin, 'Tense Situations', p. 18.

16. *International Herald Tribune*, 11 November 1978.

17. *Lettres françaises*, 30 July 1964. As we shall see this criticism prefigures later appraisal of Luc Besson's films.

3
Remakes of the 1980s and 1990s: Boom Time

As we have seen in the preceding chapters, the early 1980s saw a sudden increase in the number of French films remade in Hollywood. This proliferation is frequently attributed to the financial success of *Three Men and a Baby* (1987), Leonard Nimoy's remake of Coline Serreau's *Trois hommes et un couffin* of 1985.[1] Table 1, first published in *Variety* in April 1993, lists gross takings for a number of films and their remakes at the American box-office. The success of *Three Men and a Baby* is certainly striking when we compare it with the careers of other remakes. The film's producers, Touchstone and Silver Screen Partners, went on to produce four further remakes between 1987 and 1994 surely encouraged by the reception of *Three Men and a Baby* and it is almost certain that this phenomenal box-office success had a significant impact upon the involvement of other producers in the remake process.

However, to attribute the rise of the remake to the career of a single film is somewhat problematic. Indeed *Three Men and a Baby*, far from heralding the remake boom of the 80s, was preceded by twelve remakes including Paul Mazursky's *Down and Out in Beverly Hills* (1986), also a commercial success produced by Touchstone and Silver Screen Partners. Such claims perhaps lie in the tendency to perceive the remake as a purely commercial practice. Moreover, by ignoring the pre-history of the remake in this manner, critics seem to suggest that it is a new phenomenon, a fresh onslaught upon French culture on the part of Hollywood. Thus it is inscribed in a general history of 'American cultural invasion' while abstracted from its particular past in order to lend it increased significance.

Nevertheless, the box-office success of Nimoy's film is significant for a number of reasons. It almost certainly contributed to the rise of the remake during the late 1980s and 1990s. *Three Men and a Baby* is one of the films most frequently cited as an example of a remake (this may also of course be due to the success of Serreau's film in the French market) and this is one of the few remake pairs to receive a certain degree of scholarly attention.[2] A number of articles comparing the films were published in the years following their release and it seems very likely that this is a result of their commercial success rather than any artistic value they may be considered to possess.[3] The vast majority of these articles concentrate on the films' representations and constructions of gender and paternity/maternity. This focus is perhaps not surprising given the films' narrative concerns (and of course the gender of the French film's director), however, as I will reveal in this chapter, the significance of this type of analysis extends beyond the

Table 1

FRENCH FILMS	Gross USA Receipts (in $)	REMAKES	Gross USA Receipts (in $)
Trois hommes et un couffin	2,150,000	Three Men and a Baby	168,000,000
Le Jouet	700,000	The Toy	50,000,000
Le Retour de Martin Guerre	4,000,000	Sommersby	44,500,000
Les Fugitifs (not distributed)		Three Fugitives	40,000,000
Nikita	5,000,000	The Assassin	25,000,000
Un Éléphant ça trompe ...	1,700,000	The Woman in Red	24,000,000
La Chèvre	2,100,000	Pure Luck	22,000,000
Un Moment d'égarement	150,000	Blame it on Rio	21,000,000
Cousin, Cousine	8,500,000	Cousins	20,000,000
Le Grand Chemin	750,000	Paradise	19,000,000
L'Homme qui aimait les femmes	2,000,000	The Man who Loved Women	10,000,000
Le Grand Blond avec une ...	1,400,000	The Man with One Red Shoe	9,000,000
L' Emmerdeur	1,200,000	Buddy Buddy	7,000,000
La Vie continue	800,000	Men Don't Leave	6,100,000
Bonne Année	600,000	Happy New Year	100,000

Source: Variety, 19 April 1993.

arguments of the various articles and indeed beyond the films themselves. Many of the remake pairs of the 1980s and 1990s are concerned in some form or another with issues of gender and, more specifically, paternity. Examples include *Les Fugitifs* (1986)/*Three Fugitives* (1989), *Le Grand Chemin* (1987)/*Paradise* (1991), *Mon Père ce héros* (1991)/*My Father the Hero* (1994), *La Totale* (1991)/*True Lies* (1994), *Neuf mois* (1994)/*Nine Months* (1995) and *Les Compères* (1983)/*Father's Day* (1997). In other words, by choosing to focus upon these particular issues, these articles position themselves within, and foreground, an ongoing negotiation of gender and paternity in the remakes of the period. Through my own readings of *Trois hommes et un couffin* and *Three Men and a Baby* as well as a number of other films, the following chapter will attempt to determine why these narrative concerns re-emerge throughout the 80s and 90s in both cinematic contexts, why such narratives are so frequently part of the remake process, and what happens to them as they are transformed across cultures. This in turn will help to determine why the remake re-emerged with such force at this juncture.

Both films recount the various mishaps and complications which ensue when a baby girl is unexpectedly left in the care of three confirmed bachelors. The baby's father, Jacques (André Dussollier)/Jack (Ted Danson), unaware of the existence of his progeniture, leaves the country at the start of the narrative having promised to receive a package on behalf of a colleague. The 'package' duly arrives in the shape of a baby left by her mother, Sylvia, which is discovered by Jacques's/Jack's flat-mates, Pierre (Roland

Giraud) and Michel (Michel Boujenah)/Peter (Tom Selleck) and Michael (Steve Gut-tenberg). A second package arrives later the same day. This time it contains heroin and the films proceed to combine in rather different ways the 'female' tale of paternity and domesticity engendered by the first 'package' and the 'masculine' narrative of action introduced by the second. Indeed, despite many striking similarities in terms of narra-tive structure, dialogue and humour (for example the films share a number of sight gags built around the men's inability to cope with the baby), the films do part company quite radically in their handling of these two disparate plots. Whereas the French film dis-penses quite swiftly with the drugs plot as Michel deposits the package hidden in a nappy in a park waste-paper bin, the American version includes a quite protracted sequence depicting the three men's successful ensnaring of the drug dealers.

This is certainly symptomatic of the prevalence of action sequences in the Hollywood product (other examples include the race to the airport towards the end of the film and the increased emphasis on physical comedy). However, the shift is also revealing in its negotiation of moral codes. In *Trois hommes et un couffin* Michel hands the drugs over to the dealers who remain unpunished. Moreover, the police are shown to be ineffectual and even somewhat foolish. The *gendarme* who initially accosts Pierre as he attempts to retrieve the baby from the fleeing dealers is a rather absurd figure who rants and ges-ticulates and bears more than a passing resemblance to Louis de Funès's incarnation of the same profession in the highly popular *Les Gendarmes* film series.[4] The young police officer who follows Michel to the park as he transfers the drugs fails to realise what is going on until too late and, having lost his job, returns to the men's apartment later in the film in order to determine exactly how they disposed of the heroin.

In *Three Men and a Baby* the police are shown to be rather more authoritative fig-ures. In contrast to the diminutive *gendarme*, the officer who stops Peter sits astride a large horse (an obvious phallic symbol) thus underlining his power over Peter who is literally obliged to look up to him. Although Michael conceals the drugs inside a nappy while the police are actually present in the apartment (in contrast to the French film when this takes place *after* the police visit), any suggestion of police incompetence is effaced by the knowing air of the chief officer (whose authority is also underlined by his concern for, and ease with, baby Mary) and by the subsequent tailing of Peter and Michael of which they remain quite unaware (in the French film Pierre and Michel leave the apartment fully aware that they will be followed). Rather than simply hand over the drugs to the dealers, the three American men hatch a complicated plot which, in an extended sequence, shows them capturing the criminals at Peter's work-place. They sub-sequently hand the dealers over to the police. Thus the moral ambivalence and mockery of authority present in the French film are replaced by victory over wrongdoing, pun-ishment and an affirmation of authority in the remake.

We can find other examples of this shift from ambivalence to a far more clear-cut negotiation of 'right' and 'wrong' in the two films. For example, the note which accom-panies baby Marie/Mary explains Sylvia's reasons for abandoning her daughter. Whereas in the French film she simply states that she has gone to the United States for six months and is leaving the baby with Jacques, in the American version she attributes her decision to leave to an inability to cope and a need to spend some time alone. The French Sylvia baldly announces that she has gone for six months, her American counterpart does not give any indication of the length of her absence and begs for Jack's understanding, 'I can't handle this now, I don't know where else to turn. I hope you can both forgive me some day.' Moreover, it is striking that Mary is discovered after Peter's morning jog. In other words, she was not there when he set out and so can only have spent a short time alone on the doorstep. In contrast Marie is discovered when Pierre sets out to buy croissants suggesting that she could well have been there all night. Just as the moral ambiguities of the drugs plot are smoothed over and resolved in the remake, so the problematic connotations of a mother unwilling to look after her baby daughter are, to a certain degree, excused and explained. This shift from moral ambivalence and gentle derision of authority in the French film to apparently straightforward moral codes and affirmation of authority in the remake is not at all uncommon. Indeed, as we shall see in subsequent chapters, it is a prevailing feature of the transformation of popular French comedies in Hollywood.

As these various shifts and transformations begin to suggest, *Trois hommes et un couffin* and *Three Men and a Baby* are in many ways quite different films. Like the films discussed in the preceding chapter, the remake is far from being a simple copy of its French source. This is made immediately apparent in the opening sequence of each work. Serreau's film opens with a party in the bachelors' Paris apartment. The opening shot shows a dimly lit painting of a baby. Figures pass back and forth in front of this painting and the camera then pans slowly across the room. This is followed by another slow panning shot and then a tracking shot follows Jacques's friend (the intended recipient of the second 'package') as he makes his way towards Jacques to organise the delivery. The sequence ends with another slow pan, this time over the detritus of the meal, which culminates in a close-up on a painting of a naked woman. The move from baby to naked woman clearly provides a reverse mirroring and a prefiguring of the film's central narrative trajectory (from the sexual freedom of bachelor life to the responsibilities of childcare). However, what I particularly want to emphasise is the style and *mise en scène* of the sequence. The slow camera movements and minimal editing combine with low-key lighting and a soft jazz soundtrack to produce a languorous feel.

In marked contrast, the remake opens with a sequence showing Michael painting the murals which will adorn the entrance to their apartment. As the titles run, Michael gradually fills in the black and white outlines which represent himself and his two flatmates to produce brightly coloured cartoon figures. His work is interspersed with the comings and goings of their daily lives, in other words the arrival and departure of numerous young women. Rapid editing, accelerated motion and a lively pop soundtrack (the song of course is entitled 'Bad Boys') combine to produce an energetic, almost frenetic tone. This is continued in the ensuing party sequence. The dark, shadowy apartment of the French film is replaced by an airy, open space accentuated through high-key lighting. A great variety of shots (Michael's view through the video camera, pans, close-ups, long shots and so on), rapid editing and more pop music on the soundtrack further accelerate the pace. These opening sequences embody the style and tone of the films that follow and encapsulate the differences between them. Whereas *Three Men and a Baby* can be described relatively unproblematically as a comic film, *Trois hommes et un couffin* is somewhat darker and can perhaps best be described as comic drama/melodrama (in many ways a contradiction in terms but one which sums up the film's rather wistful

Jack (Ted Danson), Peter (Tom Selleck) and Michael (Steve Guttenberg) celebrate bachelor life in *Three Men and a Baby*.

treatment of an ostensibly comic premise). The still-life of the French interior becomes the bright cartoon of the American apartment and thus provides a spatial embodiment of the contrasting treatment of similar narrative concerns.[5]

Both films do however seem to offer problematic and partial representations of gender. Men are left 'holding the baby' while women, and more specifically mothers, are effaced by an all-encompassing paternity. Such representations are perhaps another reason for the critical response to the films. Serreau's film in particular was much criticised by American feminists for its apparent misogyny, a position no doubt reinforced by the belief that as a woman director Serreau should have 'known better'.[6] Nevertheless, without necessarily wanting to deny the limitations of the films' treatment of gender, it would be misleading to say that each one is equally, or rather *identically*, problematic. Both films are about confusion and the attempts to replace this confusion with renewed cohesion. The arrival of the baby disrupts the men's lives and the second package complicates things further. As Carolyn Durham points out, the very combination of the two separate plots introduces confusion into the narrative structure. Although this narrative confusion is ostensibly solved early in the French film as Michel rids himself of the drugs, it does in fact continue as the very act of telling the story itself creates confusion. As Durham explains, Michel and Pierre are unable to explain the presence of the baby or the adventures with the drugs to Jacques on his return. In similar fashion, Jacques's later attempts to explain things to the young police officer collapse into incoherence.[7] In the American film the two plots continue in tandem for much longer. However, rather than create more confusion, they are effectively narrativised by the men and progress in seeming narrative harmony until their respective closures.

The 'false' coherence of the remake (the two plots are after all quite separate) is extremely revealing. Although *Trois hommes et un couffin* does progress towards a form of coherence (a *modus vivendi* which will allow the men to care for the baby) the inability to tell this story adequately suggests the impossibility of fully dispelling confusion. In contrast, *Three Men and a Baby* moves smoothly towards full closure, coherently telling and combining its separate elements (indeed Peter takes firm control of the narrative, responding to the drug dealers' demands by stating 'We'll do it our way'). This contrast echoes the films' respective representations of masculinity; whereas Serreau shows us masculinity in crisis which can never fully be resolved, Nimoy shows us masculinity in confusion which can ultimately be rendered coherent.

Criticism of the films' gender politics tends to concentrate on their respective depictions of women. Both *Trois hommes et un couffin* and *Three Men and a Baby* construct narratives which very explicitly exclude women. The three men live together and women play a transitory role as they come and go for various one-night stands and social encounters. This exclusion is particularly striking in Serreau's film; whereas the opening sequence of the remake does reveal some form of relationship between Peter and Rebecca (he tells another young woman that they have an 'open' relationship but responds to another man's interest in Rebecca by insisting that they are entirely committed), the French film merely shows the fleeting encounters of the party. Moreover, when Michel suggests that they should ask Jacques's mother to care for Marie, Pierre reacts by stating that 'mothers should be left where they are,' reminding him that their cohabitation is based upon the understanding that no women should move into the apartment. In both films women are shown to be impermanent and, at worst, unreliable. This is partly revealed through their transitory roles in the men's lives but is also negotiated via their responses to the arrival of the baby.

Again, this representation of women seems rather more problematic in the French film. In Nimoy's film both Rebecca and Jack's mother refuse to take care of Mary in an attempt to force the men to accept responsibility. Although Rebecca does remind Peter that he should not assume she knows about childcare simply because she is a woman, she ultimately explains her refusal to help out by assuring him that he will manage quite well on his own. In other words, her refusal is based not so much upon her own lack of maternal instinct as upon her desire to see Peter cope alone. Similarly Jack's mother declines to help in an attempt to make Jack accept the responsibilities of fatherhood. She replies to his pleas of incapability by stating 'You were a screw-up, now you're a father.'

In contrast women in the French film show a quite undisguised reluctance to care for the child. The men's dinner party collapses into chaos when Marie wakes up and begins to cry. As the soft diegetic music and social chatter is replaced by her wails, the guests become increasingly uncomfortable. The women guests suggest that she should be returned to her bed in an obvious attempt to resume the party without her rather noisy presence. Jacques's mother also refuses to care for her granddaughter. However her decision has nothing to do with an altruistic (and highly 'maternal') attempt to improve her son's behaviour. Instead she is unable to care for Marie because she is about to set off on a Caribbean cruise with her friend Marie-Rose. Thus Jacques's mother not only fails to reveal any maternal instincts but she also shows the irresponsibility that in the remake it is left to the mother to cure. This lack of maternal feeling is extended to the various women who are called upon to participate in the care of Marie. Upon discovery of the baby Pierre rushes out to buy her food. He consults a female pharmacist who responds, not through personal knowledge of childcare, but through scientific, logical explanation. Madame Rapon, the nanny from the rather inappropriately named '*Agence seconde maman*', defines her skills in terms of the various qualifications she has achieved. Pierre, who opposes his personal experience of Marie to Madame Rapon's professional competence, hotly disputes her childcare methods. An explicit connection is made between these two women and their scientific approaches to maternity when, in response to the nanny's assertion that 'medicine is a serious business', Pierre asks, 'Have you ever heard the song that says medicine is a whore and the chemist her pimp?'

Durham attributes this rejection of women, and more specifically 'female' maternity, to a specifically French relationship between gender and culture. French feminism has typically been articulated through the concept of 'difference' in which the 'natural' specificities of the female body (female sexuality, pregnancy, childbirth and so on) have been invoked to revalorise female experience. In these terms men who wish to parent must not only prove their *ability* to care for a child they must also prove their natural *right* to do so. Durham argues that Serreau's film represents this project as a two-part process; first 'real' women must be excluded and/or proved unworthy mothers, second the men must assume these 'maternal' roles themselves.[8] In contrast, *Three Men and a Baby* draws upon American feminism and its discourse of equality. In other words, women are neither effaced nor replaced. As we have already seen, they simply deny their 'natural' ability to mother and invite the men to carry out this role instead. Although Durham acknowledges the misogyny at work in both narratives, she does claim the possibility of a slightly more optimistic reading of Nimoy's film. Women as mothers do not disappear entirely from his film and, moreover, the men's ability to integrate professional life and childcare (for example we see Peter take Mary to the construction site at which he works) suggests new and rather more progressive concepts of 'mothering' and shared parenting.[9]

Without wanting to deny the misogynistic discourses of these films, I am sceptical of any reading which posits the remake as more 'progressive' than its French counterpart. The film's comic tone and style as well as its ideological discourses which efface entirely the realities of the impact of a young child on the lives of three working adults (the men initially fail to work but do not lose their jobs or appear to suffer any financial consequences) undermine attempts to accord it a serious social message. Indeed, in many ways the French film is less problematic in this respect as it does emphasise the dull, routine nature of childcare. The sequence which follows the frantic response to Marie's arrival shows Pierre and Michel bathing, feeding and changing the baby. The repetition of these chores, along with the lack of music and the relatively slow pace of the sequence, underline the tedium of childcare and can be read as an intervention into debates about the need to reconsider the status of domestic labour. In contrast similar scenes in the remake are fast-paced, accompanied by a brisk pop soundtrack and contain various comic elements all of which downplay the drudgery of childcare and recast it as light-hearted play.

Above all, I would dispute claims about the 'progressive' nature of Nimoy's film because of its rather hysterical affirmation of heterosexual masculinity. The basic narrative premise of each film (three single men sharing an apartment) evidently raises certain problems *vis-à-vis* constructions of masculinity. *Trois hommes et un couffin* and *Three Men and a Baby* respond to this situation in quite different ways. It is striking that whereas in the French film the visiting *gendarme* obviously assumes that Michel and Pierre are gay, his suspicions only confirmed when they deny this by pointing out they share the apartment with a *third* male friend, no such conclusions are manifested in the remake. Indeed, from the outset the American film seems anxious to deny any such suggestions. The previously described opening sequence provides an overload of heterosexual signifiers as numerous women come and go from the apartment for sexual encounters with the three men. This sequence speaks volumes about the moral double standards of mainstream Hollywood production. As a 'family' film, a film aimed at and marketed for a broad audience, *Three Men and a Baby* must play down any suggestion of homosexuality and yet seems quite happy to advocate a promiscuous heterosexuality.

This process continues throughout the film and contrasts markedly with the far more ambiguous construction of masculinity in Serreau's film. Pierre's discovery of Marie in *Trois hommes et un couffin* occurs as he leaves the apartment to buy croissants. We see him enter Michel's bedroom to ask him how many croissants he would like. Michel lies in crumpled sheets, apparently naked, and asks for three or four. This entry into Michel's room and the shared breakfast as well as the suggestion of their domestic routine carry clear connotations of the couple, connotations reinforced by the sexual overtones of Michel's nakedness and crumpled bed linen. In contrast, Peter discovers Mary after a session on the rowing machine and a morning jog and he calls to Michael who emerges from his bedroom wrapped in a bathrobe. Of course Peter's emphasis on fitness and his singlet clad, well-toned body could be seen as carrying suggestions of gay sexuality. This possibility is reinforced by the persona of Tom Selleck who was subject to threats of outing in the late 80s/early 90s. However, the film explicitly rejects such connotations by showing Peter picking up a young woman while jogging in the opening sequence.

The men's approach to childcare extends these very different constructions of masculinity. As we have seen, the French men take on the routine drudgery of childcare typically deemed to be 'women's work'. The American men however incorporate childcare within a 'masculine' world of work and leisure. Peter and Jack take Mary to work, they bath and dress her on the pool table and Peter's choice of bed-time story for his surrogate daughter is an extract from *Sports Illustrated* read in a soothing, sing-song tone. Rather than transform their bachelor life-style and thus threaten their masculinity, the baby becomes an intrinsic part of it. She may dirty Jack's silk sheets and her bottles may replace the wine in the fridge, nevertheless her insertion within a straight male household is affirmed when she becomes an accessory in the pursuit of women during a game of frisbee in the park. Interestingly, and indeed rather worryingly, this affirmation of heterosexual masculinity is underlined by the men's perception of Mary as a sexual being. Michael worries about changing her nappy, 'She's a girl, should we be doing this?' and turns off the television when he hears Dr Ruth begin to talk about orgasms. It is perhaps rather surprising that this process should occur in the American film; as I will discuss later in the chapter, the sexualisation of the father/daughter relationship is a frequent trope in French culture and is rarely visible in Hollywood production. How-ever its presence here serves to reinforce the affirmation of straightforward gender constructions as even the men and Mary are situated in unproblematic gender binaries.[10]

This shift from the French film's more ambivalent construction of masculinity to the remake's assertion of straight male sexuality is made particularly apparent in the men's responses to the baby's departure. In *Three Men and a Baby* the imminent return of Sylvia and Mary to England results in Jack's admission that he misses his daughter (Peter and Michael have no hesitation in revealing their desire to have Mary back) and a rush to the airport in an attempt to retrieve her. In *Trois hommes et un couffin* the men's reac-tion is far more passive. They fail to admit that they miss Marie and instead their sadness is revealed through a variety of physical symptoms (Pierre's cold, Michel's failure to work and Jacques's depression and drunken impersonation of a pregnant woman). What these changes suggest is that whereas in Nimoy's film the male body is a site of (masculine) activity, in the French film it is a site of (feminine) passivity. In other words, the desire to keep Mary manifests itself in an acceptance and affirmation of this desire and the immediate decision to act upon it while the desire to keep Marie produces a range of uncontrolled and uncontrollable physical and emotional symptoms. This sug-gestion of neurosis is part and parcel of the problematisation of traditional masculinity which can be perceived in Serreau's film. It links to the frequent shots of the men's semi-clothed bodies (notably at the end of the film) and an emphasis on their soft, feminine or even child-like flesh to suggest a renegotiation of masculinity, masculinity in crisis as the binaries which typically define gender are broken down.

Michel (Michel Boujenah) and Pierre (Roland Giraud) suffer the effects of parenthood in *Trois hommes et un couffin*.

From this perspective critique of Serreau's apparent effacement of women and a male appropriation of female roles can be rethought and her film read as an attempt to suggest non-essential, performative and highly ambivalent gender identities. Nimoy's film on the other hand constructs the 'new man', in touch with his feelings (note the comparative readiness of Michael and Peter to admit to their feelings for Mary) and yet simultaneously active and productive. It is striking that the opening sequence, source of so many fascinating signifiers, informs us that Peter (an architect) has designed the apartment while Michael produces the murals. Jack, we later find out, has fathered Mary so each man is a producer, is engaged in an activity unproblematically cast as masculine which he then combines with the care of Mary in a cohesive whole which in no way threatens his clearly affirmed gender identity.[11] It may be true that both films show a new kind of masculinity. However whereas Nimoy's film offers us the dubious ideology of the 'new man' and thus asserts a new status quo in which men and women retain their traditional identities while taking on board some elements of femininity/masculinity (the men and Sylvia join forces to care for Mary), Serreau's film offers us a masculinity in crisis, unsure of its identity and of its relationship with feminity. Unlike the remake, the source film ends with Sylvia asleep in the cradle and the three men, bare-chested agreeing to care for Marie. The infantilisation of Sylvia and the homo-erotic connotations embodied in the men undermine any suggestion of cohesion and the film ends with an ambivalent negotiation of gender, an acknowledgment of its unstable nature which, I would argue, can be seen to be far more progressive than the sharing caring message which ends Nimoy's film.

These transformations reveal much about the different contexts of production from which these films emerged and the varying modes of reception they can be seen to invite. It is quite apparent that the films' specific constructions of gender and paternity are closely connected to the impact of feminism and the negotiation of masculinity in France and the United States in the 1980s. The cultural gap which separates these negotiations perhaps helps to explain each film's relative failure at the box-office of the country of its cinematic counterpart. Indeed, *Trois hommes et un couffin* was condemned by many American critics as evidence of the paucity of contemporary French cinema despite being put forward for an Academy Award for best foreign-language film, 'I knew the French film industry had fallen on bad times, but I didn't realise how bad until I saw *Three Men and a Cradle* which won the 1985 French Academy Award, and which is so insufferable that I wanted to cry out in protest against the stupidity on screen.'[12] Such criticism is striking as it reposes upon particular constructions of French cinema as 'art' cinema, a category to which Serreau's film clearly does not belong:

> The national cinema that once gave us Truffaut, Renoir, Resnais and Godard is now heaping its highest honors on *Three Men and a Cradle* [...] and *Subway* [...]. These two films dominated the Cesars (the French Academy Awards) a couple of months ago, and they're indicative of what is so distressingly wrong with French films today.[13]

Given the domestic success of Serreau's film it is ironic that it should be condemned by American critics as evidence of the demise of French cinema. Evidently it does not fit readily into a cinematic trajectory comprising Renoir, Truffaut et al. In other words,

it can not be easily positioned within the 'art' cinema which dominates American critical perceptions of the French product. It is worth noting that Roger Ebert criticises the
decision to remake the film first because it is a 'bad' film and second because he claims
that the French film is itself a remake of John Ford's 1948 film, *Three Godfathers*. Certainly the basic premise of Ford's Western resembles *Trois hommes et un couffin*; three
outlaws (John Wayne, Harry Carey Jr. and Pedro Armendáriz) find an abandoned baby
in the desert and attempt to take it to safety. However the films differ tremendously.
Ford's baby is a boy, his genre is the western which turns almost to tragedy as two of the
three main characters die. Above all, the film does not use the enforced parenting to suggest a renegotiation of masculinity. Instead, via a multiplication of religious allusions
and imagery, he uses the baby to bring about the men's redemption, either through a
noble death (singing hymns in the case of Carey Jr. and via a selfless suicide for
Armendáriz) or through punishment and a new beginning in New Jerusalem in the case
of Wayne.

Nevertheless it is this concentration on masculinity and paternity which makes both
remake and source so much a product of their particular context of production and
reception. Their different treatments of these themes may have curtailed their success
in the country of their source/target however it is this same focus which helps us to
understand the decision to remake Serreau's film and the films' broader cinematic success. While articulation of these concerns is culturally specific, the themes themselves
are central to both French and American cinema and society in the 1980s and 1990s
(witness the numerous remake pairs dealing with the family and/or paternity). Without
wanting to over-simplify the reasons for the predominance of these themes in cinema
of the period, I think it is fair to say that in both cultures representation and reappraisal
of masculinity emerges from the shifts in society brought about by feminism and changing gender roles both within the work-place and the family. What is striking is that the
shift from crisis to a less problematic confusion, from ambivalence to coherence visible
in the pair of films discussed so far can also be discerned in many of the other remake
pairs concerned with gender and the family. Notable examples are Gérard Lauzier's *Mon
Père ce héros* (1991) and Steve Miner's *My Father the Hero* (1994). In each of the films
divorcee André (played by Gérard Depardieu in both versions) takes his adolescent
daughter Véronique/Nicole on an expensive foreign holiday. The daughter's initial hostility to her father becomes rather more complicated when she starts to pretend that he
is her lover in an attempt to attract the attention of a teenage boy staying at the same
hotel.

Depardieu's double role is significant here. Undoubtably his role in the remake plays
upon his work in Lauzier's film. However both films extend these allusions to the actor's
previous work, to the particular connotations of his star persona and, in the case of the
Hollywood production, to specific cinematic constructions of French identity embodied in the screen presence of Depardieu. In each of the films André helps his daughter
to write a love letter and then crouches beside her, beneath the balcony of her beloved,
providing her with the expressions of sentiment that will ultimately win his affection.
These scenes recall Depardieu's role in Jean-Paul Rappeneau's *Cyrano de Bergerac* (1990)
providing a playful extension of his screen presence intelligible to both French and
American audiences due to the relative success of the film in the United States. Refer-

ences are also made to Depardieu's other major success in the American market, Peter Weir's *Green Card* (1990), as he relishes 'smelly' French cheese and plays the piano so recalling the musical abilities and gastronomic excesses of his character in the earlier film.

However, the connotations provided by the Depardieu persona in remake and source are rather different. In France the actor's career has straddled both popular genres and art or auteur cinema and, as Ginette Vincendeau points out, this has enabled him to develop and connote a 'tragic' persona, a form of masculinity in crisis, alongside his comic heroes.[14] In Lauzier's film Depardieu plays upon both of these aspects; he is a comic figure caught up in the confusion that follows his daughter's claims that he is her lover and a source of melancholy, of paternity in crisis as he struggles to come to terms with their changing relationship and his concomitant jealousy. In the remake he is reduced to pure comedy, a transformation figured through his body which is shown to be much softer, more fleshy and so less threatening than in the French film, and his high-lighted blond hair and brightly coloured shirts. He is not able to connote the duality and ambiguity inscribed in his French star image, rather his success in the United States is based upon a particular notion of Frenchness constructed through cliché and stereotype. This was exemplified in *Green Card* by his *gauloise*-smoking, steak-eating entirely non-politically correct character and the process is furthered in Miner's film as André's 'relationship' with Nicole is repeatedly ascribed to his 'Frenchness'. This construction also articulates previous American cinematic representations of French identity. Early in the film some of his fellow hotel residents compare him to Louis Jourdan and Catherine Deneuve and at the hotel's talent night Depardieu bursts into a spirited, heavily accented rendition of 'Thank Heavens for Little Girls', echoing that seminal Hollywood depiction of France, Vincente Minnelli's *Gigi* (1954) and its star, Maurice Chevalier.

André (Gérard Depardieu) and Véro (Marie Gillain) in *Mon Père ce héros*.

André (Gérard Depardieu) and Nicole (Katherine Heigl) in *My Father the Hero*.

Along with this shift in star persona, the films reveal a transition from a rather low-key *comédie de moeurs* in the French version to a far broader more physical comedy in the remake. The Hollywood transformation of *Mon Père ce héros* thus mirrors the reworking of *Trois hommes et un couffin*: ambivalent male heroes become straightforward comic figures, gentle comic drama becomes broad farce and crisis in identity becomes initial confusion and the affirmation of a new status quo. Although both films negotiate the theme of paternity via the relationship between a father and his teenage daughter they do it in remarkably different ways. While the French film represents this father/daughter dyad in terms of incipient sexuality and Oedipal conflict, the remake suggests this incestuous threat and then hastens to disavow it, reinscribing the narrative within the tribulations of single parenthood and confusion and conflict through absence or distance. Whereas the remake seems to suggest that any confusion as to the relationship between André and Nicky stems only from her lies, in the French film this confusion is revealed as an integral part of the father/daughter relationship.

Once again these transformations need to be located within specific cinematic and cultural contexts. The French film's negotiations of the incestuous possibilities of the father/daughter relationship can not be abstracted from a wider examination of these concerns in French culture. Indeed, such representations of paternal seduction can be discerned across a broad range of French cultural artefacts, for example Françoise Sagan's *Bonjour Tristesse* (1954) and Serge Gainsbourg's celebrations of his daughter in his film *Charlotte Forever* (1986) and a subsequent song, 'Lemon Incest'. Within this particular tradition the title song of *Mon Père ce héros* is not insignificant. It is performed by Marie Gillain (Véro) in a breathy, child-like voice which reinforces the similarly infantile yet suggestive lyrics ('What I like is the cherry on the cake'). This particular performance style, exemplified by the likes of Jane Birkin and Vanessa Paradis, is enduringly popular in France, suggesting a fascination with the young girl, still child-like yet resonant with sexual promise. In contrast the American film actively denies such sexual possibilities. This rather hypocritical denial (the film's narrative after all does not change) is perhaps bound up with the fact that within the hegemony of political correctness, incest and paedophilia have become the great taboos of American society (witness anxieties about the spread of child pornography on the internet). Moroever, the physical comedy of the remake and its focus on the adolescent romance suggest that as a Disney production it was aimed at a young audience making the negation of a problematic sexuality all the more important.

Above all the films' different treatment of paternity must be linked to French and American constructions of gender and the impact of feminism described earlier in this chapter. Although Lauzier's film is a popular comedy and in no way intellectualises its narrative concerns, its rather more complex exploration of the father/daughter relationship reflects the constructions of masculinity in *Trois hommes et un couffin* to suggest a masculinity in crisis, an ambivalence *vis-à-vis* gender roles in a society in which feminist politics have called into question the very limits of identity. How can you be a father, particularly the father of a daughter, in a society in which what it means to be a man or a woman is far from clear? The open-endedness of both films is perhaps promising but certainly far from unproblematically progressive. Indeed, the very choice of a young girl as object of (albeit repressed) sexual desire in Lauzier's film suggests an anxiety about new powers achieved by women and it is striking that contemporary French production is dominated by similarly youthful female actors to the detriment of more mature women.[15] The American films also engage in a renegotiation of masculinity via paternity in the light of broader social changes linked partly to the impact of feminism. As Susan Jeffords remarks, many recent Hollywood productions have tended to replace the muscular action hero with a more nurturing family man, thus creating a new space for masculinity within 'post-feminist' society.[16] Of course it would be foolhardy to overstate the case and to make sweeping claims about 'post-feminism' and so on. However, I think it is fair to say that whereas in the French films discussed so far we can see an exploration of identity in crisis linked to French feminism's focus on 'difference' and the body, in the remakes we can see an attempt to construct a 'new man', a man able to take on the different domestic and labour roles demanded by the dominant political and social agendas of American feminism. Further evidence of this shift is provided by Francis Veber's films *Les Fugitifs* and *Three Fugitives*. Whereas the source film ends with the two male heroes, one of them still in drag, and the young child disappearing over the mountains hand in hand to start a new life as a family thus suggesting ambivalent gender identities and notions of parenting, the remake closes with an action sequence, Ned having already removed his wig. The men may stay together to raise the child and thus accept new responsibilities in the absence of a mother, but they do so as 'buddies', their heterosexual masculinity is not threatened.

I will return to the question of identity and the various ways in which it is reconstructed and transformed through the remake process in later chapters. It is indubitably a theme which lies at the very heart of an analysis of the remake. The narrative concerns of a great many of these films involve some form of identity negotiation. Moreover, the very act of moving a film across cultures calls into question its own identity as 'national' product, as comedy or melodrama, as 'art' film or popular movie and so on. The particular representations of paternity and masculinity described here reveal the rootedness of this focus in specific 'national' cultures (the films' transformations of these tropes are bound up with their differing contexts of production) and its simultaneous ability to transcend these 'national' boundaries (although they may treat them differently, remake and source share almost identical narrative themes and concerns). It is this very duality, the ability to both articulate and exceed national boundaries to which we will turn in Chapter 4 but certainly it does seem apparent that, beyond material concerns, this shared emphasis (of genre and themes) and a simultaneous difference manifested in these films and indeed many of their successors can explain the re-emergence of the remake in the 1980s.

Notes

1. For example, in *The Economist*, 27 February 1993; *Empire* no. 49, July 1993; *Studio* (French version) no. 73, May 1993.

2. Over ten million people saw *Trois hommes et un couffin* in its first year of release and it proved to be one of the most successful French films of the 1980s. Indeed, until the release of *Les Visiteurs* (1993), its box-office success was exceeded by only two other French films, *La Grande Vadrouille* (1966) and *Le Corniaud* (1965). It is worth noting that all of these films are comedies.

3. These articles include Tania Modleski, 'Three Men and Baby M', *Camera Obscura* no. 17, May 1988, pp. 69–81; Raymonde Carroll, 'Film et analyse culturelle: le remake', *Contemporary French Civilization* vol. 13 no. 2, Summer/Fall 1989, pp. 346–59; Anne-Marie Picard, 'Travestissement et paternité: la masculinité remade in the USA', *Cinémas* vol. 1 nos. 1–2, Fall 1990, pp. 115–31; Carolyn A. Durham, 'Taking the Baby out of the Basket and/or Robbing the Cradle: "Remaking" Gender and Culture in Franco-American Film', *The French Review* vol. 65 no. 5, April 1992, pp. 774–84.

4. For example *Le Gendarme de St. Tropez* (Jean Girault, 1964, France/Italy) and *Le Gendarme en ballade* (Jean Girault, 1970, France/Italy).

5. In his work *French Cinema in the 1980s: Nostalgia and the Crisis of Masculinity* (Oxford: Oxford University Press, 1997), Phil Powrie points out the 'hysterical mobility' of the three French men who, once left with the baby, constantly run from one end of the apartment to the other. This perhaps reinforces the relationship between space, style and narrative set up in the opening sequence. The mellow, dark space of the apartment contains and traps the frantic reactions of the men. In other words, the comedy introduced by the arrival of the baby is played out within this dark, rather melancholic interior, echoing and reinforcing the film's combination of comedy and drama. Similarly the shift from the detailed oil paintings of the French film to these cartoon-like murals mirrors and reinforces the move from the darkly comic French film to the extremely light-hearted remake.

6. For example Durham, 'Taking the Baby out of the Basket'.

7. Ibid., pp. 775–6.

8. Ibid., pp. 777–8.

9. Ibid., p. 782. She does however stress that the film's comic emphasis undermines a reading of this nature.

10. For more discussion of this see Lucy Mazdon, 'Remaking Paternity: *Mon Père ce héros* and *My Father the Hero*', in Phil Powrie (ed.), *French Cinema of the 1990s* (Oxford: Oxford University Press, 1999).

11. This is of course extended by the previously described treatment of the drugs narrative.

12. Roger Ebert, *Chicago Sun Times*, 5 February 1986, http://www.suntimes.com/ebert/ebert-reviews/1986/05/56283.html.

13. John Hartl, http://www.film.com/film-review/1985/10269/109/default-review.html.

14. Ginette Vicendeau, 'Gérard Depardieu: The Axiom of Contemporary French Cinema', *Screen* vol. 34 no. 4, Winter 1993, pp. 343–61.

15. See Ginette Vincendeau, 'Family Plots: The Fathers and Daughters of French Cinema', *Sight and Sound* vol. 1 no. 11, March 1992, pp. 14–17.

16. Susan Jeffords, 'The Big Switch: Hollywood Masculinity in the Nineties', in Jim Collins, Ava Preacher Collins and Hilary Radner (eds), *Film Theory Goes to the Movies* (London: Routledge, 1993), pp. 196–208.

4
Remaking National Histories, Remaking National Cinemas

The negative discourses which surround the remake process establish a one-way trajectory from the 'art' of the 'French' film to the debased commercialism of the 'American' remake. Within this trajectory the French film becomes an intrinsic part of French culture and thus an important mobiliser of the national identity. The American film threatens this identity by hijacking the French 'original' and producing a popular copy. As we have seen, this vision of the remake process is manifestly simplistic. It reposes upon a well-defined differentiation between the 'French' and 'American' cinematic product, a differentiation which in turn enables the valorisation outlined above. It denies the varying forms of exchange and interaction which identify the remake process. The tropes of intertextuality and the hybrid nature of the products of an increasingly globalised cinema industry undermine national identities, and yet the nation remains a central organising concept for many critical accounts of the practice. Indeed it is one of the central paradoxes of the remake that while demonstrating the *transnationalism* which lies at the heart of cinematic production it is also mobilised to reinforce the *national* identities which continue to dominate so much discussion of film and film industries.

As we saw in Chapter 1, audiovisual production is an essential tool in the construction of French national identity. The very existence of the Centre national de la cinématographie is testimony to the importance of cinematic production and it is significant that as many countries celebrated the hundredth anniversary of cinema in 1996, celebrations of the event were held throughout France in 1995 as the birth of cinema was traced back to the Lumière brothers in 1895. Thus cinema was presented as a *French* invention, an intrinsic part of the national cultural heritage. However, it is not sufficient to simply define French national cinema in terms of the role of the CNC and its discourses. Just as definitions of the nation are complex and shifting so cinema itself is an extremely multifarious system made up of films themselves, the discourses and images which surround and penetrate them and the industrial and cultural institutions within which they are produced, distributed and exhibited. The identification of a national cinema necessarily denies this plurality as it is based upon a sense of coherence and homogeneity, defined through similarity (the traditions of French cinema) and difference (Hollywood).

However, the establishment of a specifically national cinematic identity is problematised by the location of cinematic production in what is essentially an international industry. In order to achieve commercial success films must conform to standards which, although originating in Hollywood, are now globally dominant. National cinemas are faced with the paradox of attempting to create specifically national cultural artefacts within the context of a global industry. The traditional answer to this dilemma in Europe has been the production of a 'cinema of quality', a state-subsidised art cinema which is mobilised against Hollywood's 'mass production'. These films are often based upon other national cultural artefacts (classic novels for example) and involve prestigious actors, directors and other personnel. As Ginette Vincendeau demonstrates, these films borrow Hollywood's big-budget production values while differentiating themselves through subject matter (frequently historical and/or literary) and language. As such they can be seen to form a contrast with French auteur cinema which opposes Hollywood through *mise en scène* and subject matter which tends to be non-historical/non-literary.[1]

This opposition feeds into the discourse surrounding remakes and the positing of French high cultural artefacts, copied and popularised by Hollywood. The establishment of a national 'cinema of quality' in France in opposition to American mass culture demonstrates anxieties about globalisation and the undermining of European and French identity. However, the identification of French art cinema as a specifically national product is itself problematised by the fact that these films also circulate in a global market.[2] Moroever, as we saw in Chapter 1, France does not of course produce 'high' cultural artefacts alone. It is significant that of a list of the top fifty-eight films in France between 1956 and 1996, in terms of box-office revenue, twenty-five are French and thirteen of these are comedies. The biggest grossing film in France with 17.228 million admissions is still *La Grande Vadrouille* (1966) a Franco-British comedy starring Louis de Funès, directed by Gérard Oury. The identification of a specific, homogeneous French cinematic identity, defined through the discourses of 'art' and 'quality', is not a straightforward process. So-called 'French' films are frequently the result of international, often European, co-productions. Moreover, Hollywood itself can be seen as part of French national cinema. Through its enduring penetration of overseas markets, Hollywood production has become part of the cultural landscape of these nations. Above all it is vital to note the plurality of French cinemas. Just as it is impossible to define a unique, entire identity for cinema itself, so cinematic production in France is diverse and fragmented. It is composed of both the high cultural artefacts and the popular production already referred to yet this binary identity is itself dispersed by minority cinemas. The establishment of a national cinema necessitates a form of 'internal cultural colonialism'.[3] Along with the plurality of cinematic discourses themselves, the diversity of production is denied in order to enable the construction of a dominant, national cinematic entity.

Nevertheless, just as it is vital not to deny the importance of the nation as an organising concept so we should not ignore the construction of national cinemas despite the difficulties inherent to definitions of this discursive strategy. Nations mobilise films and other cultural artefacts in order to disseminate and reinforce a specific 'national' identity. Moreover, either explicitly or implicitly films interrogate the discourses of their particular moment and place of production. In other words, however precarious definitions of the 'nation' and of 'national cinemas' may be, films can be seen to emerge from, and to enter into debate with, specific national constructions. Different cinemas establish particular cultural identities via narrative and subject matter, genre and form, stars, industrial conventions and so on. Individual films are located within, and penetrated by, discourses of the 'national', and these films in turn interpellate 'national' audiences (themselves, just like the nation, 'imagined communities'). This process is then extended through the act of consumption as different audiences make sense of the films and their 'national' identity in a variety of ways.

This brings us back to the paradox described at the beginning of this chapter. A recognition of the plural and shifting nature of national identities, cultures and consumers prohibits attempts to simply condemn the Hollywood remake as a straightforward pilfering of an intrinsically French cultural product and thus as a threat to French cultural identity. The location of both films in a global film industry along with the various forms of exchange and interaction immanent to the practice make the remake a thoroughly *transnational* undertaking. However, as we have seen the films do indeed enter into dialogue with constructions of the nation and interpellate national audiences, and the French source is frequently held up as an exemplar of French film culture so the remake also reposes upon a construction of the *national*. In Chapter 4 we will look at two pairs of films, *Le Retour de Martin Guerre* (Daniel Vigne, 1982) and *Sommersby* (Jon Amiel, 1993), and *A bout de souffle* (Jean-Luc Godard, 1959) and *Breathless* (Jim McBride, 1983) and examine the ways in which they play out this fascinating paradox via their respective (re)constructions of 'national' histories and 'national' cinemas.

Both *Le Retour de Martin Guerre* and *Sommersby* are essentially costume dramas set in a specific moment in the national past. They share the same basic narrative structure; a man, Martin Guerre (Gérard Depardieu)/Jack Sommersby (Richard Gere), leaves his village, abandoning his wife and son. Years later a man returns claiming to be Guerre/Sommersby. His identity is initially accepted and he reinserts himself into the community proving to be a vastly improved husband, father and worker. However, fellow villagers subsequently question his identity and he is tried and eventually hanged. The two films achieved success both in their country of origin and abroad. *Le Retour de Martin Guerre* was a commercial success in France and, perhaps owing to critical approbation in Anglo-Saxon countries (Depardieu was elected best actor of 1982 by the Society of American Critics), it proved to be one of the most successful foreign films of the early 1980s in the United States. *Sommersby* also achieved box-office success in both France and the United States. Evidently it must be stressed that as a subtitled work distributed in art-house cinemas, the commercial potential of Vigne's film in North America was slight when compared to that of *Sommersby*, which was supported by all the power of Hollywood distribution. Nevertheless, what these commercial trajectories do show is that the two films achieved a certain crossover between the United States and France, a fact which both suggests a certain similarity and yet at the same time complicates any identification of the films as uniquely national products. This undermining of a specifically national identity is reinforced by the fact that a major co-producer of *Sommersby* was Le Studio Canal Plus, a French production company.

Le Retour de Martin Guerre is based upon a 'true' anecdote that has a long history in French popular folk tales. The written origins of the events are found in two contemporary accounts, published in Lyon in 1561, a year after the hanging of the impostor

Arnaud du Tilh, and later in Paris in slightly altered versions. The *Arrest Memorable* was written by Jean de Coras, the judge at the trial, and the *Admiranda historia* by Guillaume Le Sueur, a clerk. Since these initial accounts the tale has been retold many times, as a play, a novel, an operetta and, most recently, a stage musical entitled *Martin Guerre* by Boublil and Schonberg. This repetition of the narrative in various forms undermines any attempt to establish a binary opposition between Vigne's film and its American remake. *Le Retour de Martin Guerre* can surely not be perceived as an 'original', copied and thus threatened by Hollywood, when it is itself preceded by numerous other versions of the tale.

Vigne's film underlines the historical roots of its narrative through its insistence on historical veracity. Vigne and his script-writer, Jean-Claude Carrière, worked alongside an historical consultant, Natalie Zemon Davis, a specialist in the society and culture of early modern France. In her own account of the film-making process, Zemon Davis stresses her role in the film's representation of its historical and social location and her desire to ensure its accuracy.[4] This attempt to create a sense of historical verisimilitude is immediately made apparent by the film's opening voice-over narrative which reveals the precise temporal and geographical location of the events related, describing them as a 'real-life story'. The spectator is thus invited to view the film not as a piece of fiction, part of cinematic myth, but as a precise account of a true historical event. This veracity is reinforced by the film's attention to the details of costume and physical location and in its depiction of the everyday life of the village community. Zemon Davis discusses her admiration for René Allio's film of 1976, *Moi, Pierre Rivière* (based upon Michel Foucault's work of the same title),[5] explaining that she hoped to emulate its social and historical realism and its contemporary relevance. This comparison is significant as it locates Vigne's film in a specific French cinematic trend, beginning in the 1970s, which produced films dealing with the past but which deliberately rejected a positivist approach to history. Rather than recount the tales of 'great' historical figures and events, these films represent the 'reality' of everyday life. It is worth noting that Vigne himself, prior to *Le Retour de Martin Guerre*, was best known for a television series, *Le Paysage français*, for which Emmanuel Le Roy Ladurie worked as historical consultant. Le Roy Ladurie is renowned for his work with the *Annales* school which pioneered the study of a history rooted in common experience.

Sommersby's location in, and treatment of, history is very different. The narrative is set in the American South immediately after the Civil War. By transposing his film from sixteenth-century France to a specifically American location, Amiel ruptures its connections to earlier accounts of the tale and so denies its historical veracity. The film is set in a certain part of the United States at a certain moment but unlike *Le Retour de Martin Guerre* it does not reveal specificities. In contrast to the opening scenes of the French film which show images of Jean de Coras, the destination and source of the narrative, coupled with the aforementioned voice-over, the opening scenes of Amiel's film give no precise information. Time and location are suggested as we see soldiers in the uniforms of the Civil War, and 'Sommersby' travels from the cold of the North to the warmth of the South. However, whereas *Le Retour de Martin Guerre* sets out to suggest the truth of its history, its status as non-fiction, *Sommersby* is closer to other cinematic representations of the period, for example *Gone With the Wind* (1939), than to verifiable historic sources. It is perhaps worth noting that some of the film's costumes were originally used in Selznick/Fleming's film.

Instead the opening scenes concentrate on close-up shots of Richard Gere (Sommersby). The use of the close-up in classical Hollywood cinema is a privileged means of gaining knowledge of the psyche of individual characters and through use of the close-up here, it is immediately demonstrated that this is to be a film centred around this individual character with whom the audience is invited to identify. This process continues throughout the film as most major encounters are constructed around shot/counter-shot, in marked contrast to *Martin Guerre* which tends to show characters within social groups.[6] Indeed the film is essentially a love story, focusing on the relationship between Sommersby and his wife (Jodie Foster) and as we shall see, it eschews many of the issues raised in *Le Retour de Martin Guerre*. However, as a romantic drama, the film can be seen to fit into Hollywood genre conventions just as the source work can be located in a specific French tradition. As such the American film is not a straightforward copy, it has become something other.

The fact that both works are 'historical' films is not insignificant in terms of their location within, and construction of, the 'nation'. Both *Le Retour de Martin Guerre* and *Sommersby* can be described as costume drama. Although, as we have seen, their general historical settings can be determined, they do not deal with specific moments or events but rather situate their narratives in identifiable historical 'periods' albeit in somewhat different ways. However the insistence of Vigne's film upon its 'true' source may cause us to question its status as costume drama; should it perhaps be situated between costume drama and documentary? Such questions are not relevant to

Sommersby: Lauren (Jodie Foster) and Jack (Richard Gere).

Sommersby which makes no claims to historical fact and presents itself as pure fiction. Yet it should be stressed that however much history films may strive for veracity, adhering to what Marc Ferro terms 'the erudite tradition' of historical authenticity,[7] they remain fictions. However reliable their source materials may be, however many historians they may consult, the production of history films necessarily involves an imaginary reconstruction of the past. They are 'fictions' of the past, intrinsically rooted in the present in which they are produced and as such they are both representations of history and part of history themselves.

The history film's use of culturally specific references helps to explain their important role in constructions of myths of the nation. Representations of a 'national' past can be mobilised to underwrite the 'national' present. Through a complex process of coercion and consent, the history film becomes a site for the struggle over understanding. Our understanding of our collective past has traditionally been closely linked to popular memory (witness the early oral accounts of the life of Martin Guerre). Film and television usurp this role as they present images of the collective past to a 'national' audience and this is vital to the process of nation building; indeed a central part of the process of becoming a nation involves telling people what to remember and what to forget. Such a 'stifling' of popular memory entails a battle for the past and the attempted construction of a framework within which to understand the present. Yet, somewhat paradoxically, history films can also enable popular memory as they make visible people and events of the past that have otherwise been ignored. Certainly it should be stressed that films now play a crucial role in our understanding of our individual and collective past. Popular cinematic representations of history make available knowledge (albeit partial) hitherto reserved for the specialist.

Indubitably the relationship between cinema and history is both complex, and vital to representations of the nation and the national past. Both *Le Retour de Martin Guerre* and *Sommersby*, despite their differing emphasis on historical authenticity, should be perceived as fictions which, in various ways, interrogate and mobilise aspects of national myth and identity. The variations between the films in historical and geographical location are important in terms of the position of the two films within the cinematic traditions from which they emerge but also in terms of the specific cultural references upon which they draw and the version of the national past and present to which they can be seen to give voice. It is striking that while the source film appears to emerge from other forms of historical discourse (the contemporary accounts of the trial, the work of the *Annales* School, the research of Zemon Davis and so on) the remake draws heavily upon earlier *cinematic* representations of history. This is not to deny the attributes shared by Vigne's film and a number of other historical films described previously. However the shift from the quasi-cinéma vérité style of the source film to the lush melodrama of the remake suggests an articulation of rather different historical sources.

Certainly the references to other Hollywood films about the post-Civil War period in *Sommersby* are far from surprising; this is a key moment in American history frequently represented in cinematic production. However, the relations between *Le Retour de Martin Guerre* and other historical films merit a closer look for although it does seem that the film draws more explicitly on *non-cinematic* sources, the history, or rather 'heritage' film was beginning to emerge as a dominant force in France by the early 1980s. This begs the question as to whether its ostensible drawing on non-cinematic sources in fact masks a much closer connection to other filmic constructions of the past.

The 'heritage' film became a central feature of French cinematic production throughout the 1980s and on into the 1990s. Its hegemonic status is revealed by its ability to compete with, and indeed surpass, the domestic comedies and thrillers so long dominant at the French box-office.[8] Although the heritage genre is not easily defined, incorporating as it does a number of contrasting films, it is generally true that it will focus on some important aspect of the 'national' culture (a literary text or a 'great' figure or event of the past) and it will place much emphasis on high production values and visual spectacle. Noteworthy examples include Claude Berri's *Germinal* of 1993, *Jean de Florette* and its sequel, *Manon des Sources* (1986), Jean-Claude Rappeneau's *Cyrano de Bergerac* (1990) and his later film, *Le Hussard sur le toit* (1995). This genre, or sub-genre, is particularly striking in terms of a discussion of national cinemas. It can be located in a particular French cinematic trajectory reaching back to the *tradition de qualité* of the post-war period. Moreover, it became central to the construction and articulation of French cinematic and cultural identity during the 80s and 90s. It was actively supported and promoted by successive French governments, attracting significant sums of money via the *avance sur recettes* and other forms of subsidy, and, as we saw in Chapter 1, it was a vital tool in the struggle against Hollywood.[9]

However, just like the remake process the heritage genre reveals the problematic nature of definitions of the national. The development of the heritage film in France was mirrored by the production of similar types of film in Britain and elsewhere (for example, the highly successful Merchant-Ivory adaptations of a number of novels by E. M. Forster). In other words, like the remake the heritage film reveals a tension between articulations of the national and its location in a transnational film industry. The rather worrying nostalgia of a great many of these films suggests a recourse to hegemonic visions of the past in the face of an increasingly uncertain future which again resembles the defence of French cinema and culture in the face of global culture industries.

So *Le Retour de Martin Guerre* is far from being an isolated example of French filmic representations of history. Instead it emerges during a period when such representations, via the heritage genre, began to dominate the French cinematic landscape. However, it is my opinion that Vigne's work can not be described in terms of, nor inserted within, the hegemony of the heritage film. It does indeed, as Guy Austin points out, feature extensive exterior locations, numerous extras and rich soundtrack music and photography, all of which recall the heritage genre.[10] However, in contrast to the sweeping spectacle of films such as *Cyrano de Bergerac* and *Le Hussard sur le toit* the film remains anchored in the harsh realities of medieval peasant life. The cinematography is drained of colour, suggesting the dirt and poverty of the village. There are no obvious heroes in Vigne's film; the story tells of 'Martin' yet he remains at best an ambiguous figure. Above all, the film does not present the unifying vision of an uncontested national past which, it seems to me, lies at the heart of the heritage project. Instead it is a film shot through with the uncertainty and unknowability of identity. Vigne's film may well herald the emergent heritage genre but its connection to this body of work is I believe, tenuous.

The events of *Le Retour de Martin Guerre* take place between 1542 and 1560, a time during which France was involved in wars with Spain and the struggle between Catholicism and Protestantism. Evidently the Jacobin notion of a centralised national identity, forged by the Revolution, was not in existence at this time. This is a period during which French identities were in a process of construction. Central to this struggle for identity was religion and it is significant that the film informs us that Jean de Coras was a Protestant, killed during the notorious massacre of Saint Bartholomew in 1572, twelve years after the trial of Martin Guerre; the instability of these times, the struggle for identity through religion, is thus underlined. However, Vigne and Carrière articulate this pre-Revolutionary moment through a post-Revolutionary ideology of liberty and universal human rights. Zemon Davis points out that the court scene is historically erroneous. The film depicts an open court, filled with the villagers and other spectators despite the fact that courts at this time were not open to the public and were thus far more forbidding than that shown in the film. Furthermore, a contrast is established between the superstition of the village priest and the rationality of Coras. However, Zemon Davis points out that Coras did indeed believe in the devil and stated in his own account of the events that Arnaud du Tilh had conjured up a spirit in order to acquire his knowledge of Martin Guerre. She claims that Coras was presented as a Protestant man of the Enlightenment, feeding in to a tendency in France to think of Protestantism in terms of the rational tolerance of Pierre Bayle rather than the zeal and doctrines of Calvin.[11] It would seem that the film presents a moment in the nation's past from the perspective of subsequent French history. In this way the film enables an interrogation of the

Martin (Gérard Depardieu) defends his identity in court in *Le Retour de Martin Guerre*.

antecedents and foundations of a unified national identity based upon rationalism, liberty and justice.

Le Retour de Martin Guerre examines the very constitution of identity. Is identity determined through vision, the sight of Martin's bodily presence as he returns to the village, through the touch of the blind woman in the courtroom, or through writing, Bertrande's signature? Each of these affirmations of identity is ultimately proved false and thus the film seems to suggest the instability of identity, its inessential and hence performative nature. Arnaud du Tilh, the imposter, proves that identity can be assumed by anyone. He is simultaneously Arnaud, Pansette and Martin and he fulfils the role of the latter more successfully than the 'first' Martin Guerre, finally filling the leggings made for him by his wife. This usurpation of the 'original' Martin provides an interesting allegory of the history film; the history film is fiction which tries to persuade the spectator of its authenticity just as Martin/Depardieu must persuade the villagers of *his* identity.

Vigne's film can then be understood as a metaphor for the very construction of national identity, its instability and temporality, a metaphor which underlines and reinforces the previously discussed interrogation of a specifically French history and identity. Just as national identity is based upon similarity and difference so the acceptance of 'Martin's' identity as he returns to the village is founded both upon his similarity to the original Martin and upon difference, as, 'forgetting' names and faces he points out to what extent people have changed. The film's articulation of identity as liminal and inherently unstable can be seen to coincide with the construction of national identity. National cultures may present themselves as stable and enduring but this is a necessary misrecognition. Instead they are in a constant process of construction, never fully formed and always shifting. This notion of the liminality of national identity is underlined by the interrogation of French history and identity in *Le Retour de Martin Guerre*. It is surely not insignificant that the film was produced as the Socialist government came to power in France, heralding a period of both continuity (the reassertion of the French democratic tradition and cultural heritage) and change (a new plurality and a shift in what it meant to be French). Thus the film's very interrogation of the instability of identity enabled readings emerging from a 'micro' context of similar interrogation while at the same time engaging with a 'macro' context of long-standing tradition through the depiction of history.[12]

Jon Amiel's film, *Sommersby*, is also set in a time of uncertainty and change, the immediate aftermath of the American Civil War. In terms of the mobilisation of national myths and the film's identity as a national artefact this is a significant choice. The Civil War and the reconstruction period which followed it can be seen as founding moments in the construction of American identity. Unlike *Le Retour de Martin Guerre* which focuses on a community, Amiel's film concentrates on an individual, the supposed Jack Sommersby. The film plays upon the American tradition of individualism and individual effort, constructing a heroic representation of the enlightened saviour. Despite a similar narrative structure based upon the dissembling of identity, *Sommersby* differs from Vigne's film in that it does not attempt to question the construction of identity. This is perhaps significant in that the film emerges from an American society based upon the notion of the melting pot, the right to plurality and difference. 'Jack's' new identity serves as a metaphor for the reconstruction of American society and the enabling of this multi-cultural society. He represents the American capitalist dream that every man and woman can become what he or she wants to be through individual effort; identity is something to be earned.

The representation of this conception of identity is reinforced by the significant difference in the ending of the two films. In Vigne's film the first Martin Guerre returns underlining the doubling and dissemination of identity that is a central theme of the film. We learn that Arnaud du Tilh is an imposter and yet his effective assumption of the role of Martin demonstrates the performative nature of identity. In *Sommersby* the opening scenes show the supposed Jack burying a body which we later learn is the real Jack Sommersby. The doubling of identity is not an issue in this film; indeed in an early scene we see Laurel, Jack's wife, putting out a photograph of her husband, suggesting that identity can in some way be fixed and that such doubling is implausible. Horace Townsend earns the right to assume the identity of Jack Sommersby through his hard work and sacrifice on behalf of the village and his family. At the end of the film Townsend/Sommersby is hanged like Arnaud du Tilh. However, he is hanged for the past crimes of Sommersby, having chosen to retain the identity to which he has given rebirth through his attainment of peace and prosperity for the village community. The film does seem to suggest a certain complicity on the part of Jack's wife in his deception. Early scenes showing them looking at their reflections in a shaving mirror and her words 'Who is this man sitting in my kitchen?' suggest that she does not 'know' him but chooses to accept his identity. This is reinforced at the end of the film when she abandons her attempts to prove that he is Horace Townsend in order to save his life, accepting his right to take on the identity of her dead husband. Amiel's film represents identity as something to be earned, a discourse that can indubitably be located within the ideology of an American capitalist meritocracy where what you are, or what you become, supposedly depends upon how hard you are prepared to work.

It is perhaps somewhat paradoxical that Amiel's film shows Jack Sommersby earning his identity within the ideological context of a libertarian, capitalist society and yet at the same time represents him as a founder of the self-same society. The film's rather uncomfortable racial politics suggest that through the endeavours of the white hero, blacks and whites begin to work together establishing the beginnings of the 'melting pot' culture. In contrast to the priest in *Martin Guerre*, superstition here does not emanate from the Reverend but from those Southerners who refuse to accept the rebirth enabled by Jack and the construction of a 'new' American identity. By depicting them as the 'bad' characters, Amiel reinforces the film's affirmation of the foundation of a specific ideological construction of American society. It is perhaps significant that just as *Le Retour de Martin Guerre* was produced as the Socialists came to power in France so *Sommersby* was released as Bill Clinton became President in the United States after years of Republican rule. In a review of the film in *Sight and Sound*, Jason Drake describes Jack Sommersby as a 'Clintonesque figure',[13] a comparison reinforced by Richard Gere's vocal support for Clinton prior to the presidential elections. Clinton based his campaign upon an ideology of rebirth and renewal for American society, thus, just as *Martin Guerre* engages with both a micro and a macro national context, so *Sommersby*'s articulation of these themes can be seen to voice myths of the national past and to emerge from a specific national present. Indeed by making visible the process of renewal after the Civil War and the foundations of an enduring vision of American identity, the film enabled a viewing which gave a sense of anchorage and stability to contemporary plans for renewal.

It is not insignificant that both films interrogate moments of great upheaval and social change in the national past. *Sommersby* is manifestly set in the period of reconstruction which followed the American Civil War and, as suggested above, *Le Retour de Martin Guerre* can be seen to represent the period prior to the French Revolution in terms of Revolutionary and post-Revolutionary discourses of enlightenment, liberty and justice. Pierre Sorlin describes both these events as 'original shocks' or 'starting points' against which subsequent history is defined.[14] Constant interrogation emphasises their central position in national history and identity; since the earliest days of cinema there have been about 800 American films on the Civil War and forty French films on the Revolution.[15] Significantly Sorlin only cites films dealing explicitly with these events, ignoring those films which interrogate them implicitly. Marc Ferro discusses cinematic representations of history in terms of their 'non-visible areas of reality' which, he claims, can reveal as much as, or perhaps more than, their manifest content.[16] The French Revolution can similarly be described as the latent content of *Martin Guerre* as the film depicts and/or suggests those aspects of French society which can be seen to pre-date and indeed give rise to the Revolution; the Wars of Religion which led to the establishment of an absolute monarchy, the enlightenment tradition, and the three 'estates' which made up French society prior to the Revolution: clergy (the *curé*), nobility (de Coras) and the third estate (including wealthy peasants such as the Guerre family).

Both the Revolution and the Civil War are founding moments in the establishment of national identity. France was not a nation-state before the Revolution; indeed the creation of a unified nation was a central legacy of the Revolutionary period. The Civil War can be seen to have a similar role in American history. Although the popular image of this war is of a battle to emancipate Southern slaves, like the French Revolution the Civil War was a bourgeois revolution. The war may have brought about the freedom of the slaves but it also established the political hegemony of the Northern industrial and financial bourgeoisie and laid the foundations for the emergent capitalist nation-state. Both the French Revolution and the American Civil War led to the overthrow of old feudal systems and the ensuing dominance of industrial capitalism. Each then has resonances in the other culture (perhaps helping to explain the success of *Martin Guerre* and *Sommersby* both in France and the United States). Yet at the same time these events were founding moments in the construction of the individual nation-state and as such are firmly rooted in the national past. Indeed, not only have France and the United States constructed their respective national identities via these founding events, but as we have seen their differing concepts of democracy and revolution have also long formed the corner-stone of Franco-American relations. It becomes vital to interrogate these moments as they are simultaneously used to underwrite the national present (witness the use of the Revolution as a founding myth by the French Socialist party during the early 1980s) and threatened, as an increasing globalisation led to a crisis in democratic traditions throughout the 1980s. The mobilisation of the Revolution of 1789 and the

Civil War in *Le Retour de Martin Guerre* and *Sommersby* demonstrates the location of these films within a 'national' culture and their articulation of national myths. A striking image in both films shows young children staring at a gibbet. This occurs at the beginning of *Sommersby* as 'Jack' makes his way back to the village and at the end of *Le Retour de Martin Guerre* as preparations are made for the hanging of 'Martin'. The different narrative location of this image in each film underlines their contrasting trajectories and treatment of history/identity. Whereas the remake moves towards cohesion and renewal so suggesting a unifying version of the past (the film's closing images show the prosperity which is the legacy of 'Jack's' efforts), the source film ends in death and disarray leaving us with a fractured, violent vision of history.

Despite their obvious differences both of these films can be seen to articulate concerns about the national present through their representations of the national past. They are part of a wide cinematic tradition of historical drama which can be seen to shape collective memories, represent specific histories and reconstruct national identities. As Anne Friedberg points out, cinema offers an ideal site for this type of interrogation and reconstruction of the past as through its 'mobilized, virtual gaze' it enables boundless travel through space and time.[17] She claims that in the act of cinema viewing the past is uprooted and becomes a part of the present, and that by so bringing the past into the present, cinema radically changed the way people experienced both their collective and personal past. The history film is an exceptionally privileged site for the articulation and interrogation of national identities. As *Le Retour de Martin Guerre* and its American remake demonstrate, they enable a focus on moments in the national past which in turn enable representation and/or critique of national myths and the construction of national identities, which can then make possible a fresh understanding of contemporary society.

This account of these two films serves to demonstrate some of the complex ways in which cinema mobilises national identity and is itself mobilised as part of that identity, underlining both the position of the films within specific national cinematic industries and their exchange and interpenetration. Furthermore, the films' differing articulations of the nation demonstrate once again the highly reductive nature of accounts of the remake as a straightforward copy of a French 'original' and as a threat to a specifically French national identity. The French film and its remake are separate artefacts; indeed the production of a remake can be seen to create a new audience for the work upon which it was based, witness *Le Retour de Martin Guerre* which was re-released on video in Britain as 'the film remade as *Sommersby*'. It does then seem that in the case of the cinematic remake, reworking and adaptation within another national context can be seen as an extension, an addition to the source film rather than as an explicit threat to its identity and the identity of its country of production.

History is a privileged site for representations and interrogations of national identity. However, as we have seen, many other aspects of cinematic production and cinematic culture can also be mobilised to construct or 'narrate' the nation. I will now turn to *A bout de souffle* (Jean-Luc Godard, 1960) and its remake of 1983, *Breathless* (Jim McBride), in order to examine to what extent each of these films can be seen to constitute and/or transgress a particular national aesthetic. In other words, in what ways do they bolster up or undermine the hegemonic cinema so central to the construction of national cultural identity?

Godard's film had an immediate and enduring impact on cinematic culture, both in France and beyond. Although the first full-length film of Godard's career, *A bout de souf-fle* was his most successful work in terms of the box-office, attracting almost 260,000 spectators in the seven weeks of its first run in Paris in March 1960. It was also a criti-cal success, inciting much comment upon its innovation and transgression of the established codes of contemporary French cinema. Godard himself stressed this inno-vation and its centrality to his project in *A bout de souffle*, 'What I wanted to do was to take a conventional story and then remake, in different ways, all the cinema which had come before.'[18] The film has since been canonised as a seminal work of the *nouvelle vague*, consequently the film is commonly perceived as an exemplar of a typically French or European 'art' cinema, a high cultural artefact. This is perhaps especially true of exter-nal perceptions of *A bout de souffle*, for outside France the *nouvelle vague* tends to be defined quite straightforwardly as 'art' cinema, ignoring the complexities and diversity of the works subsumed under this title and their interrogation of the very concept of traditional 'art' cinema through the development of the *politique des auteurs*.

By describing Godard's film as 'art' cinema, critics conveniently situate it in a specifi-cally French and European tradition of great art and high culture. We have already acknowledged the problematic nature of any attempts to posit clearly defined 'French' or 'European', 'art' or 'popular' cinemas. Nevertheless such discourses merit mention at this juncture as both within its country of production and abroad, critical debate has incorporated *A bout de souffle* within the broad context of 'art' cinema. Cinema can be perceived as a tripartite structure consisting of the commercial cinema, art cinema (which is at once both within and without commercial production), and experimental or avant-garde cinema. Pamela Falkenberg describes these divisions as the classical nar-rative cinema, the art cinema and the modernist cinema.[19] Godard's film can be seen to originate in the third category along with much of his later work. The film was produced on an extremely modest budget; 40 million francs at 1959 value or approximately half the average budget for French production of that period. Although this money was pro-vided by producer Georges de Beauregard, Godard had almost complete control of the project. He refused to use the machinery of the studio, preferring to shoot in natural light using a hand-held camera. The film's intertextuality, including allusions to high cultural artefacts such as Patricia's quotation of Faulkner's *Wild Palms*, made 'high' cul-tural demands upon the audience. Experiments with dialogue and editing refused the coherence of a classical narrative trajectory. As a result he overturned many of the tra-ditions of French art cinema, situating his work outside this genre and producing an innovative and independent 'modernist' work.

However, unlike his later works which remained within avant-garde or experimental cinema, *A bout de souffle* was subsequently critically appropriated as an art cinema arte-fact. Its relative commercial success began this process and, as Godard's innovation influenced later films and became accepted cinematic practice, so it became the semi-nal film of the *nouvelle vague* and part of a different cinematic field. Indeed, the early success of the New Wave films led producers to screen them in mainstream cinemas, so relocating them within commercial production. However, this strategy proved ineffi-cient as audiences rejected their experimentation and by 1963 very few of the so-called New Wave films were exhibited at all. Significantly, many of the directors involved in this work, for example Truffaut and Chabrol, later joined mainstream production. Somewhat paradoxically, early distribution practices shifted many of the films of the *nouvelle vague* from the avant-garde into the domain of commercial art cinema while also contributing to the demise of the 'movement'.

Nevertheless, through this location within the *nouvelle vague* and a French art/auteur cinema, Godard's film has been accorded a specifically French cinematic identity. The very term *nouvelle vague* confers homogeneity upon a group of films and directors which was in reality quite disparate. Moreover, by grouping works within a 'movement' which is commonly perceived as inherently and uniquely French, critical discourse, both within France and beyond, enables the description of these films as national products and ignores the complications to which this definition gives rise. The New Wave was seen by critics to rejuvenate French cinematic production, establishing a new 'French' identity and reasserting aesthetic dominance, 'Ten years ago the best cinema in the world was Italian. [...] Today the best cinema in the world is unquestionably French.'[20]

This appropriation and incorporation of *A bout de souffle* within a European art cinema and a French national cinema demands deconstruction. We have already seen that the film is highly intertextual. However its intertexts are not only the 'high' cultural items already referred to but also, and indeed more importantly, a welter of popular cultural artefacts. Godard's film demonstrates a fascination with the popular icons of contemporary France; the girlfriend visited by Michel in the early scenes of the film smokes Lucky Strikes and listens to Radio Luxembourg, Michel's drive from Marseilles to Paris suggests a new concept of France based upon tourism and the recent availability of the car.

The most striking and recurrent intertexts of *A bout de souffle* are its references to Hollywood cinema. The film's roots are evidently situated in the gangster films of the 1930s and 1940s and in film noir, a genre or style which was highly popular in the United States during the early days of Godard's work as a film critic and cinema spectator. These roots are made explicit by the film's opening dedication. The introductory quotation to Truffaut's script, upon which the film was based, was from Stendhal and part of a specifically French high cultural tradition. In contrast, Godard dedicates his film to Monogram Pictures, a small American production company specialising in B movies, low budget westerns and crime series. Godard very deliberately names his intertexts, shifting his film from the domain of the specifically French to something other derived from mass culture and Hollywood.

The film's narrative borrows from the same genres, presenting as it does a criminal anti-hero doomed to failure and death by his love for a dangerous woman.[21] Godard himself commented upon the film's faithfulness to its Hollywood models, particularly in terms of its ending, 'The ending caused me some problems. Should the hero die? [...] In the end I decided that as my intention was to make a normal gangster film I shouldn't necessarily contradict the genre: the guy would have to die.'[22] *A bout de souffle* contains abundant references to American mass culture and Hollywood cinema. Michel is obsessed with both, the former typified by American cars and the latter by Humphrey Bogart. His love for Patricia, an American woman, is bound up with these desires; he wants the woman to go with the car and the films. This identification of Patricia with American mass culture is made explicit by the telephone conversation during which

A bout de souffle: Michel (Jean-Paul Belmondo) and Patricia (Jean Seberg) on the Champs Elysées.

Michel refers to '*une belle américaine*', meaning a car. Patricia overhears and assumes that it is to her that he is referring. Michel models himself upon Bogart, frequently running his finger across his lips in a gesture copied from his cinematic hero. The film depicts Michel outside a cinema which is showing *The Harder They Fall* (Mark Robson, 1956), gazing at a photograph of Bogart, running his fingers across his lips. The scene inter-cuts between Belmondo and Bogart, each in medium close-up and, as Steve Smith points out, filling the frame despite the diminutive size of the photo, and establishing an identification between the two.[23] Michel/Belmondo both is and isn't Bogart. He wears the fedora of the gangster and yet sports it at a jaunty angle, transgressing gangster style while at the same time imitating it. The film takes place within the city, preferred location of the gangster film and film noir, yet here the city is not Los Angeles but Paris. Nevertheless, it is this imitation which propels the narrative; in enacting this imitation Michel must remain in Paris, must pursue Patricia, must die. In other words, he must fulfil the role of a noir/gangster hero, he must be Bogey. The film both transgresses and copies the codes of its cinematic intertexts but it is this imitation which decides the direction of the narrative.

This outline of *A bout de souffle*'s Hollywood intertexts serves to demonstrate the film's relationship with American popular culture. Evidently these 'Americanisms' problematise attempts to locate Godard's film within a specifically French art cinema. The film overtly borrows from and imitates cinematic genres which are neither French nor a part of high culture and so its own identity is called into question. Godard was not the

A bout de souffle: Michel (Jean-Paul Belmondo).

only French director of the period to seek his cinematic roots in American mass culture (and as we shall see in Chapter 6 he was certainly not the last). Indeed, such influence was apparent in many French films of the 1950s and 1960s, particularly the '*polars*' or '*séries noires*' which were often adapted from translations of popular American detective stories and which were strongly influenced by the conventions of film noir. Among these films were those of Jean-Pierre Melville, for example *Bob le Flambeur* of 1956. Godard openly refers to this film in *A bout de souffle* during the scene in Tolmatchoff's travel agency and Melville appears in Godard's work as the writer Parvulesco. By situating his film within this wider intertextuality, Godard further undermines notions of a specifically French cinema and at the same time interrogates this tradition of influence.

The reappraisal of American directors and the development of auteur theory, to which Godard was so central, are significant in terms of attempts to describe *A bout de souffle* and other so-called New Wave films as part of a specifically French 'art' cinema. The work of the *Cahiers* critics undermined some of the long-standing oppositions between a French cinema of quality and American mass culture. Indeed, by identifying the personal within the products of Hollywood the critics enabled a re-examination of the very concept of mass culture and its impact. This is not to suggest that they praised mass production as such; rather, they questioned the overarching definition of Hollywood as mass entertainment, and appropriated some of its directors for the domain of high culture. The *politique des auteurs* did not discard the notion of 'mass' and 'high' culture, indeed it was at the root of subsequent polarisations of French cinematic production into 'art' (the work of the individual auteur) and 'popular entertainment' (mass production unmarked by the particular genius of the director), a fact which adds to the problematic nature of attempts to locate Godard's film in either category. Nevertheless, it did attempt to posit a more dialectical understanding of the relationship between the two, an understanding which would undermine traditional perceptions of Hollywood and France as always and already positioned on either side of the cultural fence.

It does then seem a dangerous venture to describe *A bout de souffle* as part of a specifically French cinematic aesthetic or indeed as a 'high' cultural artefact. Godard's film deliberately rejects the French cinematic tradition which precedes and surrounds it, instead seeking explicit intertexts in the films of Hollywood. Its national specificities (Paris, its 'star', Belmondo) are both imitations and transgressions of the codes of Hollywood genre cinema and so they lose their national specificity, becoming liminal, something at once both French and other. Similarly, the film is situated on the cusp of high and popular cinemas. Its experimentation and innovation seem to situate it within the context of avant-garde and/or art cinema yet its imitation of Hollywood production and its popular cultural references relocate it within commercial entertainment. It would seem that the identification of *A bout de souffle* as a uniquely French 'art' film is symptomatic of a retrospective homogenisation of the diversity of the work of the New Wave period (paradoxically arising from the polarisation in French production instigated by the discourses of auteurism). The 'movement's' impact on French cinematic production was such that it is now frequently perceived as a founding moment in a specifically French aesthetic of film. As a result the fragmentation and shifting identities of both the 'movement' itself and of individual works are denied.

In contrast, Jim McBride's *Breathless* tends to be critically located within the industrial and aesthetic traditions of Hollywood. Comment on the film frequently draws a clear distinction between the 'art' of *A bout de souffle* and the commercial nature of the remake. McBride's use of an established star (Richard Gere) in contrast to the (then) relatively unknown Belmondo, colour film stock and sophisticated production values, and the film's 'simplification' of Godard's dialogue and narrative are cited in order to justify descriptions of *Breathless* as 'pure Hollywood', 'Curiously McBride's film resembles an old Hollywood classic that a beginner named Godard would dig up in order to make, in 1959, a superb "remake" which would change everything.'[24] This location of *Breathless* within Hollywood commercialism underpins a subsequent set of oppositions between Godard's film as 'high culture' and 'original production' and the remake as 'debased mass culture' and 'copy' or reproduction.

McBride's film *is* a reproduction; it follows Godard's narrative closely and it was released in France as *A bout de souffle made in USA* so drawing explicit attention to its status as remake and its 'Americanisation' of a French cinematic work (the title also refers to Godard's film of 1966, *Made in U.S.A.*). However, the relationship between the two films is far less straightforward than these oppositions would suggest. It should be remembered that *Breathless* is a reproduction of a reproduction; it reappropriates for Hollywood Godard's own appropriation and transformation of a specific Hollywood tradition. Pamela Falkenberg sees the films in terms of their attempts to transform the commercial cinema in which they are situated through transformation of another cinematic tradition. In other words, both films function as reproductions while performing an equivalent if inverse rewriting.[25] Evidently the films cannot be perceived of in terms of 'original' and 'copy', as both perform an act of reproduction or transformation. Moreover, the description of *Breathless* as a typical product of Hollywood is itself problematic. At the time of the making of this film, Jim McBride was not part of the Hollywood 'mainstream'. Rather he emerged from American 'underground' production; in *David Holzman's Diary* (1967) for example he chose the format of a film diary, a determinedly non-commercial cinema, in order to attempt a demystification of cinéma vérité. As such he can be seen to engage in an experimentation and innovation not unlike that of Godard.

It is significant that McBride's career as a director began during the 1960s, the time of the *nouvelle vague*. The films of this period had an important impact upon Hollywood which was searching for novelty in order to counteract the dangers posed by the decline of the studio system and the advent of television. The techniques of the New Wave influenced many of those working at this time and helped to create the aesthetic developments subsequently dubbed the 'New Hollywood'. *Breathless* must be situated within these changes and as part of a Hollywood production much influenced by European 'art' cinema; as such its status as pure Hollywood 'mass entertainment' becomes untenable.

This is not to deny out of hand the film's identity as a product of Hollywood. Its use of an established star, its narrative based upon an outlawed 'anti-hero' and the fulfilment of heterosexual love, and its privileging of action above dialogue all serve to link it to a specifically Hollywood tradition which is located both in the past (the gangster films of the 30s and 40s) and the present (action films of the late 70s and early 80s). Yet these same features can also be seen to transgress the codes of mainstream Hollywood production. The narrative remains partly open, there is no full resolution. The closing scenes of the film depict Jesse (Gere) dancing in front of the armed police who have come to arrest/shoot him. As he bends down to pick up a gun the image freezes, fixing him in this parodic gesture of dance and (potential) death. The film neither depicts his death nor the resolution of the narrative of desire. Monica (Valerie Kaprisky) runs towards him as he dances but is excluded from the final freeze-frame. The film's portrayal of heterosexual sex, while linking it to a Hollywood tradition which refuses depiction of non-heterosexual or transgressive sexual activity, serves at the same time to marginalise it as its 18 certificate distances it from the 'family' films which are central to mainstream Hollywood production.

It is not insignificant that McBride's film is much admired by director Quentin Tarantino.[26] Tarantino's own work (for example *Reservoir Dogs*, 1991 and *Pulp Fiction*, 1994) has enjoyed both critical and commercial success, locating it within and without mainstream American production. Like *Breathless* his films quote and incorporate other popular cultural artefacts while depicting graphic scenes of violence (in contrast to the sexual activity portrayed in McBride's film) which preclude them from the 'family' audience. *Pulp Fiction* quotes briefly from both *Breathless* and Godard's *Bande à part* (1964), establishing a relationship which underlines the necessity of perceiving McBride's film as part of a non-Hollywood tradition which is situated within both popular and commercial cinema. Just as *A bout de souffle* can be seen as both French and not French, art and entertainment, so *Breathless* can be seen to shift between the discourses of Hollywood, European art cinema and American independent production. Interesting comparisons can be drawn with Gus Van Sant's 1998 remake, *Psycho*. His film provoked a great deal of critical hostility; it was an affront to Hitchcock's classic 'original' and, as a more or less shot-for-shot copy, was deemed by many to be a rather pointless exercise. However, Van Sant himself described the film as a homage to cinema, an experiment which makes us re-view Hitchcock's film and rethink the very notion of (re)production. He draws parallels with the works of Marcel Duchamps and Andy Warhol, aligning his critically condemned film with the traditions of 'high' art. He laments the fact that the studios marketed his film as a conventional thriller so undermining the intellectual project of his work.[27] McBride's film can also be seen as a homage to *A bout de souffle*, a taking to extremes of Tarantino's admiring quotations and a means of making us reconsider the source film and the act of reproduction itself. However like the remake of *Psycho*, these discourses are inevitably curtailed by subsequent distribution and consumption of the film.

Breathless can perhaps most usefully be seen as a simulation or simulacrum, as a copy which no longer possesses a referent, the object of a 'hyperreality' in which 'reality' and the 'past' have been eclipsed and disappeared.[28] The referent to which *Breathless* alludes is *A bout de souffle*, itself a simulation. The remake is then the representation of a representation, its authorial expression a hyperexpression modelled upon Godard's expression which in turn remodels its own defunct referents. This eclipsing of the past and reality, this constant recycling of images, was remarked upon by Serge Daney in his review of McBride's film:

> There is something fascinating about the way American cinema always, everywhere, knows how to recuperate and recycle ideas, making them anodyne and timeless. *A bout de souffle*, like all Godard's films, is an old, dated film. *Breathless*, like all American films is already ageless. It has no wrinkles, it's true, but then it never will have.[29]

The discourses of postmodernism seem especially pertinent to a discussion of *Breathless*. McBride's film is pastiche, the fragmentation and incorporation of both *A bout de souffle* (the simulation of simulation) and what Fredric Jameson calls the 'whole "degraded" landscape of schlock and kitsch'.[30] Jesse is fascinated with the songs of Jerry Lee Lewis and the *Silver Surfer* comic strips. This mirrors Michel's identification with Bogart yet Jesse's imitation is two-fold and entirely depthless as he models himself on both Michel and his American heroes. Moreover, unlike Godard, McBride does not attempt to reappropriate these artefacts for high culture. They are pure simulacrum, the representation of objects without referent, a flatness or depthlessness which Jameson describes as the 'supreme formal feature of all the postmodernisms'.[31]

This depthlessness is made explicit during a scene in which Monica is followed by a police officer who is in turn followed by Jesse. This three-way chase mimics that of *A bout de souffle*, yet here its circular and hence parodic nature is reinforced by the painted representations of Los Angeles in front of which it takes place. Similarly, in an earlier scene Monica waits for a bus in front of a sign which reads 'Hollywood Wax Museum. Mingle with the Stars'. This juxtaposition of the film's female 'star' and an advertisement

Jesse (Richard Gere) in front of painted murals in *Breathless*.

for copies of the stars invokes both the film's identity as a 'copy' and its postmodern depthlessness. Indeed, the double simulation of *Breathless* is apparent in the film's cinematic quotations. Its principal intertext is *A bout de souffle*, yet, just as Godard's film refers to Hollywood production of the 1930s and 1940s, so *Breathless* contains elements of these same works. This is manifest in the film's narrative (which follows closely that of Godard) and in explicit reference to earlier films. For example, Monica and Jesse hide in a cinema and mimic the action shown on the screen. The film projected is *Gun Crazy* (Joseph H. Lewis, 1950), which tells the story of a man and a woman who set off on a trail of armed robbery and murder, in other words the story of Jesse and Monica. Significantly it was produced by Monogram Pictures and so McBride underlines the reproductive trajectory of his film; *Breathless* simulates *A bout de souffle* which simulates Hollywood crime films which are in turn simulated by *Breathless*.

Jesse/Gere himself becomes a highly postmodern artefact in this film. Jameson perceives representations of the human figure as sites for a postmodern 'waning of effect': the repudiation of depth and authenticity in favour of multiple surfaces. Human figures are 'commodified and transformed into their own images'.[32] Jesse is a mass of fetishised icons; the film's opening scene focuses on the steel toe-caps of his boots. Significantly he does not change his clothes until his arrival in Los Angeles and his realisation that he is wanted by the police. Here he purchases a new set of clothes from a second-hand store which he then wears throughout the rest of the film. He becomes these clothes which are at once new (to him) and old (second-hand); like the film Jesse is pastiche, 'blank parody, a statue with blind eyeballs'.[33] Like Michel, Jesse wears a hat in bed. However, Michel wears a fedora which recalls and transgresses Bogart and in retrospect recalls Belmondo's roles in later films such as Jacques Deray's *Borsalino* (1969). Michel imitates but his imitation can be seen to possess an identifiable referent. Jesse wears a hat and as such imitates Michel and yet the hat he wears is an exaggerated sombrero, an artefact of touristic kitsch and an image with no stable referent.

Breathless can almost be viewed as a textbook of postmodern style. It is not insignificant that a scene from the film takes place in Los Angeles' Westin Bonaventure Hotel, a construction which Jameson describes as a 'full-blown postmodern building'.[34] The film can then be located within a contemporary tradition of postmodern cinematic production typified by focus on parody and/or pastiche, intertextuality and bricolage. This identity complicates attempts to define McBride's film as part of Hollywood mass production. As we have seen, the film's intertexts are both 'art' (French film) and 'popular' (comic strips, rock and roll) and as such it must be situated between these two taxonomies. Indeed it establishes a dialectical relationship between them and as such performs one of the central features of postmodern style, namely the effacement of the frontier between high culture and so-called mass or commercial culture.

This perception of *Breathless* as a postmodern artefact also complicates attempts to describe the film as part of a specifically national aesthetic. Postmodernism emerged in the era of global capitalism, and as a product of a global industry, namely Hollywood, McBride's film should be situated within the global/local nexus outlined earlier in this chapter. It is indeed possible to see *A bout de souffle* as part of a European (local) modernism and *Breathless* as part of a globalised postmodernism, a perception which can be borne out by the films' respective endings. Michel may imitate his cinematic heroes but this imitation causes his death and so he fulfils his filmic destiny. The fragmentation of imitation finds a certain coherence. Jesse however is not seen to die; the film closes with his 'performance', coherence is denied. The (albeit limited) resolution of the source film is replaced by continuing fragmentation and non-resolution in the remake.

Identification of *A bout de souffle* and its American remake as products of a specific national aesthetic is highly problematic. Indeed it seems that it may be more productive to discuss them in terms of the global/local nexus so central to current theories of the postmodern. The identities commonly attributed to the films are part of an intricate process of appropriation and rewriting; *A bout de souffle* has been appropriated for art cinema and the logic of the discourses of this tradition means that its 'remake' must be dismissed as commercial reproduction. The films are at once different and the same. Both shift between high and popular cultures, indigenous and 'other' cinemas. Moreover, description of Godard's film as 'modernist' may be deemed unacceptable. Its sheer intertextuality and experimentation may situate it within the postmodern thus again eroding the simple binary relationship between the two films.[35] So it is evident that rather than describe these films solely in terms of their location within a particular national aesthetic, it is vital to examine their position on the cusp of various cinematic aesthetics and identities.

Nevertheless, the tendency to appropriate *A bout de souffle* for an 'art' cinema which is seen as intrinsically French, and to confine *Breathless* to an American 'popular' cinema, has enabled the location of these films within specific national contexts. Both films were involved in a renewal of a cinematic aesthetic which could be perceived as 'national' (the *nouvelle vague*'s overturning of the traditions of the *cinéma de qualité*, and the innovations of the 'New Hollywood' of the 1970s). However, this renewal took place through a rejection of the dominant 'national' cinema and a recourse to other non-national cinematic traditions. In other words, although each film may be located within the trajectory of a particular national cinema, this identity is evidently rendered highly complex by the hybrid nature of the films' intertexts and aesthetics. Ultimately these films can be seen as a microcosm of cinema's relation to discourses of the nation. They emerge from specific cultures at specific times and engage with aspects of this culture, yet they also reveal and articulate discourse external to the moment and the place of production. Furthermore, their identity as 'national' product is fixed not so much by their moment of production but by subsequent moments of reception; *A bout de souffle* set out to overturn everything which identified a 'French' film yet it is now described as a central work in the history of French cinema.

This leads us back to where we started this chapter. French source films are often described as intrinsically 'national' products enabling condemnation of the remake as an act of violence against the 'national' culture. However, as the films discussed in this chapter demonstrate, the cinematic mobilisation of the 'nation' and of national identities is never this simple; films articulate national and non-national discourses in thoroughly complex ways. Moreover, to condemn the remake as an explicit attack is to deny the transformation which necessarily occurs as films shift between cultures, as they are both reproduced and re-consumed. What emerges from analysis of these French films and their remakes is a negotiation of identity which undermines any attempt to position them in the fixed binaries of France/Hollywood, art/popular, original/copy. The construction and deconstruction of identity lies at the heart of the narrative concerns of many of the films discussed so far and, as we shall see in subsequent chapters, it resurfaces in varying forms in a number of others. Moreover, the very act of remaking simultaneously underwrites and undermines filmic identity as the 'national' product becomes something other only to be reinvoked as a 'national' artefact in critical discourse. If this national identity can be threatened, if it needs to be defended, then perhaps it is not as inviolable as such discourses suggest. What is certain is that as a form of cross-cultural exchange, the remake provides a privileged point of access for this very necessary reconsideration of the nation and its relation to cinema and of the various oppositions between high and popular cultural forms which result from a positing of distinct national cultures.

Notes

1. Ginette Vincendeau, 'Unsettling Memories', *Sight and Sound* vol. 5 no. 7, July 1995, pp. 30–2.

2. Stephen Neale, 'Art Cinema as Institution', *Screen* vol. 22 no. 1, 1981, pp. 11–39.

3. Andrew Higson, 'The Concept of National Cinema', *Screen* vol. 30 no. 4, Autumn 1989, p. 44.

4. Ed Benson, 'Martin Guerre, the Historian and the Filmmakers: An Interview with Natalie Zemon Davis', *Film and History* vol. 13 no. 3, September 1983, pp. 49–65.

5. Michel Foucault, *Moi, Pierre Rivière, ayant égorgé ma mère, ma soeur et mon frère* (Paris: Gallimard, 1973).

6. Ginette Vincendeau, 'Hijacked', *Sight and Sound* vol. 3 no. 7, July 1993, pp. 22–5.

7. Marc Ferro, *Cinéma et histoire*, 2nd edn (Paris: Gallimard, 1993).

8. See Phil Powrie, 'Heritage, History, and "New Realism": French Cinema in the 1990s', in Phil Powrie (ed.), *French Cinema in the 1990s: Continuity and Difference* (Oxford: Oxford University Press, 1999), pp. 1–21.

9. See Guy Austin, *Contemporary French Cinema: An Introduction* (Manchester: Manchester University Press, 1996).

10. Ibid., p. 143.

11. Benson, 'Martin Guerre, the Historian and the Filmmaker', p. 62.

12. Interesting links can be established between this film and *La Reine Margot* (Patrice Chéreau, 1995) which depicted the massacre of Saint Bartholomew and the intrigues in the French court which preceded and accompanied it, and which can also be seen to interrogate this pre-Revolutionary moment from the perspective of the 1980s/1990s.

13. Jason Drake, Review of *Sommersby*, *Sight and Sound* vol. 3 no. 5, May 1993, p. 56.

14. Pierre Sorlin, *The Film in History: Restaging the Past* (Oxford: Blackwell, 1980), pp. 45–7.

15. Ibid., p. 47. The contrast in numbers can be explained by Hollywood's much greater production.

16. Ferro, *Cinéma et histoire*, p. 61.

17. Anne Friedberg, *Window Shopping: Cinema and the Postmodern* (Berkeley: University of California Press, 1993).

18. Alain Bergala (ed.), *Jean-Luc Godard par Jean-Luc Godard* (Paris: Cahiers du cinéma–Éditions de l'étoile, 1985), p. 218.

19. Pamela Falkenberg, 'Hollywood and the Art Cinema as a Bipolar Modeling System: *A bout de souffle* and *Breathless*', *Wide Angle* vol. 7 no. 3, 1985, pp. 44–53.

20. Jean Dutourd, *Carrefour*, 23 March 1960.

21. Although Patricia is not a typical *femme fatale* she is equally dangerous. Michel refuses to leave Paris because of his love for her and so he can not escape capture and death. She also displays some of the narcissism of noir women, asking Michel to describe her best features and repeatedly examining her reflection in the mirror during the long scene in her bedroom.

22. Bergala, *Jean-Luc Godard par Jean-Luc Godard*, p. 218.

23. Steve Smith, 'Godard and Film Noir: A Reading of *A bout de souffle*', *Nottingham French Studies* vol. 32, 1993, pp. 65–73.

24. *Télérama* no. 1745, 22 June 1983.

25. Falkenberg, 'Hollywood and the Art Cinema', p. 44.

26. See 'My Heroes by Quentin Tarantino', *Guardian*, 2 February 1995, p. 28.

27. Nicolas Saada, '*Psycho* 1998 de Gus Van Sant: l'originale copie', *Synopsis* no. 2, Spring 1999, pp. 74–5.

28. See Jean Baudrillard, *Simulacres et simulation* (Paris: Éditions. Galilée, 1981).

29. *Libération*, 24 June 1983.

30. Fredric Jameson, *Postmodernism or the Cultural Logic of Late Capitalism* (London: Verso, 1991), p. 2.

31. Ibid., p. 9.

32. Ibid., pp. 11–12.

33. Ibid., p. 17.

34. Ibid., p. 38.

35. Of course we should also be aware of the highly problematic nature of definitions of the postmodern.

5
Remaking Comedy

The remakes of the 1980s and 1990s have been dominated by comedy. Of the thirty-three films remade between 1980 and 1998, twenty can be seen to identify in some way with this genre. These films include domestic comedies such as *Trois hommes et un couffin* (1985) and *Three Men and a Baby* (1987), the action/spy spoofs *La Totale* (1991) and *True Lies* (1994), and romantic comedies such as *Cousin, Cousine* (1975) and *Cousins* (1989). Significant within this group of films is the work of Francis Veber; seven of the French films remade during this period were written and/or directed by Veber, he was both the script-writer and the director of *Les Fugitifs* (1986) and its remake of 1989, *Three Fugitives* and he has written the screenplay for a projected remake of his 1998 hit, *Le Dîner des cons*.

These figures beg the question as to why comedies should prove such a fruitful source for the remaking process. As we have seen, comedy is an eminently popular genre in France, often achieving great commercial success. *Les Visiteurs* of 1993, directed by Jean-Marie Poiré, demolished almost all previous French box-office records achieving 13,634,523 admissions in its first year of release. *Gazon Maudit*, directed by Josiane Balasko and released in 1995, proved the second most popular film in France that year, selling over four million tickets. The films selected for remaking tend also to be commercial successes in their country of production: for example, *Un Éléphant ça trompe énormément* (Yves Robert, 1976) attracted over 500,000 spectators in France during its first four weeks of release. The commercial success of these films demonstrates the ability of 'national' comedies to challenge Hollywood productions at the French box-office. Indeed as Ginette Vincendeau points out, although French cinema is conventionally perceived in terms of dramatic trends such as Poetic Realism and auteur cinema, as one of the only domestic genres to resist Hollywood it is perhaps comedy which best identifies French 'national' cinema.[1]

This commercial success is further emphasised by the endurance of the genre in French cinematic production. A significant amount of silent production involved comics such as André Deed and Max Linder and early sound films were influenced by comic genres derived from both the theatre and the music-hall. Since the post-war period the popularity of domestic comedies has continued through the work of actors and/or directors such as Jacques Tati, Louis de Funès, Bourvil and, more recently, Yves Robert, Gérard Oury, Claude Zidi, Jean-Marie Poiré and, of course, Francis Veber. As we have seen, the prevalence and the commercial success of this genre in France evidently undermine the constructions of French cinematic production as high art which are so common in much critique of the remake process. As Vincendeau remarks, these works are not 'art' films, nor are their directors considered to be auteurs despite the fact that in some cases the director is also the script-writer and even the star of the film.[2] As a result, comic films are frequently dismissed by French critics, in many cases the same critics who condemn the hegemony of Hollywood production challenged by these comedies. This critical disregard is apparent in the general absence of any sustained analysis of domestic comedy in the pages of *Positif* and *Cahiers du cinéma*, the principal 'serious' French cinema journals. Yet it is these popular films which are most frequently selected for remaking, rendering somewhat paradoxical calls for the protection of French 'art' in the face of Hollywood. It would seem that it is not French 'art' which is 'under threat' from the remake but rather those popular domestic genres often despised by the critics.

Despite commercial success in their country of production, French comedies generally fail to achieve equal success in the United States. This failure is demonstrated by the striking disparity between North American box-office takings for individual comedies and those for their subsequent remakes. Both *Le Grand Blond avec une chaussure noire* (Yves Robert, 1972) and *Un Éléphant ça trompe énormément* (Yves Robert, 1976) made approximately $1.5 million in the United States while *The Man with One Red Shoe* (Stan Dragoti, 1985, a remake of *Le Grand blond avec une chaussure noire*) made $9 million and *The Woman in Red* (Gene Wilder, 1984, a remake of *Un Éléphant ça trompe énormément*) made over $24 million. Despite the significant gap between the box-office receipts of the French productions and those of their American counterparts, these figures compare quite favourably with the commercial trajectories of many French films released in the American market.

Nevertheless, the French films do fail to match the profits made by the American productions and there are a number of reasons for this. As we have seen, distribution and exhibition practices, as well as the resistance of American audiences to non-English language productions, will all help to determine the career of a French film in the American market. Moreover, coupled with these factors it has become a critical commonplace to claim that comedies are intrinsically unexportable. Perhaps more than any other genre, comedy is said to be highly culturally specific; that which proves amusing to an audience in Paris will invariably fail to raise a laugh among spectators in New York. The apparent inability of much comedy to transcend national boundaries is thus seen to explain the frequency of the comic remake. The domestic success of French cinematic comedies demonstrates their potential to American producers and they are subsequently remade according to the comic norms and conventions of Hollywood. It is not insignificant that both *The Woman in Red* and *The Man with One Red Shoe* were co-produced by Victor Drai and based upon films directed by Yves Robert. The source of *The Man with One Red Shoe* was released four years before that of *The Woman in Red* suggesting that the box-office success of Wilder's film proved the viability of Robert's work as remake material and prompted Drai to set in motion the later production.

However, an initial viewing of these pairs of films tends to problematise this description of comedy. The plots of both of these films and indeed many of their jokes and gags appear to undergo little change during the remake process. In the first pair of films (*Un Éléphant.../The Woman...*) a middle-aged married man spots a young woman in a red dress 'dancing' over an air vent, her skirt raised, and he subsequently becomes besotted with her. The rest of the film deals with his attempts to find the woman, arrange a date and ultimately take her to bed. Both films begin and end with the male protagonist standing outside the woman's window having been forced to hide due to the arrival of her husband. As crowds of people, television cameras, journalists and the emergency services look on, the man jumps into a safety net below. In the second pair of films (*Le Grand Blond…/The Man…*) the chief of Secret Services realises that a colleague is attempting to steal his job. In order to undermine his plans he arranges for him to investigate a 'nobody', picked out from the crowd at an airport. The chosen individual (the man with one red/black shoe) is a violinist. The film then follows attempts on the part of the colleague and his team to discover the identity and the aims of this apparent spy. Both films end with a romance between the chosen man and the young female spy set to pursue him.

These similarities in plot structure can simply be seen to reinforce condemnations of the remake as a straightforward copy. However such similarities should not be abstracted from broader notions of intertextuality and the hybridity of comic genres. Comedy can take many forms; indeed it is extremely difficult to define even the characteristics of Hollywood comedy or French cinematic comedy. The very diversity of the French comedies chosen for remaking suggests the impossibility of constructing limits and boundaries for any description of the genre. This fluidity is carried through to the films themselves. Consider the following reviews of *Un Éléphant ça trompe énormément* (released in the United States as *Pardon mon affaire*):

> *Pardon mon affaire* […] is a peculiarly Gallic version of the *Seven Year Itch* comedy genre. A quicksilver amalgam of American screwball comedy and a dash of French boudoir hi-jinks, the comedy is as light and as fluffy as an expertly made soufflé.[3]

> Yves Robert has modelled his new film on *The Seven Year Itch*, a fact signalled by Etienne's first enticing glimpse of Charlotte walking over a hot-air grille …, and later confirmed by an occasional borrowed plot device, notably the wife's discovery of her husband's amorous activities through an involuntary television appearance.[4]

These reviews demonstrate the unfeasibility of establishing straightforward definitions of 'French' comedy, clearly distinct from the work of Hollywood. Whether or not Yves Robert consciously drew upon Billy Wilder's film of 1955 is not at issue here. Rather it is vital to perceive Robert's film as a highly intertextual artefact which enables a similarly intertextual reading on the part of its spectators and which thus complicates attempts to describe it as an unproblematically 'French' comedy. As heterosexual romantic comedies, both films can be inserted into an enduring comic tradition and more specifically, the remake can be located within a revival of this genre in Hollywood during the 1980s.[5]

Comic cinematic themes and plots are not necessarily entirely culturally specific or unexportable as our earlier comparison of *Trois hommes et un couffin* and *Three Men and a Baby* makes only too clear. Certainly the depiction of a middle-aged man's attraction to, or relationship with, a younger woman is a common comic theme. Consider Tom Ewell's pursuit of Marilyn Monroe in *The Seven Year Itch* (Billy Wilder, 1955), John Cleese's romantic involvement with Jamie Lee Curtis in *A Fish Called Wanda* (Charles

Crichton, 1988) and two other pairs of remakes which deal with a similar older man/younger woman dyad, *Un Moment d'égarement* (1977)/*Blame it on Rio* (1983) and *Mon Père ce héros* (1991)/*My Father the Hero* (1994). Similarly the comic caper/mistaken identity plot of *Le Grand Blond avec une chaussure noire* and *The Man with One Red Shoe* has been frequently reworked in both Hollywood and French cinematic production. A notable example of this is provided by a later pair of remakes, *La Totale* (1991) and *True Lies* (1994).

Similarities between these pairs of films should not then be dismissed as mere evidence of copying and 'unoriginality'. Furthermore, descriptions of comic genres as clearly culturally defined and unexportable should be problematised. Cinematic comedy is both fluid and hybrid; films from different cinematic cultures will draw upon similar themes and motifs, reworking them in a thoroughly intertextual fashion. Victor Drai demonstrates this commonality as he describes his selection of films for the remake process, ' "I first look for solid stories and universal themes, things that any culture can relate to or that Americans can especially appreciate. Provincial, culture-specific approaches just don't work." '[6] Nevertheless, as the review from the *Hollywood Reporter* reveals, there is something 'Gallic' about the French films; in other words there are differences between the French film and its remake, in the way narratives are structured, in film and acting styles, in ideological content and so on. *The Woman in Red* and *The Man with One Red Shoe* and their source films are at once both different and 'the same'. What these films share and the ways in which they differ can tell us much about the comic traditions and the broader cultural discourses of the cinematic contexts from which they emerge.

As I have already indicated, both of these remakes were co-produced by Victor Drai, a French national resident in the United States. Drai resists the sterility and negativity associated with the remake, claiming that these films are not in fact remakes at all but 'translations'. He states that rather than simply copying the French source films, the Hollywood productions rework their plots and motifs according to the cinematic conventions of the target culture:

> 'My films are not remakes at all. [...] The basic situations are retained but the comedy styles are completely different. French audiences, who are accustomed to working harder than American audiences, like cerebral farce and become angry if you give them a lot of physical comedy in their domestic films. American audiences, who prefer to be simply entertained, for the most part like a much broader physical type of comedy, and have difficulty sitting through a lot of cerebral comedy. This is not to say that French audiences are more intelligent than American audiences. It's just that the habits are different.'[7]

The broad nature of Drai's descriptions of French and American comic traditions is somewhat simplistic. One need only consider the sight gags of the films of Jacques Tati or the wordy comedy of Woody Allen to understand that neither 'national' cinema can be seen to focus exclusively on either physical or cerebral comedy. Nevertheless it is perhaps not insignificant that the work of Tati, in contrast to so much French domestic comedy, found an audience in the United States, while the films of Woody Allen continue to attract larger audiences in France than in their country of production.

Certainly there are various reasons for these successes, not least, in the case of Tati, the lack of a linguistic barrier due to the physicality of his comedy. However, they also reinforce Drai's descriptions of a strong tradition of cerebral comedy in France and the contrasting popularity of physical comedy in the United States. Analysis of *Trois hommes et un couffin* and *Three Men and a Baby* in Chapter 3 revealed an increased emphasis on action and physical humour in the American film and this type of shift is also visible in a number of other comic remakes. It is striking that the publicity poster for *My Father the Hero* showed a decidedly unathletic Depardieu on a pair of water-skis unlike the poster for the French film which showed a medium close-up of a rather wistful Depardieu and his daughter. This publicity emphasised the increased physical comedy of the remake and the rather more serious negotiation of the father/daughter relationship which lies at the heart of the source. The two films were marketed in quite different ways and surely attracted different types of spectator. In the words of a journalist writing in *Le Film français*, 'It's a well known fact – all French films, even comedies, talk about serious things.'[8]

It is certainly true that without in any way being intellectual films, both *Un Éléphant ça trompe énormément* and *Le Grand blond avec une chaussure noire* are quite verbose comedies with a strong emphasis on dialogue. This is particularly true of *Un Éléphant....* The film opens with a voice-over from the central protagonist, Etienne (Jean Rochefort), and this voice-over recurs throughout the film, providing a commentary on the action and linking together different sequences. The language used by Etienne for these voice-overs is strikingly flowery and somewhat self-conscious. In contrast, the voice-over provided by Teddy (Gene Wilder), the main protagonist of *The Woman in Red*, is both far less frequent and is couched in a more prosaic register. Consider for example the closing voice-over of each film. As Etienne falls towards the waiting safety net, we hear him say, 'Néanmoins, j'ai pris sur moi de tomber posément. ... A vrai dire, je n'étais qu'au début de mon ascension (Nevertheless, I took it upon myself to fall gracefully. ... To tell the truth, I was only at the beginning of my ascent).' We also hear the voice of Teddy as he falls, but in contrast he simply remarks upon his own foolishness, the lesson he has or has not learnt. In the French film the language itself is foregrounded, whereas in the American work the words merely provide a commentary on the action.

This verbosity is also displayed in the films' differing attitudes towards language and action. These can be exemplified through reference to a sequence from *Un Éléphant.../The Woman...* in which the male protagonists set out on horseback in search of the woman in red. In the source film the entire sequence lasts for just under two minutes. However, the vast majority (seventy-five seconds, thirteen frames) is taken up with a scene shot in Etienne's home in which he pulls on his riding boots under the amused gaze of his wife and his godmother. This then cuts to a much shorter scene (thirty seconds, seven frames) showing him on a horse, setting out to begin his search. These scenes are accompanied by Etienne's voice-over, indeed it is language that is privileged here rather than action, the humour emanates from the irony of his commentary on his endeavours. Etienne's rather pompous, romantic account of the events forms a striking contrast with the palpable absurdity of his actions (reinforced by his wife's amusement which he interprets as intrigue) and reveals him as a naive or fallible narrator/protagonist. Throughout most of the sequence the camera remains still. At one point it pans from right to left to follow a group of horses as they gallop across the frame, however it ultimately comes to rest upon Etienne as he and his horse move slowly forward towards the camera. This lack of mobility echoes the foregrounding of linguistic over physical comedy at this juncture.

In contrast, the equivalent sequence in the second film focuses upon Teddy's rather unsuccessful attempts to ride a horse. Although the sequence is of approximately the same length as that of the French film, it takes place entirely at the riding stables and the park. Apart from the final frame of the sequence, the action is not accompanied by Teddy's voice-over suggesting that here it is action that is privileged rather than language. Indeed the humour emanates from Teddy's inability to control his horse. This is underscored in the frames depicting his attempts to urge his mount to leave the stables. As the sequence cuts between Teddy and a bemused riding instructor in a classic shot/reverse shot structure, so the viewer is invited to identify with the latter's amusement at the physical exploits portrayed.

A similar disparity between physical and linguistic comedy can be perceived in *Le Grand blond avec une chaussure noire* and *The Man with One Red Shoe*. The American production involves far more action and physical gags than its French counterpart. For example, the first film opens with a sequence depicting a French spy undergoing a lie detector test in New York. The questions posed by his captors reveal that he has been arrested in possession of heroin. The sequence is brief (sixty-seven seconds) and is composed of fourteen frames which cut between close-ups on the lie detector and the spy's face and hands, and zooms out to medium shots of the spy and his interlocutors. The high-key lighting and the lack of music reinforce this relative simplicity of structure. In contrast, the second film opens with an extended action sequence set in Morocco, depicting the planting of cocaine upon an American agent and his subsequent arrest by the Moroccan authorities. This sequence is both much longer than its French equivalent (three minutes and fifty-three seconds) and possesses a far more complex structure. The forty-one frames reveal a great variety of camera angles (straight on, high angle and low angle), camera distances (ranging from long shots through to close-ups) and camera movements (tracking shots, crane shots, pans and tilts) as well as a certain distortion of the frame achieved through Dragoti's decision to film via mirrors (Maddy's reflection in the car's wing mirror), binoculars (point-of-view shots) and through wire fences. This complexity is heightened by the tense rhythm of the non-diegetic music which accompanies the sequence and the varied use of lighting to suggest both bright sunlight and contrasting shadow. The length of this extract, coupled with the very fact that it opens the narrative, underlines the centrality of physical comedy or action in the film, in marked contrast to the French production. Moreover, the formal complexity described above underscores the action displayed, increasing tension and pace.

Perhaps most striking of all is the different handling of the chase sequence that takes place towards the end of both of these films. In *Le Grand blond ...* this sequence is quite brief, lasting only eighty seconds. After the initial frames which show François (Pierre Richard) setting off in pursuit of the car containing Christine (Mireille Darc), the scene cuts to a medium shot of the front of the car followed by a long shot which tracks backwards as the car moves down the street towards the camera. A further medium shot of the front of the car shows Christine grabbing the steering wheel and this then cuts to a long, high-angle shot of the car as it enters a tunnel clearly marked with a no-entry sign. The camera zooms in on this sign and remains static as we hear the car crash and see the sign detach itself from the tunnel due to the impact. The relative formal simplicity of this sequence (there is no music, lighting is high key, and there are few changes in camera angle or movement) echoes the depiction of the chase in which the climax of the action (the crash and Christine's subsequent escape) is suggested rather than made visible.

In *The Man with One Red Shoe* the sequence is far longer. It uses cross-cutting to move between the actual chase and events occurring simultaneously in Richard's (Tom Hanks) apartment, thus heightening a sense of action, movement and speed. The total length of the sequence is seven minutes and thirty-five seconds and of this well over six minutes are devoted to the chase alone. Like the film's opening sequence, this extract displays a formal complexity which reinforces the frenetic action portrayed. Particularly notable are the rapid editing (ninety-four cuts in the final five minutes), and the great variety of camera angles (for example the different point-of-view shots which switch between the various characters and their contrasting perspectives creating a sense of dis-orientation and dizziness which both reinforces and duplicates the energetic on-screen activity). Both films do then employ that mainstay of action cinema, the car chase, yet whereas the French film downplays the event, displaying little visible action, the American production exploits the chase to such an extent that it becomes one of the most prolonged sequences of the film.

None of these films can be seen to belong solely or unproblematically to a single tradition of either physical or verbal comedy. All the films exploit each of these comic forms to a greater or lesser extent. Indeed it is significant that the later horse riding sequence in *Un Éléphant…/The Woman…* in which Etienne/Teddy finally catches up with Charlotte albeit somewhat clumsily, is of an almost equal length in both films, is composed of a similar number of frames, and uses similar camera angles and distances, and dialogue, suggesting that neither film can be said to eschew either verbal or physical humour entirely. However, it seems clear that Drai's distinctions between a cerebral French comedy and a physical American comedy can be seen to apply here in terms of the different emphases exemplified by the sequences described above. It should be noted that such differences can not be reduced to aesthetic trends alone; the inferior budgets available to the French productions would tend to preclude the type of complex action sequences present in *The Man with One Red Shoe*. Nevertheless, without wanting to over-generalise, it is apparent that these French films belong to a tradition of linguistic humour, a fact exemplified by the following review of *Un Éléphant ça trompe énormément*:

> … the film is made up of too many over long sequences […] and there is an attempt to hide this slowness through an emphasis on dialogue. Words flourish and, forty years on, the legacy of Prévert and Jeanson continues to gently poison French comedy.[9]

A further distinction between the two pairs of films can be perceived in the remakes' streamlining or 'literalising' of narrative. It is a critical commonplace to define classical Hollywood production in terms of clear causality in contrast to the ambiguity of French auteur cinema. We have seen examples of this distinction in a number of films already discussed and this streamlining is particularly evident in *The Woman in Red*. The various subplots and digressions of *Un Éléphant ça trompe énormément* are either discarded (Simon's relationship with his mother) or minimised (the departure and return of the wife of Bouly/Joe and the 'relationship' between the wife of Etienne/Teddy and Lucien/Shelly). The result in the American film is a far more straightforward linear narrative and a consequent change in emphasis. The French film, due to its development of the characters of Etienne's friends, can be seen to be as much about the relationships between these protagonists as about Etienne's pursuit of the woman. It is not insignificant that the film's opening credits appear over the tennis match between the four friends, about five minutes into the film. This would seem to suggest that all that has preceded this moment (Etienne's first sighting of Charlotte [Anny Duperey], his initial attempts to set up a date with her and the resulting lies to his wife) is in some way a prelude to the film's principal concern, male friendship. In contrast, the remake focuses almost exclusively upon Teddy's pursuit of Charlotte (Kelly Le Brock). The French film is far more episodic in structure than its American counterpart; it eschews a single linear narrative in favour of a series of digressions or plural narratives. As such it can be perceived as simultaneously romantic comedy, sex farce and male 'buddy' movie, it has no single genre identification.

Etienne (Jean Rochefort), Bouly (Victor Lanoux), Claude (Claude Brasseur) and Simon (Guy Bedos) play tennis in *Un Éléphant ça trompe énormément*.

The Hollywood version is far less open. It is structured around a dominant goal-oriented narrative and so can be more straightforwardly defined as sex farce/romantic comedy. This description is reinforced by the emphasis upon Teddy's pursuit of Charlotte and by other plot devices. For example, in an early scene Teddy overhears a colleague making a telephone call. He becomes uncomfortable and annoyed as he understands the conversation as sexual *double entendres*, a common source of humour in the sex farce. In a later scene Teddy's wife, Didi (Judith Ivey), accidentally fires a gun as they discuss Joe's infidelity. This scene also occurs in the French film yet there are telling differences. Didi fires the gun into Teddy's underpants and subsequently, as he responds to the telephone call which he had hoped would enable him to spend the evening with Charlotte, she sits beside him with the gun placed on his lap, pointing towards his genitals. Evidently both the underpants and the position of the gun suggest the penis, Teddy's sexual desires and the possible consequences of his deviation. This scene can in fact be seen to reinforce the sexual comedy of the film. Indeed the very linear structure of the film supports its definition as sex farce/romantic comedy. As Richard Dyer explains, there is an interesting similarity in the way both male sexuality and narrative are frequently described. Male sexuality is said to be goal oriented, seduction and foreplay are merely the means of achieving an orgasm. Likewise, the underlying structure of most narratives in Western fiction is about the pursuit of a goal and its attainment, often through possession.[10] Whereas the French production constantly shifts its emphasis away from Etienne's desire for the woman in red, the remake remains far more centred upon this single story. The linear progress of the narrative echoes the attempt to attain Charlotte and thus the film's status as romantic/sex comedy.

A similar 'streamlining' can be discerned in the films' depiction of character. French cinematic production tends to be character rather than action based, a trend influenced as we have seen by both aesthetic conventions and comparatively limited material conditions. Certainly it is true that the two French films discussed here, along with a number of the films analysed in earlier chapters, engage in a far more complex character development than their American counterparts. This is exemplified in the depiction of Etienne's friends described a moment ago. These protagonists not only figure more prominently in the narrative but they are also portrayed in more detail; for example we witness the hypochondria of Simon (Guy Bedos) and the flamboyant dress sense of Claude (Claude Brasseur).

The contrast between the depiction of Bouly (Victor Lanoux) in the source film and Joe (Joseph Bologna) in the remake is particularly striking. While Joe is portrayed in terms of stereotypical machismo (he chases other women and becomes angry when his wife leaves him), Bouly is a somewhat more complex character. He also flirts with other women yet his reactions to his wife's departure range from violent anger to tears and melancholy. Indeed the film plays upon this contrast; as he discovers that his wife and children have left home Bouly wears a T-shirt bearing the words *bisoo bisoo* (kiss kiss) and two 'lipstick kisses'. This mark of an inveterate playboy forms an amusing contrast with the close-up on his soft, rather babyish face and his tearful reaction. The disparity between the heterosexually 'macho' goings on of the four friends (sports, ribald humour, chasing other women) and some distinctly 'non-macho' character traits (Bouly's inability to cope with his wife's departure, Simon's hypochondria and overly close relationship with his mother, Claude's homosexuality) suggests an ambiguity not present in the remake where these characters are far less developed (and again recalls Serreau's 'three men'). These incongruities are also an important source of humour; we are invited to laugh at the characters' self-deception and thus a certain critique is implied. By choosing not to develop these ambiguities, the remake eschews irony and to a great extent the male friends become mere ciphers, amusing examples of the consequences of sexual infidelity.

Of course such differences have a significance which extends far beyond formal or generic concerns. The narrative transformations which take place as the French film is remade in Hollywood are indicative of contrasting articulations of, and work upon, ideological structures. Both productions can be described as romantic/sex comedies, however the emphasis upon male friendship in *Un Éléphant ça trompe énormément* necessitates the insertion of this work into a tradition of male 'buddy' movies which both explore and articulate constructions of masculinity. Indeed, the film can be seen to negotiate a sense of masculinity in crisis and thus in many ways becomes a direct precursor to Coline Serreau's later treatment of similar themes. Each of the four male protagonists is in some way infantilised. Consider again Simon's dependent yet problematic relationship with his mother, Bouly's inability to cope with his wife's departure and the visual emphasis on the soft, child-like aspects of his body, Claude's disavowal of his homosexuality, and Etienne's attempted rejection of marital responsibility. Moreover, each lacks self-knowledge and displays dishonesty both towards the self and others. This is nowhere more apparent than in the irony of Etienne's voice-over narrative. This depiction of flawed masculinity and the concomitant suggestion of a failure to accept the full weight of patriarchal authority, reveal the film's articulation of a crisis in masculinity which can be seen to emerge from the particular socio-historical context of its moment of production. By 1976, the year of the film's release, the women's movement in France had achieved a certain status and currency which furthered the calling into question of traditional gender roles. Moreover, the social upheavals of the late 1960s, including changes in sexual mores, had given way to a period of relative reflection, an attempt to come to terms with these transformations. Thus the 'mid-life crisis' of Etienne and his friends emanates from, and works upon, a similar 'mid-life crisis' in gender identities and sexual conventions in France at that time. It is also significant that the 1970s saw French society beginning to face up to the relative nature of its own position in the global economy (a process which, as we have seen, continued throughout the 1980s); witness the onset of recession, the undermining of long-established hierarchies through the events of May 1968, and the disappearance of both the French colonial empire and the strong 'patriarch', De Gaulle. The film's representation of frail masculinities seems to negotiate a similar oscillation in the social structures of patriarchal authority at the time of its production.

By concentrating upon Teddy's pursuit of Charlotte and marginalising other narratives, *The Woman in Red* positions itself firmly within a tradition of romantic comedy/sex farce. Indeed, in contrast to the French film, it can be seen to explore masculine (hetero) sexuality rather than broader issues of identity (a process again continued in *Trois hommes et un couffin/ Three Men and a Baby*). With this in mind the film's relationships with former romantic comedies, particularly *The Seven Year Itch*, are especially revealing. As Steve Neale and Frank Krutnik point out, whereas the screwball romantic comedies produced in Hollywood during the 1930s and 1940s would concentrate on the heterosexual couple and thus on both male and female desires, the sex comedies of the 1950s and 1960s would frequently focus upon male sexual fantasy with marriage posited both as a threat to this desire and the means of its eventual containment.[11] *The Woman in Red* renegotiates the latter concerns in the context of post-feminist and post-'sexual revolution' society. In other words, a society in which male heterosexual desire is confused by the contradictions apparent in the growing power of women through feminist politics and their increasing reification in the products of consumerism. This confusion is clearly visible in the film. In their discussion of *The Seven Year Itch*, Bruce Babington and Peter William Evans remark:

> Brilliant but limited, *The Seven Year Itch* is capable of anatomising the poverty of male categorisation of women, while finding it difficult to escape some of the limitations it castigates in its characters. There are neither female nor male voices of maturity in the film; without them the comedy of desire is denied the ballast of exemplary ideals of living.[12]

This criticism can also be applied to *The Woman in Red* which both displays and mocks male reification of women and yet reinforces it through its own formal structures. Whereas the French film simultaneously diffuses and critiques Etienne's perception of Charlotte through its deployment of irony, the remake tends to reinforce Teddy's objectified vision of women. In *Un Éléphant ça trompe énormément* Etienne's wife is pursued by a young student, a subplot which is developed at some length. The emphasis on this digression undermines Etienne's image of his wife (as he sits in the airport imagining her waiting for him she is in fact in the process of fending off her suitor) and suggests the possibility of sexual relationships between older women and younger men which contrasts with and also ridicules Etienne's liaison with Charlotte. By downplaying this subplot the remake reduces Judith so that she becomes no more than Teddy's wife, the obstacle to his affair with Charlotte, and disavows the sexual possibilities made visible in the French film.

   This confusion is nowhere more apparent than in the representation of Charlotte herself. Certainly both films can be seen to reify her, to present her as the object of Teddy's/Etienne's gaze, and by implication, that of the heterosexual male viewer. However, this process becomes far more extended in the American film as a sequence is devoted to a modelling assignment in which Charlotte is presented in various poses while Teddy looks on. Moreover, it is not insignificant that in both films Charlotte is initially nameless; she is 'the woman in red'/'*la femme en rouge*'. Unlike the Marilyn Monroe character in *The Seven Year Itch* she does eventually receive a name, suggesting that she is more than just reified 'woman', the object of male desire. However, the remake's confusion is underlined by the decision to both name Charlotte and yet deny this name through the film's title.

   The film's articulation of masculine sexuality displays an ambivalence bound up with ideological configurations in the United States in the 1980s. The establishment of the women's movement, which by this point had shifted from the margins of political debate

to the centre, meant the vacillation of traditional male perceptions of women. This, coupled with the continuing reification of women as sex objects in the media, suggested a
crisis in masculine sexuality revealed in *The Woman in Red*. The film seems to want to
have it both ways; whereas the Tom Ewell character in *The Seven Year Itch* renounces an
affair with 'the girl' through fear, Teddy simply fails to consummate the relationship
through mischance. In other words, the film disavows marital fidelity and at the same
time recuperates it. As such *The Woman in Red* harks back to earlier comedies in which
marriage would ultimately circumscribe illicit desire, alludes to the absence of moral
strictures of *Un Éléphant ça trompe énormément,* and prefigures the Hollywood
romances of the late 1980s in which marriage would once again be invoked, this time as
protection against AIDS, the danger of non-monogamous, non-heterosexual sexuality.
This conservative revisionism of sexual possibilities is underlined by Teddy's dismissal
of Charlotte as a 'piece of ass' at the end of the film. The return of her husband shows
her to be inimical to both romance *and* monogamy and she is verbally 'punished', a
somewhat disturbing double standard which suggests, albeit fleetingly, the attacks upon
active female sexuality displayed in films such as *Fatal Attraction* (Adrian Lyne, 1987)
and *Basic Instinct* (Paul Verhoeven, 1991).

The streamlining described above is perhaps not quite so apparent in *The Man with
One Red Shoe*. As we have discussed, the film introduces gags and action sequences not
present in the French film, thus in some way it complicates the initial narrative structure. However the film can be seen to reduce the ambiguity present in the French
production through its tendency to 'literalise', to introduce clear-cut narrative motiv-
ation and causality. Consider for example the opening scenes of the film described
above. The drug smuggling plot which sets the narrative in motion is made visible and
is hence far more literal than the equivalent incident in the French film. An ensuing scene

Teddy (Gene Wilder) flees from Charlotte's (Kelly le Brock) apartment in *The Woman in Red*.

represents Ross (Charles Durning), the chief of the CIA, explaining to his assistant, Brown (Ed Herrmann) that he has tried to set up Cooper through this incident. In contrast the French film neither shows the smuggling incident nor does it make clear who is responsible for it; both Toulouse (Rochefort), the Secret Service chief, and Milan (Bernard Blier), his 'opponent', deny their involvement. Similarly, in *Le Grand Blond avec une chaussure noire* we do not learn how the spies identify François. In contrast this is made clear in the remake as Maddy (Daryl Hannah) removes Richard's wallet at the airport. This insistence upon causality and the consequent reduction in ambiguity are reinforced by the limited diegetic time (Cooper points out that they have only forty-six hours and eighteen minutes to discover Richard's role before the Senate hearing), and an ensuing increase in pace, heightened by action sequences and rapid editing. Both films are goal oriented, however causality is better established in the remake and the narrative moves towards its goal at a much quicker pace.

The contrasts in character depiction identified in *The Woman in Red* and *Un Éléphant...* can also be perceived in *Le Grand Blond ...* and *The Man with One Red Shoe*, particularly in the characters of Toulouse/Ross and Milan/Cooper. Whereas Ross and Cooper are portrayed as stereotypical 'bad' characters whose aims, to remain/become the chief of the CIA, are clear-cut, and who eventually receive their comeuppance, Rochefort and Milan are far more ambivalent. We are told that the two men are 'friends' (Toulouse sends Milan a case of wine for his birthday) so complicating their status as rivals. Both Blier and Rochefort play their characters with subtlety and a low key style; there is none of the blustering and shouting of the typical comic villain. This echoes the film's low key tone and emphasis on bathos, or the rendering extraordinary of the entirely ordinary. Perhaps most striking of all are the homo-erotic suggestions surrounding Toulouse. His apartment is filled with Greek-style statues of naked men, he lives alone with his mother, and as he stands on his balcony he is seen to gaze at a semi-clad male runner in the park below. While the equation of a stereotypical homosexuality and improbity is somewhat problematic, the mixed undercurrents suggested by these character depictions do reinforce the relative ambiguity of the French films.

These contrasts in character portrayal are visible in the central protagonists of both pairs of films. This is partly due to acting styles; Rochefort's wordy, rather self-regarding performance as Etienne creates a humorous paradox between his image of himself and of events and these same events as they actually occur. In contrast, Wilder emphasises Teddy's nervousness via his various mannerisms, tending to invite sympathy rather than mockery. Pierre Richard interprets François as a clumsy fool, a fact made immediately apparent as he battles with a sweet and its wrapper during the early scenes in the airport. Hanks' portrayal of Richard is that of a more conventional Hollywood hero. He breaks his tooth not due to mishap but because his friend Morris has given him a 'joke' nut. These differences are particularly striking in the films' 'seduction' scenes. Whereas that between François and Christine is shot through with physical gags, the equivalent scene between Richard and Maddy is a far more traditional 'romantic' sequence. As a result the gag involving the catching of the woman's hair in the male protagonist's zip that features in both films, seems somewhat out of place in the remake. Nevertheless, as part of a Hollywood tradition which tends to eschew ambiguity in favour of clear oppositions between good and evil, it is perhaps not surprising that Hanks' 'heroic' qualities should be emphasised. He resists an affair with his best friend's wife far more vociferously than François (the latter has sex with Paulette, Hanks spurns the advances of Paula), he is shown to be a philanthropic figure, giving music lessons to underprivileged children, and unlike the discordant composition of François, his romantic melody seduces Maddy. Indeed the romance between these two characters is emphasised far more strongly than that between François and Christine in *Le Grand Blond avec une chaussure noire*. Maddy and Richard meet towards the beginning of the narrative (Christine and François meet only about forty-five minutes into the film), and Maddy is shown to be a more sympathetic character. Unlike Christine she does not begin to care for her eventual lover only after the seduction scene, instead she is seen to express concern for his well-being early on in the narrative and pauses to admire one of his childhood photographs as she searches his home.

Comedy aims to subvert or transgress particular conventions yet, as Neale and Krutnik point out, this subversion is contained by the very fact that it is a built-in feature of the comic.[13] This is unquestionably significant in terms of these particular pairs of films; all four are comedies and each can be seen to transgress certain norms and conventions yet in different ways and to a varying extent. Like the films discussed in Chapter 3, the two French comedies both represent a playful attitude towards moral codes and ethics, revealingly absent from the American remakes. Despite his status as 'hero', François engages in an affair with his best friend's wife. Richard on the other hand, sleeps with Paula only once and then, we are told, because 'she got him drunk'. He is a victim rather than a perpetrator of this infidelity and so his role as hero is untainted. Similarly, in *Un Éléphant ça trompe énormément* Etienne ultimately goes to bed with Charlotte. In contrast, the 'sex' scene between Teddy and Charlotte is reduced to farce as he throws his underpants onto a lamp and wallows around on her water bed and the arrival of her husband prevents the consummation of the affair. Thus the representation of a sexual infidelity which is acceptable within the context of French cinema and culture is, when reworked in Hollywood, denied and recast as a moral lesson. Both films play upon the fantasies of middle-aged men yet whereas Robert's film follows this through to its logical conclusion, the remake chooses not to depict a sexual act which would sully Wilder's role as 'hero' and make the film unacceptable to a broad audience.[14]

Plot changes in *The Man with One Red Shoe* also reveal subversions and recuperations that differ sharply from those of *Le Grand Blond avec une chaussure noire*. In the French film, the central villain, Toulouse, goes unpunished. Moreover, the film's closing scenes show him watching a slide of François as he leaves the country and suggesting that he will employ him as a secret agent upon his return; neither is Toulouse punished nor is François, the innocent victim, entirely free. In the Hollywood remake, Cooper is arrested as he runs into the Senate hearing and Ross is demoted, his job given to Brown, the instigator of Richard's continuing protection. The Senate hearing itself is highly significant; by representing governmental investigation of CIA malpractice at the beginning of the film, the remake reinforces constructions of the United States as the land of democracy and justice and confines the film's events to comic action, eschewing any hint of social critique. As such it plays upon former cinematic representations of the Senate as both symbol of legitimacy and malpractice (for example, *All the President's Men*, Alan J. Pakula, 1976, and *Mr Smith Goes to Washington*, Frank Capra, 1939) here recuperating it for bourgeois ideology as a site of justice. This relationship becomes all the more interesting when we consider that the film was released shortly before the revelation of the Irangate affair and the consequent vacillation in American Republican structures. The French film closes with a subtitle containing an extract from the penal code which affirms the right of each individual to privacy, a right belied by the events of the narrative. As such the film can be inserted into a French cinematic tradition of social critique, an identity reinforced by the ambivalent nature of the film's closure. Indeed it is fair to say that whereas the Hollywood film ultimately only transgresses aesthetic norms through its parody of the spy thriller, the French production subverts both aesthetic conventions and ideological structures through its implicit critique of the overweening power of state-controlled Secret Services.

Each of the films can be seen to subvert certain conventions yet in contrasting ways. It should be stressed that none of the productions can be said to be particularly adventurous or transgressive in terms of their ideological work or indeed their formal attributes. As we have seen, the French films make less attempt to contain the reversals and upheavals they set in motion than do their American counterparts, a difference closely linked to the context of production and reception of each film. Nevertheless, like many popular comedies, each of the films ultimately resists far-reaching transgression, containing their playfulness within the comic form itself. Above all, what these differences indicate once again is the process of transformation which takes place as a film is remade in Hollywood. Despite the similarities discussed earlier in this chapter, it is apparent that these French films and their remakes are in many ways quite separate artefacts. Certainly each should be seen as a hybrid structure yet, as they emanate from different cinematic, cultural and temporal contexts, so their reworking of genre conventions, of formal features and of cultural codes will alter. The films do not only emanate from different contexts, they are also made for different audiences. This is especially clear in the case of *The Woman in Red*, which was widely marketed on the basis of its Stevie Wonder soundtrack in an attempt to attract a youth audience, an audience unlikely to view a French production centred upon the exploits of a group of middle-aged men.

The films are at once both 'different' and the 'same'. They draw upon those films which precede and surround them (for example the various Hollywood romantic comedies cited earlier). The similarities between these films and other comic remakes and their sources are particularly striking. The negotiations of masculinity shared by *Trois Hommes et un couffin*/*Three Men and a Baby* and *Un Éléphant ça trompe énormément*/*The Woman in Red* and the moral ambiguities/recuperations of *Mon Père ce héros*/*My Father the Hero* and *Le Grand blond avec une chaussure noire*/*The Man with One Red Shoe* reveal again the absolute necessity of contextualising the remake. In other words, rather than simply condemn particular films as copies of their French source, we need to understand the ways in which these films draw upon and rework a whole host of cinematic and cultural discourses. In terms of comedy this is especially important. The very act of remaking a French film in Hollywood reveals the cultural difference which separates French and American comic traditions and yet simultaneously undermines claims as to the unbridgeable nature of this gap. It is striking that in both *Trois Hommes et un couffin* and *Un Éléphant ça trompe énormément* male friendships take centre stage in contrast to an emphasis on action and plot in their remakes. The 'buddy' movie is a genre or sub-genre more commonly associated with Hollywood production and while these films differ from 'buddy' films such as *Lethal Weapon* (Richard Donner, 1987) and its various sequels, they do share its exploration of male friendship. Once again it would seem that attempts to posit straightforward 'national' definitions of cinematic production are undermined. Once again the remake reveals the transnational, decidedly unstable nature of both film comedy and cinematic production more widely.

Notes

1. Ginette Vincendeau (ed.), *Encyclopedia of European Cinema* (London: Cassell/BFI, 1995), p. 88. The popular success of Robert's films is suggested by their respective sequels, *Le Retour du grand blond* (Yves Robert, 1974) and *Nous irons tous au paradis* (Yves Robert, 1977).

2. A case in point is Josiane Balasko's *Gazon Maudit*. Discussing her highly successful film, Balasko complained about French critical disregard for popular production stating, 'People say I make commercial cinema, but I write my own scripts, I direct them, I write plays … I am an auteur. Many directors of popular French films are auteurs' (Ginette Vincendeau, 'Twist and Farce', *Sight and Sound* vol. 6 no. 4, April 1996, pp. 24–6). Her stance is somewhat paradoxical; while decrying the critical hegemony of 'art' cinema in France she seems also to want to insert her own work into that tradition through her claims to auteur status. However, it should be stressed that the films under discussion are significant as popular comedies and not because of any claims to auteurism made by, or on behalf of, their directors.

3. *Hollywood Reporter* vol. 247 no. 7, 24 June 1977, p. 2.

4. *Monthly Film Bulletin* vol. 45 no. 530, March 1978, p. 50.

5. For example *Splash* (Ron Howard, 1984), *Romancing the Stone* (Robert Zemeckis, 1984), *Something Wild* (Jonathan Demme, 1986), *Blind Date* (Norman Jewison, 1987), *Moonstruck* (Norman Jewison, 1987), *When Harry Met Sally* (Rob Reiner, 1989).

6. Cited in Marc Mancini, 'French Film Remakes', *Contemporary French Civilization* vol. 13 no. 1, Winter/Spring 1989, pp. 32–46.

7. Bill Desowitz, 'Drai Says He Produces French Translations', *Hollywood Reporter* vol. 267, 5 July 1984, p. 4.

8. 'My Father: comment faire d'un père deux coups', *Le Film français* no. 2511, 17 June 1994, p. 4.

9. *Positif* no. 188, December 1976, p. 74. This review is striking for, as previously described, such attention to popular comedy is only too rare in 'serious' journals such as *Positif*. It is also somewhat surprising that the review should criticise the film's verbosity, the lack of physical humour which is often seen to characterise popular comedy. This criticism of a 'French' comic tradition perhaps reinforces the journal's disdain for the indigenous popular product, its tendency to construct a national cinema of 'art' and 'quality' drama.

10. Richard Dyer, *The Matter of Images: Essays on Representations* (London: Routledge, 1993), p. 120.

11. Steve Neale and Frank Krutnik, *Popular Film and Television Comedy* (London: Routledge, 1990). Consider for example *Pillow Talk* (Michael Gordon, 1959), *That*

Touch of Mink (Delbert Mann, 1962) and *Sex and the Single Girl* (Richard Quine, 1964).

12. Bruce Babington and Peter William Evans, *Affairs to Remember: The Hollywood Comedy of the Sexes* (Manchester: Manchester University Press, 1989), p. 220.

13. Neale and Krutnik, *Popular Film and Television Comedy*, p. 93.

14. It is significant that Robert's film was released in the United States as *Pardon mon Affaire*, so marking it unequivocally as French and perhaps making its moral attitudes more acceptable to American audiences (just as the underlining of Depardieu's nationality in *My Father the Hero* enabled the suggestion of incest). It is also worth noting that the film was first given an X certificate for release in Britain and was subsequently re-certified as AA. As the film does not actually depict any scenes of sex and violence this, along with the changes in the remake, does suggest something about Anglo-Saxon attitudes to marital infidelity, or at least its representation.

6
Remaking the Thriller

I began this book by citing Barry Norman's review of John Badham's *The Assassin* (released in the United States as *The Point of No Return*). Norman condemned the film as 'sensationalist pap' so aligning himself with the vast majority of critical accounts of the remake. We have seen that this type of critique is closely bound up with particular perceptions of French and American cinema and the relationship between the two and that it tells us very little about the films themselves. However, in this case such condemnation seems especially misleading. Norman's review establishes a hierarchy between a quality French 'original' (Luc Besson's *Nikita*) and a debased Hollywood 'copy' and yet the two films are remarkably similar. Indeed, of all the remake pairs analysed in this book, they are perhaps the films which, at first viewing, seem to be the most alike. Moreover, to position either film in terms of the France/America, high culture/popular culture oppositions upon which Norman's critique rests proves extremely problematic. As we shall see in Chapter 6, Besson's film is in many ways an active attempt to break down these very oppositions, a process that surely undermines condemnation of its Hollywood remake.

Like *Trois hommes et un couffin* and *Three Men and a Baby*, *Nikita* and *The Assassin* are an extremely well-known remake pair. This is largely a result of the box-office (and indeed cult) success of Besson's film. The film was seen by over 3.7 million spectators in France and around 3 million in the USA. Its cult status is revealed by the frequency with which it appears at student film club screenings (evidence of its appeal to a young audience) and its broader popularity and cultural impact can be traced not just in the Hollywood remake but also in a version made in Hong Kong in 1991 (*Black Cat* directed by Stephen Shin) and a television serial (which has itself achieved cult status) entitled *La Femme Nikita* (directed by Reza Badiyi and George Bloomfield), first shown on USA Network on 13 January 1997. The remaking of the film in Hong Kong is striking as Besson's film recalls the work of directors such as John Woo. Like *Nikita*, Woo's films show alienated and often brutal central characters and graphic violence. Films such as *The Killer* (1989) and *Bullet in the Head* (1990) have also achieved a cult following in the United States suggesting a close, circular (and inter-cultural) relationship between these films, Besson's work and its various remakes.

Both *Nikita* and *The Assassin* tell the story of a drug addict (Nikita, played by Anne Parillaud/Maggie, played by Bridget Fonda) who, after killing a police officer during a raid on a pharmacy, is arrested and sentenced to life imprisonment (in the French version) and to death (in the remake). After faking her death through an apparently lethal injection, a representative of the state (Bob, played by Tchéky Karyo/Gabriel Byrne) offers her a new life as a government trained assassin. The films show her training and her first assignment which, despite serious problems, she completes successfully. She is then released, armed with a new identity. She meets a young man (Marco, played by Jean-Hugues Anglade/JP, played by Dermot Mulroney) with whom she sets up home. The rest of the film traces her developing relationship with Marco/JP (and, importantly, Bob) and her subsequent assignments. Besson's film ends with the disappearance of Nikita. Badham's film closes, apparently more positively, with Maggie's escape from the state and her role as assassin.

Before looking more closely at the two films and the relationship between them, it is worth considering the particular industrial and aesthetic contexts from which they emerge. *Nikita* is Besson's fourth full-length feature. It was preceded by *Le Dernier Combat* (1983), *Subway* (1985) and *Le Grand Bleu* (1988). Besson's work has often been described in terms of the so-called *cinéma du look*. This term was coined to describe a style of film-making which appeared in the 1980s and is exemplified by the work of directors such as Besson, Jean-Jacques Beineix and Léos Carax. Rather like the *nouvelle vague* this terminology is somewhat problematic as it tends to group together films and directors who in many ways are quite disparate. Nevertheless, it is fair to say that the work of these three directors shares an emphasis on visual style, references to other (frequently popular) cultural forms and an exploration of the alienation and disaffection of youthful protagonists in disturbing (often urban) locations. All three directors have been much criticised by the French critical establishment for their 'superficial' and 'populist' films. Like the comedies discussed in Chapter 5, their films have earned critical opprobrium and/or silence as they fail to fit easily within the trajectories of French cinema. Their references to advertising, music videos and comic strips distance them from the canons of 'high culture' while their apparent lack of realism, and more importantly, ideology undermine the social concerns which have typically identified so much 'serious' French cinema.

Besson's work has been particularly subject to criticism.[1] His enormous popularity with cinema audiences and critical acclaim from popular film journals such as *Première*, have been matched by condemnation from highbrow journals such as *Cahiers du cinéma* and *Positif*. It is striking, given the focus of this book, that Besson's work (notably *Nikita*) has been described by many critics as too 'American'. The pyrotechnics and spectacular action of *Nikita* were seen by many as little more than an imitation of Hollywood production and as such it undermined the *différence* so central to the maintenance of a national cinema.

Besson's contempt for the critical establishment and their reactions to his film is revealed in the work which followed *Nikita*. *Le Grand Bleu* (1988) remained a French production (despite an initial, and apparently inadvertent sale of production rights to Warren Beatty), but distribution rights were sold to Fox (who cut the already abridged French version), the film featured American actors (notably Rosanna Arquette) and some of the dialogue was in English. Although *Nikita*, his next film, was a Franco-Italian co-production shot in France, in French and featuring French actors, Besson's sixth and seventh features were far more 'international' in scope.[2] Both *Léon* (1994) and *Le Cinquième Élément* (1997) are entirely French productions (the former was financed by Gaumont and Besson's own production company, Les Films du Dauphin, the latter by

Gaumont alone), yet distribution rights were sold to American companies, both are shot in English, feature British and American actors and are set in a version of New York. The budgets for each film vastly outstripped typical costs for French production. *Le Cinquième Élément* cost over 500 million francs ($90 million), money which it recouped through pre-production sales before shooting started. In other words, the films' industrial and material trajectories were far closer to Hollywood production than French cinema of the period and Besson was quite explicit about his desire to compete actively with big-budget American cinema.

The style and narrative of each film extend this process. Like *Nikita* both feature spectacular displays of violence. *Léon* tells the story of a 'cleaner' or 'hit-man' (extending the role played by Jean Reno in *Nikita* and Harvey Keitel in *The Assassin* but also recalling a similar role played by Keitel in *Pulp Fiction*) and is set in the archetypal Hollywood Mafia location of New York's Little Italy.[3] *Le Cinquième Élément* draws even more explicitly on American cinematic traditions. It is a science fiction film that recounts the attempt to thwart the destruction of the planet by an alien body. The film recalls a host of other 'alien invasion' films, from the B movies of the 50s to recent blockbusters such as *Independence Day* (Roland Emmerich, 1996). Elaborate special effects were produced by Digital Domain (a company co-owned by James Cameron, renowned for his exploitation of digital technology) again producing a cinematic spectacle distinct from most French production.[4] Moreover, the film starred Bruce Willis, the archetypal Hollywood action hero.

Besson played Hollywood at its own game, using large budgets to reproduce the style and extensive marketing campaigns of the typical blockbuster. His efforts were not in vain as his films performed extremely well, both in France and overseas. *Le Cinquième Élément* was the most successful film in France in 1997, with over 7.5 million box-office admissions, beating Disney's *The Hunchback of Notre Dame* (1996) and Barry Sonnenfeld's intergalactic action–comedy extravaganza, *Men in Black* (1997), into second and third place with 6.7 million and 5.6 million admissions respectively. Gérard Pirès's *Taxi*, produced by Besson, proved a great hit at the French box-office in 1998 and significantly achieved wide-scale release in Britain in 1999 (accompanied by the tag-line 'Hollywood doesn't make them like this any more'), the first French film to be distributed in this fashion for over thirty years.[5] This would seem to be a rather paradoxical state of affairs. Here we have French films beating their American competitors at the (international) box-office, reaping huge profits for the French film industry and yet still finding themselves condemned by the very same critics who so decry the impact and influence of Hollywood production. It is perhaps not surprising, given this situation and Besson's aforementioned contempt for it, that his eighth film, released in France in 1999, should be a version of the story of Joan of Arc. Besson recounts the story of this great *national* icon in English using many of the conventions of *American* action cinema.

Of course the irony of this situation is particularly striking when we consider again Barry Norman's critique of *The Assassin*. If *Nikita* is indeed already *too* 'American' why should critics (and Norman, although British, mirrored many French critical responses) oppose an ongoing Americanisation in the form of the remake? Such accounts of *Nikita* also beg the question as to why American producers should bother to remake the film. If the film is 'American' in style, narrative and so on, why should it not simply be released in the United States' market in a manner akin to any other 'American' film? Certainly linguistic issues provide one response to this question. We have already seen the general reluctance to release/watch dubbed or subtitled films in the United States. However, unlike many French films, language does not play a major role in *Nikita* (indeed this is one of the factors which links it to Hollywood production). Verbal communication is limited and fraught with difficulties in the film; Nikita's early utterances consist of little more than anguished wailing, demented screaming and a robotic drone as she repeats the words of the investigating officer. Communication is instead carried out through action (especially violence) and physical gestures (Nikita's seduction of Marco involves her ravenous consumption of the ravioli purchased earlier and a sudden pounce – her only words are 'J'ai très envie', 'I really want it'). Besson's film is perhaps not as linguistically inimical to the American market as many of its French counterparts, surely another factor in its relative success with Anglo-American audiences. Nevertheless, the remake went ahead.

The answer ultimately lies in the cultural specificities of Besson's films which, despite critical claims to the contrary, bear clear traces of their French cinematic origins. If we take the example of *Le Cinquième Élément*, arguably his most 'American' film, we can find much evidence of its connections to French culture. Costumes were designed by Jean-Paul Gaultier, one of the best-known contemporary French designers both through his cat-walk and ready-to-wear collections and his work on other films, notably Peter Greenaway's *The Cook, the Thief, his Wife and her Lover* (1989), Pedro Almodóvar's *Kika* (1993) and Jeunet and Caro's *La Cité des enfants perdus* (1995). In Britain Gaultier himself of course has come to represent the iconic French man through his heavily accented performances on cult television programme *Eurotrash* (Channel Four/Rapido). The film's visual style was much influenced by *bande dessinée* (comic strips), a highly popular and innovative form of cultural production in France. Besson has described the influence of two graphic artists on his teenage imagination, Jean Giraud (known as Moebius and renowned for his comic *Metal Hurlant* or *Heavy Metal*) and Jean-Claude Mézières (famous in France for his series featuring Valerian, the Spatio-Temporal Agent). Both artists worked with Besson during the pre-production of the film and produced designs for cityscapes, interiors and vehicles.[6] Perhaps most strikingly the film transgresses (to a certain degree) many of the ideological codes of mainstream Hollywood production through its portrayal and exploration of highly ambiguous gender/sexual identities. Consider again the hysterical repudiation of any connotation of homosexuality in Nimoy's *Three Men and a Baby* and compare this with the polymorphous, excessive figure of Ruby Rhod (Chris Tucker) or the highly sexualised yet simultaneously genderless cyborg of Leeloo (Milla Jovovich) in Besson's film.

Léon also reveals its French cultural origins in a number of ways. Léon is a cleaner, a hit man or gangster yet, in a gesture reminiscent of Michel/Jesse's dressing up in *A bout de souffle* and *Breathless* he both borrows and transforms the gangster dress code. As Stella Bruzzi points out, 'Léon's look is gangster anti-fashion.'[7] He wears a hat but the gangster fedora becomes a wool skull-cap, his braces cover T-shirts and vests, his pleated trousers are too short and fail to meet his heavy boots, while his coat on the other hand, is far too big and hangs, scarecrow-like, off his rigid body. Through this transformation of the gangster look, Besson appropriates a particular cinematic convention and reworks

Les Diaboliques: Christina (Véra Clouzot) and Nicole (Simone Signoret) plot.

it according to his own narrative and thematic concerns. Léon is both hit man (the hat, the coat, the boots) and innocent child (the too-short trousers and simple vests). Just as, unusually, we see the 'cleaner' in his domestic setting, as simultaneously professional and 'individual', so his clothes reflect the various components of his identity.

This reconstitution of the generic codes of the gangster film is not of course specifically French *per se*. However, it does reveal much about Besson's particular narrative concerns and it is in the repetition and reworking of these themes and concerns that we can perhaps see most clearly the distinctions between his films and the Hollywood production they appear to emulate. Throughout his work we can see an exploration of alienation, fragmented individuals lost and/or trapped in a (frequently dystopic) urban environment. Thus Fred's existence and apparent death in the Métro in *Subway* echoes Nikita's entrapment in the sterile spaces of the government training facilities in *Nikita*. Similarly the father/daughter relationship of Nikita and Bob is echoed in the burgeoning love between Léon and Mathilda (Natalie Portman) which progresses from a child/parent relationship to a chaste and yet somewhat disconcerting passion. We have already seen that this dyad is a key theme in French cultural production and it is perhaps not surprising that the adult/child relationship in *Léon* provoked much criticism and led to the cutting of a particular sequence at the behest of the film's American distributors, Columbia. As Susan Hayward remarks, Besson was furious at this reaction which, he believed, reduced his film's exploration of 'pure love' to sexuality.[8] He re-released the film in France in 1996 as a 'director's cut' with the offending scene (along with one or two others extending the emphasis of the Léon/Mathilda relationship) reincorporated. This reaction and Besson's subsequent gesture speak volumes about different cultural responses to the representation of child sexuality and its potential connotations of incest and paedophilia. However, they also reveal Besson's insistence on his *personal* vision, his desire to express his individual concerns and his refusal to have his film curtailed by distributors or critics despite his avowed intention to succeed at the box-office.

These connections between Besson's various features are enhanced by his tendency to work repeatedly with the same personnel. Eric Serra has scored all his full-length films, Carlo Varini was director of photography on his first three features, Thierry Arbogast took over for the next three (with the exception of *Atlantis*), and a small group of actors reappear in a number of films. For example, Jean Reno has featured in all of his films apart from *Atlantis* and *Le Cinquième Élément*, Gary Oldman starred in both *Léon* and *Le Cinquième Élément*, Jean Bouise appeared in his first four features but died during the filming of *Nikita*. These two aspects of Besson's work, his tendency to rework again and again a small number of themes and his close affiliation with a small group of technicians and actors, recall two of the most prominent moments in French film history, the *nouvelle vague* and the Poetic Realist films of the 1930s. Despite his rather disingenuous claims to be 'no more' than a film-maker and his disdain for the discourses of cinephilia,[9] Besson can indeed be perceived as an auteur. Now, this is not an attempt to reclaim Besson for the canons of art and high culture. As we saw in Chapter 5, it is vital to discuss popular films in their own terms. To attempt to relocate them within some construction of 'great' French cinema would be to reinforce oppositions which this book has so far shown to be almost untenable. Nevertheless, Besson's reworking of particular tropes does recall the discourses of auteurism so central to the advent of the films of the *nouvelle vague* and this in turn problematises attempts to see his films as 'just' an imitation of Hollywood production. Similarly his re-employment of a small group of personnel recalls similar working practices in the 1930s. The role of Alexandre Trauner, one of the key designers of the 1930s, as set designer on *Subway* underlines this association. Trauner is particularly well known for his reconstruction of the Barbès Métro in Marcel Carné's *Les Portes de la nuit* (1946). His reconstruction of this reconstruction in Besson's film thus explicitly recalls his earlier work and reveals Besson's debt to his cinematic predecessors.

It would seem then that Besson's work is at once French and not-French, American and not-American. Without a doubt its emphasis on visual spectacle (arguably at the expense of narrative and characterisation) mirrors the conventions of the Hollywood action movie. However, its references to earlier forms of French production along with its exploration of themes rarely visible in mainstream Hollywood production mark it as distinctly French and/or European. Like *A bout de souffle* and *Breathless*, Besson's films are highly intertextual artefacts. This may increase their appeal as they provide a multitude of cinematic and cultural references available to a number of audiences, however it also helps us to understand the decision to remake *Nikita* which is not as 'American' as many critics have suggested. Rather it is a liminal film which in many ways invokes both French and American cultural discourses. This very intertextuality suggests an open-endedness, a plurality of meaning which surely makes the text eminently suitable for reproduction.

The relationship between *Nikita* and its American remake is indubitably bound up with the films' generic identities. Both are action thrillers and as such part of a genre which, as we saw in Chapter 4, has long played a central role in French and American cinematic production. Indeed, the thriller genre lies at the very heart of Franco-American cultural exchange. The significance of the Hollywood thriller in all its various forms (gangster films, film noir, contemporary action thrillers and so on) is well known. However, the genre is also extremely prominent in French film history. As Ginette Vincendeau points out, its origins can be perceived in the nineteenth-century noir novels of Eugene Sue (*Les Mystères de Paris*) and the realism of Balzac, Victor Hugo and Zola, as well as later crime fiction such as the *Arsène Lupin* novels of Maurice Leblanc and the *Maigret* series of Georges Simenon.[10] The popularity of the literary *policier* continued after the Second World War with Marcel Duhamel's *série noire* imprint at Gallimard which included translations of American crime fiction by writers such as Jim Thompson along with French works written in the style of their American counterparts often under American pseudonyms. The cinematic roots of the genre can be found in silent crime series such as *Fantômas* (1913–14) and *Les Vampires* (1915–16) both directed by Louis Feuillade, as well as the Simenon adaptations of the 30s and 40s and various other examples of the genre including *Pépé le Moko* and Pierre Chenal's *Le Dernier Tournant* (1939). It is worth stressing that both these films were the source of various remakes and both emerged from crime fiction (Chenal's film was based on James M. Cain's *The Postman Always Rings Twice*). In other words, they clearly demonstrate the inter-cultural (novel to film) and 'inter-national' (United States to France and vice versa) nature of the thriller genre.

The cinematic thriller or *policier* became extremely popular in France in the 1950s following the commercial and critical success of Jacques Becker's *Touchez pas au Grisbi* (1954), *Bob le Flambeur* (Jean-Pierre Melville, 1956) and *Du Rififi chez les hommes* (Jules Dassin, 1955). The genre has continued to be reworked ever since, either through comedy (Claude Zidi's *Les Ripoux*, 1984) or through more explicitly political critique as in the films of Alain Corneau and Costa-Gavras in the 1970s, or of course in the *cinéma du look* of the 80s and 90s. These films were heavily influenced by American cultural products, both via the pulp fiction translated for the *série noire* and via Hollywood gangster films and film noir. Nevertheless, it would be highly misleading to describe the genre in France as a simple reflection of its American counterpart. As our discussion of *A bout de souffle* revealed, the Hollywood gangster film/thriller played a key role in the reinvention of French cinema carried out by the film-makers of the *nouvelle vague*. As the *policier* or *polar* became a central French genre so it transformed traditions and conventions borrowed from Hollywood. Alain Corneau's *Série Noire* (1983) is based on a short story by Jim Thompson but it is set in the suburban wastelands of contemporary Paris and reveals the social isolation of characters in this location. Melville's *Bob le Flambeur* is set in a distinct urban location like so many of its American counterparts. However here, as in *A bout de souffle*, the location is not San Francisco or Los Angeles but a very specific part of Paris, Montmartre/Pigalle, an area firmly delineated as working class. The opening shots of the film swoop down from the Sacré Coeur via the funicular railway through the streets of Montmartre to Pigalle below. The camera takes us down into this community, confining us within it just as the film's protagonists are confined to this space, to its bars, nightclubs and apartments. By leaving this space and raiding the casino at Deauville they achieve only death and capture. Like Pépé le Moko's Casbah, it is both place of safety and prison.

Nikita and *The Assassin* are thus representative of genre conventions which are at once highly prominent in their respective industries and illustrative of the relations of exchange and influence between the two. *Nikita* draws on the traditions of the Hollywood thriller while through its connections to Besson's other work and the *cinéma du look* it reveals a *French* transformation of these traditions. *The Assassin* also reworks the conventions of Hollywood (it can for example be linked to Badham's earlier articulations of the genre in films such as *War Games*, 1983, *Stakeout*, 1987 and *Bird on a Wire*, 1990) while evidently borrowing from French sources through its status as remake.

What perhaps distinguishes both films from other examples of the thriller genre is the central role of women, women who are not straightforward *femmes fatales* (although this is one connotation they embody) but who are active, aggressive 'women with guns'. This is perhaps less surprising in the remake than in its French source. As Yvonne Tasker demonstrates, the heroine of the Hollywood action cinema of the 80s and 90s has tended to move from her position as subsidiary character within the narrative to the central role of 'action heroine'.[11] The role of Maggie in the 'action thriller' *The Assassin* can then be compared to female roles in films such as *Alien* (Ridley Scott, 1979), *Blue Steel* (Kathryn Bigelow, 1990), *Terminator 2: Judgement Day* (James Cameron, 1991) and *Thelma and Louise* (Ridley Scott, 1991). The role of Nikita is striking because a similar trajectory can not be traced in French cinema of the period. Indeed not only is there no real depiction of 'women with guns' in the films which surround and precede *Nikita*, roles for women in France since the 1980s have been characterised by an increasing emphasis on youthful beauty and/or an overt femininity.[12]

It is worth comparing these women to those present in another pair of remakes, *Les Diaboliques* and *Diabolique* (Jeremiah Chechik, 1996). These films are also thrillers and also feature women as killers and/or victims. Like *Nikita*, Clouzot's film draws upon both French and American cinematic traditions. It achieved critical and popular acclaim in France and overseas (helped as we have seen by wide-scale distribution in Britain). The film was based on a novel by French crime writers Boileau and Narcejac (who also provided the source for Hitchcock's *Vertigo*) and many contemporary reviews described it in terms of Hitchcock's work.[13] Like *Nikita* it gives a pessimistic vision of French society via its depiction of the uncaring teachers at work in their dilapidated boarding school.[14]

Unlike its source film, Chechik's remake proved a box-office flop despite its extended action sequences (notably the closing scenes) and the presence of stars such as Sharon Stone and Kathy Bates. Carolyn Durham describes an article published in *Le Nouvel Observateur* in which one of the film's producers claims that as American audiences have never seen the 'original' film, Chechik's work is in fact not a remake at all.[15] Of course this remark is rather misleading; as Durham points out some American spectators have seen Clouzot's film and may well watch *Diabolique* in order to compare it to its 'classic' source. The remark is also interesting as in many ways the film actually seems to foreground its status as remake. It is a curious hybrid of genres (the thriller, the 'action' movie, the 'female buddy' film, horror and so on) producing a rather uncertain cine-

Léon: Léon (Jean Réno).

matic identity which recalls its indebtedness to other texts. Moreover its temporal location is highly uncertain. Modern technology (computers, video cameras) is combined with Sharon Stone's 50s dress style and Isabelle Adjani's Victorian gothic look to create a strangely ambivalent temporality which perhaps underlines the relationship between this late 1990s artefact and its 1950s source.

The film's significance here lies in its representation of female 'buddies' who are at once victims and killers, sites of passivity and 'action women'. The film parades its contemporary retake on Clouzot's film in the politically correct, breast cancer surviving body of Kathy Bates' detective. The female betrayal of the French film is here set in motion and then resolved as the central characters (Stone and Adjani) join forces to kill the abusive husband/lover with the blessing of Bates' detective. This disavowal of female treachery in favour of an all-action sisterhood is perhaps the film's major weakness. Clouzot's film is typically dark (and arguably misogynistic). Christine (Véra Clouzot) dies of fear upon seeing her husband's 'body' emerging from a bath. Her 'friend' (Simone Signoret) is arrested with her lover (Christine's husband, played by Paul Meurisse) by the male detective. In other words, both women ultimately remain victims of men. The transformation of this ending in the remake undermines the film's narrative of betrayal and, as we have seen, smacks of political correctness. However, it is also striking as it recalls the trajectory from victim to victor through female bonding in other Hollywood films of the period (notably *Thelma and Louise*) and the gradual progress of women's roles from subsidiary characters to central action heroine outlined a moment ago.

If we turn our attention again to Nikita and Maggie, we can see both roles as a positive response to the advances of feminism. Maggie extends a tradition visible elsewhere in American cinema (in *Diabolique* for example) while the muscular Nikita imitates her Hollywood sisters in order to transform the depiction of women in French production.

However, while a reading of this nature is perhaps tempting, a closer look at the two films can reveal a rather less optimistic account of female identity. Indeed, the films' respective constructions of gender and their depictions of their central heroines provide one of the key distinctions between the two works. Durham argues that the films are more or less identical.[16] As we shall now see, this claim is far from true.

Central to the narrative of Besson's film is an exploration of the process of becoming a woman or, more generally, becoming human. The films' contrasting titles are here revealing. Whereas the title of the source film suggests an emphasis on the identity of its eponymous heroine, the British title of the remake (*The Assassin*) underlines her role or profession in the film while the American title (*Point of No Return*) emphasises the narrative. Certainly the process of becoming, the transformation (or its failure) which lies at the heart of *Nikita*, becomes something rather different in the remake. We first see Nikita during the raid on the pharmacy in the film's opening sequence. She is more or less passive, curled up listening to a walkman while her male friends attack the police and are themselves shot to death. She is reduced to her desire for drugs, her only words are 'J'en veux' (I want some) and, as the police officer approaches her at the close of the sequence, an ambiguous 'Il n'y en a plus?' (Isn't there/aren't there any left?). Her voice here is gentle and she seems unthreatening, almost child-like as she crouches on the floor with her headphones on. However, we are immediately disabused of this image as she takes out a gun and shoots the police officer in the head. We next see her at the police station. She responds to the investigating officer's questions in a grating robot-like voice, repeating his words and then telling him her name before stabbing him in the hand with a pencil. She reacts violently to her prison sentence, screaming and struggling with her guards who have difficulty in controlling her. She is then shown awaiting an injection which she believes to be lethal. She is colourless, dressed in a white robe with harsh lighting emphasising the pallor of her skin. She weeps uncontrollably, calling for her mother and the scene then cuts to her awakening in a bright, white, empty room.

The film's opening sequences thus reveal the unknowability of their central character. She is drug addict, killer, victim and child. Her only name is Nikita which bears traces of Eastern Europe and yet ultimately remains rootless and indeed genderless (we have no idea, and will never discover, where she is from). She is reduced to a series of almost bestial needs or reactions (the desire for drugs, her violence) and yet also displays a touching childishness (her calls for her mother). As she is controlled and confined by her captors so she seems to be drained of these identities (her pale skin, the white robes) and finds herself in a similarly anonymous, empty space. She represents both an excess of identities and a lack which will appear to be filled as the film progresses.

This instability of identity, our inability to know who or what she is, recalls the central characters of Besson's other films. Nikita's androgny coupled with the processes of construction that form her new identities resemble the gendered cyborg Leeloo in *Le Cinquième Élément*. Her combination of violence and child-like innocence mirrors Léon. Nikita, Léon and Fred (in *Subway*) have no real past (and, in most cases, no future). They are no more than their on-screen presence and yet the plurality of this presence makes any attempt at 'knowing' them highly problematic. Each of these films shows these multifarious and apparently alienated characters finding some form of fulfilment and/or humanity within the threatening context of a dangerous and confining diegetic space. In each case this fulfilment will be curtailed or contained, suggesting a clear distinction between Besson's cinematic vision and the more optimistic outlook of many of the Hollywood films he appears to emulate.

As she becomes an assassin so Nikita learns to become a woman. She visits Amande (played by Jeanne Moreau, an archetypally 'feminine' French star) and receives lessons in 'femininity and the means of taking advantage of it'. We see her in front of her mirror applying the make-up that will transform her from androgynous being to extremely feminised woman thus revealing the constructed nature of gender identity. She then leaves for the restaurant with Bob and, as she kills her targets and escapes through the kitchens, she shows herself to be both woman and highly trained assassin; she has apparently become something other, the product of Bob, Amande and the training institution.

Besson seems then to underline the constructed nature of identity. Nikita appears to have no easily definable identity until she is arrested and a new persona is created for her. This narrative of transformation is in itself not unfamiliar. Indeed it echoes the Cinderella-like myths which have long played an important role in Western cultural production. Nevertheless, Besson's treatment of the theme here is fascinating as Nikita's transformation is never fully achieved, her multiple personae are never entirely contained. She leaves the institution armed with a number of new identities constructed for her. She is a trained assassin with a code name (Joséphine) and she is 'Marie', a nurse. In other words, she has (supposedly) become something other through the agency of the state and, more importantly, Bob. This representation of Nikita as 'object' constructed by the patriarch (Bob as representative of the state) evidently undermines optimistic readings of the film as a narrative of female agency and transgression. Indeed Nikita's early transgression is contained and punished by Bob and she becomes a killer

Nikita: Nikita (Anne Parillaud).

in his control and a 'daughter' subject to his authority. Susan Hayward extends this argument to claim Nikita as an extension of the phallus. Her fetishisation and the equation of her body with the guns she carries complete, in Hayward's words, 'the supreme male fantasy. [...] Women become guns (i.e., phallus). The dream of narcissus is complete.'[17]

While I would agree that the film does fetishise Nikita, frequently positioning her as the object of the gaze particularly when she engages in state-controlled violence, to see her as no more than Bob's construct is misleading. After leaving the institution armed with her new identities she goes to a supermarket. Despite her newly learned femininity, she proves incapable of shopping, following another woman around the store and loading her trolley with the same products in an attempt to imitate this 'female' role. She meets Marco, the cashier, and invites him back to her home. As we saw earlier in the chapter, she seduces him in a very forthright manner. This reveals an active sexuality that both recalls the *femme fatale* of Hollywood noir and undermines her status as 'passive' female. The elemental nature of the seduction (combined with her distinctly 'unfeminine' eating habits) and her explicit declaration of her desire for Marco recall her need for drugs and her uncontrolled behaviour in the film's opening sequences. Despite Bob and Amande's training her former identities continue to resurface.

This plurality is suggested by the film's constant vacillation between domestic spaces and/or the romance narrative and Nikita's role as killer and the conventions of the thriller genre. It is striking that each of her major missions interrupts scenes of domestic life and occurs within a domestic space. Her first killing takes place in a restaurant but she escapes through the kitchen, she learns of her next assignment as she lies in bed with Marco eating her breakfast and the work involves her disguising herself as a chamber maid and carrying a tray to a hotel bedroom. Here Besson makes the combination of the details of domesticity and the paraphernalia of violence quite explicit as he shows her accomplices attaching timers and explosives to coffee pots, fruit juice and so on. Violence and food become one and Nikita's own earlier breakfast is recalled. It is perhaps significant that after her final, abortive mission Nikita returns home to take a shower and go to bed. In other words, she renounces her identity as assassin and seems to embrace fully the home and romance she has created with Marco. This combination of domesticity and death underwrites the film's gendering of violence (Nikita's assassination of a woman from a bathroom dressed only in vest and knickers reinforces her fetishisation and reminds us of the novelty of women with guns in French cinema) while simultaneously extending the various identities on display in the film. Again, we are not sure who or what Nikita is. Is she killer, lover or (unsuccessful) housewife?

Unlike Nikita, Maggie does not have to learn to become a woman (or indeed a human). Instead she acquires the etiquette and charm which will enable her to pass in any social situation. Amanda (Anne Bancroft) makes her smile and repeat 'I never did mind about the little things' and she learns table manners and deportment. Whereas Nikita is transformed from unknowable, androgynous, cyborg-like being to ultra-feminine killer, Maggie is transformed from violent tom-boy to sophisticated, elegant assassin. In other words, the instability of identity that lies at the heart of Besson's film disappears from the remake and is replaced by the Cinderella narrative described earlier. This is underlined by the film's opening sequence which, although it follows the narrative of *Nikita* almost exactly, includes specificities of place and person which efface the ambiguity of the source text. The film opens with an aerial pan over a city which we are told is Washington, DC. Maggie is no more communicative than her French sister yet her voice does not have the robot/animal qualities of Nikita and her name is clearly recognisable. She too is dehumanised as she awaits her injection yet here this is a very real, very culturally specific process. The lethal injection she expects is, as we know, part of the judicial system in many American states. Her dehumanisation as she is strapped to the machine could perhaps be seen as an implicit criticism of the death penalty but as we know where she is and recognise what is happening to her it does not have the disorienting potential of the equivalent scene in Besson's film. This difference is further emphasised in later sequences. Maggie is surrounded by other people in the training facility. The building is far less alienating than the stark spaces shown in *Nikita* and her efforts are accompanied by a relatively upbeat soundtrack.

Above all Maggie does not connote the plural identities embodied in Nikita. As she is questioned by the investigating officer upon arrival at the police station we see things from her point of view. A cloudy, unfocused shot reveals her confusion and allows some degree of identification between protagonist and spectator. We later learn of her love for the music of Nina Simone, a passion which suggests a humanity and a past largely absent from Nikita. We do not witness her transformation from tom-boy to feminine woman. Whereas we watch Nikita paint her face and are thus always already aware of the unstable nature of her new identity, Maggie simply goes upstairs to Amanda's room and redescends a changed woman. All traces of her earlier aggression have disappeared and the success of her transformation is revealed when, after her first mission, one of her would-be assassins follows her and upon seeing her little black dress clad body assumes that she must be innocent.

Traces of Nikita's earlier identities constantly re-emerge, threatening the apparent cohesion of the identities created for her by Bob. In contrast Maggie shows no sign of her former life. After the bathroom killing she tells JP that she did something bad in her past for which she will always pay. In other words she explains and excuses her earlier crimes and fully embraces her new, more feminine, more loving self. It is worth pointing out that during their final mission both women have to disguise themselves as their victim. Nikita dresses up as a man, recalling and reinforcing her continuing gender ambivalence. Maggie on the other hand dresses up as an exaggeratedly feminine woman complete with blonde wig and red leather mini-skirt. Thus she reinforces the complete effacement of her earlier androgyny.

These differences become most apparent in the films' respective endings. Besson's film closes with the disappearance of Nikita. Bob arrives at her apartment to find Marco who tells him that he knows of her identity as assassin. Both men express their grief at her departure and the film ends. In the remake Bob arrives at Maggie's home to be told by JP that she has disappeared and that although he does not know 'what' she is, he loved her anyway. JP gives Bob her Nina Simone record and asks him if he likes Nina (the name of the singer of course but also Maggie's code name). Bob replies that he loves her and leaves the apartment. Maggie then reappears, walking back towards the apartment and JP. Bob sees her and calls the agency to say that she has died. A close-up shows Bob watching her and she then turns to see that he has disappeared.

This transformation is significant for a number of reasons. First it reinforces claims

Maggie (Bridget Fonda) in *The Assassin* (*Point of No Return*).

about the tendency in Hollywood cinema for 'happy' endings in contrast to the ambivalence of many French productions. We can assume that Maggie is now free to start a new life with JP but Nikita's fate is far from clear. Second, and more importantly, this transformation reinforces the films' different negotiations of identity and their representations of their female protagonists. As we have seen, positive readings of either woman as a response to the advances of feminism are undermined by their fetishisation (both are the objects of a powerful male gaze via the surveillance of Bob and their constant positioning as focus of the spectatorial look) and the role of Bob in their apparent empowerment. Yes they become killers, action heroines, women with guns, but they do this through Bob's (and thus the patriarchal state's) agency and are subject to his control. His continuing impact upon their lives and identities is revealed when, in the guise of Uncle Bob, he invents a childhood for Maggie/Nikita. It is worth noting that whereas in the remake Bob describes a romanticised vision of Maggie on a black horse, an image which extends his relatively unproblematic erotic desire for her, in the source film Bob tells of a little girl who used to imitate frogs. In other words, the parent/child relationship is emphasised in Besson's film; Bob is both father and potential lover (a combination, as we know, present in many French cultural artefacts but generally absent from, or concealed in their American counterparts) and this in turn extends further the film's multiplication of identity.

Susan Hayward argues that the disappearance of Nikita at the end of Besson's feature is a corroboration of the film's problematic gender politics. Nikita disappears because of her very excess (of identity), her transgression of gender boundaries, '... she threatens the very thing that secures masculinity (the binary gender division).'[18] In other words, her very plurality of identity and her appropriation of typically masculine traits ultimately lead to her effacement and relocation within a typically 'feminine' gender role. Hayward adds that Nikita's effacement of identity (through her transformation in the training institution) is confirmed by her own disappearance. In other words, her apparent agency becomes a collaboration in her own erasure. In these terms the ending of The Assassin should be read as rather less problematic. Instead of disappearing, Maggie remains and is liberated from the control of the state.

However, while such accounts of the film are suggestive, I think they become precarious when we consider again the themes and representations described in this chapter. Maggie may well escape at the end of the film but she does this only with Bob's blessing. It is striking that while Bob and JP discuss Maggie in the film's closing scenes, we see in the background a large photograph of her face. The film's final image is a close-up on this same photograph thus Maggie is reduced to pure object. The fetishisation of her body demonstrated throughout the film culminates in this image. She becomes silent image (the object of the men's conversation) and the empowerment suggested by her 'escape' is undermined. Moreover our last sight of the 'living' Maggie shows her as the object of Bob's gaze as he watches her from his car. When she turns to look at him, to appropriate the gaze for herself, he has of course disappeared. It is also worth noting that Maggie's 'escape' and her ability to fully inhabit her new-found identity are not only a consequence of Bob's decision to let her go but also the result of her relationship with JP. In other words, she is able to be the woman she thinks she want to be (feminine rather than a tom-boy, loving rather than aggressive) through heterosexual love and, once again, the support of a man. In this respect Maggie echoes Leeloo, Besson's later heroine, as she also finds (and saves) humanity through a heterosexual love affair.

The ending of Nikita can, as Hayward reveals, be seen to undermine female empowerment/agency in similar fashion. However, this reading is problematised by the plurality of identity revealed throughout the film. Unlike Maggie, Nikita never fully embraces either of the identities created for her by Bob; she is never fully (or straightforwardly) assassin or 'woman'. She is perhaps 'made absent' by Bob at the beginning of the film as he attempts to replace her initial identities with those constructed in the training institution. Yet, as we have seen, these earlier selves are never contained, they resurface throughout the narrative and ultimately Nikita disappears through her own agency. She rejects the identities offered by either Bob or Marco. Indeed she can be seen to return to her former self. She emerges from nowhere at the outset of the film and disappears at the end. We do not know what she is at the beginning and are left equally uncertain as the film closes. Her plurality, her unknowability and, ultimately, her absence break down the binaries described by Hayward. Certainly Nikita is fetishised object of the gaze but she also has the ability to exceed that role and in the end, remove herself from our sight and from the clearly delineated roles offered to her by Bob and Marco.

So it would seem that *Nikita* and *The Assassin* are not identical at all. Without a doubt they share a plethora of traits, including narrative structure, genre, dialogue and *mise en scène*. Indeed, like Besson's later films they are representative of the various forms of exchange and interpenetration between different 'national' film industries. Their allegiance to the thriller genre positions them within a particular form of Franco-American traffic which has played an important role in the construction of both these cinemas. Moreover, their representation of action women, women with guns, recalls and/or transforms many of the films and discourses which surround and penetrate them. Nevertheless, they remain separate artefacts as they negotiate their shared concerns in rather different ways. Certainly Besson's exploration of identity and its instability can be located within his own particular body of work. However, as we have seen elsewhere, it is also a concern central to many of the remake pairs and the broader cinematic contexts from which they emerge. It is to these concerns and the ways in which they can be seen to symbolise the remake process itself that we shall turn in Chapter 7.

Notes

1. See Susan Hayward, *Luc Besson* (Manchester: Manchester University Press, 1998) for examples of this type of critique.

2. His fifth feature, *Atlantis* (1991) is a documentary-style film of marine life accompanied by an imaginative score. It is a Franco-Italian co-production and its lack of dialogue, actors or indeed narrative limit its relevance to a discussion of the 'Americanisation' or 'transnationalism' visible in his later films.

3. The connections between Besson's films, the remakes and other American productions are nicely illustrated in a review of *The Assassin* from the *Washington Post*, 19 March 1993. Desson Howe praises Keitel's role and suggests that he should star in a 'spinoff movie called "Victor the Cleaner"'. He goes on to say 'It would be exactly the kind of cult hit Warner Bros. is trying to crib. Perhaps they'd better wait for it to come out in France first.' The film did of course come out in France first in the guise of *Léon* but with Jean Reno in the title role while Harvey Keitel reprised his role in comic fashion in *Pulp Fiction*.

4. See Susan Hayward, 'Besson's "Mission Elastoplast": *Le Cinquième Élément*', in Phil Powrie (ed.), *French Cinema in the 1990s: Continuity and Difference* (Oxford: Oxford University Press, 1999), pp. 246–57, for a useful analysis of the film's use of digital technology. Hayward suggests that, unlike many Hollywood directors, Besson uses technology to drive the narrative rather than for its visual effect alone. In this sense he uses American technology in a distinctly European fashion.

5. It is striking that the last two French language films to be given wide-scale distribution in Britain, *Les Diaboliques* (Clouzot, 1954) and *Du Rififi chez les hommes* (Jules Dassin, 1955), are both examples of the thriller genre.

6. See Nigel Floyd, 'Infinite City', *Sight and Sound* vol. 7 no. 6, June 1997, pp. 6–9.

7. Stella Bruzzi, *Undressing Cinema: Clothing and Identity in the Movies* (London: Routledge, 1997), p. 91.

8. Hayward, *Luc Besson*, pp. 65–6.

9. See ibid., pp. 1–23.

10. Ginette Vincendeau, 'France 1945–65 and Hollywood: The *Policier* as Inter-National Text', *Screen* vol. 33 no. 1, Spring 1992, pp. 50–80.

11. Yvonne Tasker, *Spectacular Bodies: Gender, Genre and the Action Cinema* (London: Routledge, 1993), pp. 132–52.

12. Witness the popularity of actors such as Emmanuelle Béart, Sophie Marceau and Charlotte Gainsbourg. Marceau and Gainsbourg are particularly revealing as both became prominent as adolescents.

13. In a letter sent to Hitchcock shortly after the release of *Psycho*, a man informs him that since seeing *Les Diaboliques* his daughter could not take a bath and having seen *Psycho* she could now not take a shower. He asked Hitchcock what he should do with his daughter. The director's reply: 'Send her to the dry cleaners'!

14. This of course recalls Clouzot's earlier work, notably *Le Salaire de la peur*.

15. Carolyn Durham, *Double Takes: Culture and Gender in French Films and their American Remakes* (Hanover: University Press of New England, 1998), p. 180.

16. Ibid., pp. 175–6.

17. Susan Hayward, *French National Cinema* (London: Routledge, 1993), p. 293.

18. Hayward, *Luc Besson*, p. 114.

7
Remaking Identities

The preceding chapters have shown that issues of identity lie at the very heart of the remake. Critique of the practice tends to be centred around attempts to define straightforward national and cultural identities for both French and American cinema and yet the very act of remaking a film calls these identities into question, revealing the instabilities and hybridity which constitute the filmic text. The films themselves extend this process through their own explorations of identity. Through genre (the transformation of comedy), representations of history (the negotiations of accounts of the 'national' past), constructions of gender and sexuality and so on, the remake and its source continue the process which their very status as cinematic texts sets in motion. Their questioning of issues of identity can most certainly not be abstracted from the broader cinematic contexts from which they emerge. We have already seen that the articulations of the past in *Le Retour de Martin Guerre* and *Sommersby* emerge from, precede and/or extend similar constructions in other filmic texts (the heritage film for example) just as the representations of gender and paternity in *Trois hommes et un couffin* and its remake are closely linked to a host of other French and American films including a number of other remake pairs. What is perhaps unique about the remake is the way in which these narrative or formal explorations mirror the very films' own revelation of the instability of identity. Daniel Vigne's film shows the volatile nature of interpretations of the past while through its reproduction as *Sommersby* it is itself revealed as an open-ended, thoroughly plural text. Chapter 7 will look at two pairs of films, *La Totale* (Claude Zidi, 1991) and its remake of 1993, *True Lies* (James Cameron) and *La Cage aux folles* (Edouard Molinaro, 1978) and *The Birdcage* (Mike Nicholls, 1996) in order to explore further the various ways in which these multiple explorations of identity take place. Of course these issues have already been addressed in earlier chapters. Nevertheless I believe that these pairs of films are particularly interesting and merit closer analysis as identity is absolutely central to their respective narratives and to the transformations they undergo through adaptation. As such I will suggest that they can in many ways be seen as metaphors for the remake process itself.

Like so many of the films already discussed, *La Totale* and *True Lies* are popular cinematic works. Indeed both are clearly marked as non-high cultural artefacts by virtue of their very genre (at least within their countries of production; the cultural status of a French film released in the United States is, as we know, liable to alter). *La Totale* is a comedy and hence part of one of the most commercially successful indigenous French cinematic genres, a genre which is almost invariably ignored by the French critical establishment. *True Lies* is essentially an action film, a film of spectacle. Yvonne Tasker pointedly describes these films as 'dumb movies for dumb people', claiming that their emphasis on spectacle has tended to their exclusion from critical esteem.[1] Tasker's own work is part of a recent move to accord action cinema just such critical attention, however her comments underline the non-high cultural status of action cinema such as *True Lies*.

The films share an almost identical narrative structure. In each, the hero, François (Thierry Lhermitte) and Harry (Arnold Schwarzenegger), pretends to lead a routine existence employed in a dull nine-to-five job. However this is a cover for his true occupation as a secret agent. In both films the hero finds his marriage in trouble as his wife, Hélène (Miou-Miou)/Helen (Jamie Lee Curtis), longing for excitement and unaware of her husband's true identity, falls for the lies of a car salesman who claims to be a secret agent. François/Harry discovers this liaison and captures both wife and would-be paramour, subsequently involving Hélène/Helen in a 'spoof' covert operation which turns to reality when they are captured by the Arab terrorists whose illegal transport of arms, and plans to detonate a large explosive device which will threaten 'national' security, have been jeopardised by the hero. Both films also contain a narrative centred on a rebellious offspring – the hero's daughter in *True Lies*, a son in *La Totale*. In both films the various strands of the narrative are resolved: the terrorists' plans are thwarted and harmony is restored in the hero's marriage and family. The narrative similarities are extended by many identical gags (for example Hélène's/Helen's elimination of numerous villains as she drops a machine gun down the stairs causing it to fire as it hits each step), jokes (the play on the contrasts between the hero's assumed identity and the dangerous reality of his true function) and even dialogues.

Nevertheless, the films are not identical artefacts. They belong to very different genres, or as José Arroyo points out, they use different combinations of elements from various genres.[2] *La Totale* is essentially a domestic comedy; it focuses primarily on the family plot, indeed around two-thirds of the film involves François's attempts to deal with the exploits of his wife and son, and the Arab narrative is manifestly a subplot. In contrast *True Lies* is primarily an action film, a film of spectacle; like the French production it is a comedy but it is a comedy of action, many of the comic moments arise from Harry's daring feats, for example as he chases the motor-cycle riding villain through a hotel lobby on horseback. Here the Arab plot is given much more prominence, indeed the film opens as Harry breaks into a Swiss château on the trail of the villains and within five minutes an extended action sequence begins, involving a high speed car chase and escape on skis. Compare this to the opening of *La Totale* which centres on the family plot via a planned birthday party for the hero.

While it would be quite wrong to see the comedy of either film as either purely physical or purely linguistic, these differences in emphasis do situate each work within the specific comic traditions outlined in Chapter 5. Indeed each should be located within a particular 'national' cinematic trajectory; thus *La Totale* can be seen to intersect with a French tradition of 'social' comedy, films which mock social norms and hierarchies. Ginette Vincendeau identifies three features which she claims can justify the enduring popularity of domestic film comedy in France, '... its overwhelming maleness, which has gone hand in hand with the hegemony of male stars at the box office [...]; the importance of language and word-play in French culture; and the taste for deriding social and regional types'.[3] *La Totale* can be seen to share each of these attributes; the narrative centres on Thierry Lhermitte, and the relationship he shares with his wife is to all intents and purposes equalled by the all-male relationship he shares with his buddy Albert (Eddy Mitchell). Much of the film's humour arises from language, and the narrative sets out to mock social types and institutions such as the petty-bourgeois *fonctionnaire* and the middle-class family, resident in the Parisian suburbs. Both Vincendeau's definitions and the film itself reveal close affinities between *La Totale* and *Trois hommes et un couffin*.

True Lies also forms part of a specific cinematic tradition, the Hollywood action blockbuster, or the cinema of spectacle. As we have seen, big-budget action movies became an integral part of Hollywood production during the 1980s. Films such as *First Blood* (Ted Kotcheff, 1982), *Die Hard* (John McTiernan, 1988), *Lethal Weapon* (Richard Donner, 1987) and *RoboCop* (Paul Verhoeven, 1987) reaped huge profits at the box-office, both in their country of production and on the international market. Indeed their commercial success was demonstrated and entrenched by the various sequels and franchises to which they gave rise. The popularity of these films spawned a new type of star, the 'muscular' action hero exemplified by the likes of Jean-Claude Van Damme, Chuck Norris, Sylvester Stallone and, of course, Arnold Schwarzenegger. Achieving prominence through the action film, these stars then guaranteed the continuing success of the genre as their star images and box-office appeal developed throughout the decade. The action cinema became increasingly centred upon spectacle achieved through elaborate special effects, a shift which made the presence of a star somewhat less vital to a film's commercial appeal. In films such as *Mission Impossible* (Brian de Palma, 1996), *Twister* (Jan de Bont, 1996) and *Independence Day* (Roland Emmerich, 1996) spectacular action and special effects are so integral that they become the very driving force, and the principal attraction, of the films. *True Lies* evidently straddles the two genres; it is both muscular action cinema, played out in the presence of Schwarzenegger, and it is cinema of spectacle, as revealed by the film's multiple (and highly sophisticated) use of special effects. Thus this film can be situated in a recent tradition of action/spectacular cinema which can itself be located within a long-standing Hollywood tradition of spectacle and 'attractions' (the 'tricks' and 'exoticisms' of early cinema and the experiments with CinemaScope, 3D and so on in the 1950s).

The popularity and endurance of particular cinematic forms and genres are of course closely bound up with the contemporary aesthetic and industrial context. Both films should then be located in a national history of production *and* the contemporary conjuncture. *La Totale* is part of a series of French domestic/social comedies produced during the 1980s and 1990s which often had their roots in the *café-théâtre* of the 1970s. These comedies would tend to be set in recognisable, everyday locations, using an earthy, naturalistic language based upon contemporary slang. They were frequently more sexually explicit than their comic predecessors and they satirised social institutions and norms. Films such as *Les Bronzés* (Patrice Leconte, 1978), *Le Père Noël est une ordure* (Jean-Marie Poiré, 1982), *Les Hommes préfèrent les grosses* (Jean-Marie Poiré, 1981) and *Les Ripoux* (Claude Zidi, 1984) proved successful at the domestic box-office, ensuring the continuing production of such comedies, often involving the same personnel. Unquestionably, *La Totale* forms part of this particular comic conjuncture. As we shall see, the film is manifestly rooted in the *café-théâtre* tradition. Its parody of the spy genre is coupled with a satiric portrait of conventional petty-bourgeois life-styles and its use of language and dialogue is both inventive and naturalistic.

The very fact that, unlike its remake, *La Totale* is *not* a spectacular film is also significant in terms of its production context. The film emerges from a French or European cinema industry which as we know lacks the finance and the necessary material infrastructure for the type of special effects displayed in *True Lies* (whose budget reputedly reached $120 million). This material lack is reinforced by the fact that *La Totale* was co-produced by the television company TF1, clearly with an eventual televisual screening in mind.[4] The spectacular display of films such as *True Lies* is designed for wide-screen cinema viewing with dolby stereo sound. Lacking finance, and in some ways circumscribed by its future televisual career, *La Totale* forsakes special effects in favour of concentration on narrative, character and dialogue.

As part of the action cinema/cinema of spectacle dominant in Hollywood throughout the 1980s and 1990s, *True Lies* is also an integral part of its specific production context. As we saw in Chapter 1, the big-budget hit, the blockbuster, has become a staple feature of Hollywood's enduring success, in many respects the key to its survival in the face of the changes brought about by the demise of the big studios and the competition emanating from new media such as television, video and, more recently, information technology. The importance of the blockbuster has increased as the Hollywood studios have become part of large multimedia conglomerates, anxious to diversify the cinematic product across a range of media. This wide-scale 'synergy' is predicated on the blockbuster, which necessitates significant financial investment both for production costs and intense marketing. Perhaps somewhat paradoxically, synergy developed through other media products or other films both helps to ensure a market for the expensive blockbuster and at the same time depends upon big-budget productions for its existence (low- or medium-budget films will not give rise to this sort of diversification). Not surprisingly then, film budgets rose steadily during the 1980s and, as the budget of *True Lies* indicates, these figures continue to escalate.[5]

An important feature of these material and aesthetic developments was the increased power of the film star. Although many of the early 'New Hollywood' blockbusters (*Jaws*, 1975, *Star Wars*, 1977) were not star vehicles, the development of synergy and escalating budgets saw a dramatic rise in the role of the star, a fact evidenced by the escalation in star salaries.[6] Films began to be produced and marketed on the basis of the stars they involved, indeed stars became franchises in their own right. Thus *True Lies* was advertised as both a James Cameron film, drawing upon the success of his earlier films, *Terminator 2* and *Aliens*, and as an Arnold Schwarzenegger vehicle. Posters and the video cover featured a close-up still of the star's face in a 'tough' glare familiar from his previous roles. Significantly, the film was not marketed as a remake. *La Totale* was not distributed in the United States and would have been unknown to the vast majority of the remake's audience. As a result *True Lies* could be inserted unproblematically into a specifically Hollywood tradition of action/spectacle films and Schwarzenegger vehicles; its status as a remake, without being actively denied, became irrelevant.

Despite their location in specific temporal, material and aesthetic conjunctures, neither film can be straightforwardly described in terms of a single genre. Certainly *La*

Totale is essentially a domestic/social comedy and *True Lies* is primarily a comedy of action/spectacle, however their generic identities are highly complex. Each features elements of the domestic comedy (the family narrative), the spy genre (the hero's identity as secret agent), the action film (the hero's exploits as he attempts to thwart the terrorists) and the buddy movie (the hero's relationship with his male partner). This bricolage or combination of different genres is an increasingly common feature of contemporary popular cinema, both in Hollywood and elsewhere (Besson's films are evident examples). Unquestionably the synergy discussed above is an important part of this process; blockbusters are no longer considered to be discreet entities but rather elements of an extended media process involving sequels and related multimedia products. Yvonne Tasker perceives this hybridity as a central feature of the so-called New Hollywood, claiming that repetition is now at the very heart of narrative significance and pleasure, 'Hybridity [...] allows films to both draw on and redefine a range of genres, through the forging of new associations between them.'[7]

This intertextuality is especially knowing in *True Lies*. Although both films incorporate elements of various genres, this process is repeatedly stressed in the American production in a manner that is not apparent in the French source. For example, both films draw upon the James Bond cinema cycle; the hero is shown to be a suit-wearing secret agent, attractive to women and in possession of various ingenious gadgets. However, this reference is stressed in *True Lies* during the opening sequence as Harry enters a Swiss château dressed in a dinner jacket, demonstrates his ability to speak various languages, tangos with the beautiful (and 'exotic') villainess and is then chased by villains on skis.

This insistent intertextuality is not restricted to Bond films alone. *True Lies* also makes frequent references to other action movies, particularly those starring Arnold Schwarzenegger. Towards the end of the film, as the Secret Service helicopter arrives at the terrorists' hideout, Harry emerges from a mass of burning buildings, framed by a red sky in a scene strongly reminiscent of the apocalyptic landscape of *Terminator*. 'I thought this would be your work,' says Albert (Tom Arnold), Harry's colleague; it is the work of the Terminator, the action hero. Similarly the transformation of Helen (Jamie Lee Curtis) is resonant of previous action films. As she is transformed from dowdy housewife to 'sexy' accomplice so she echoes the action women described in Chapter 6, the strong heroines of Cameron's previous films (Sigourney Weaver in *Aliens* and Linda Hamilton in *Terminator* and *Terminator 2*) as well as her own roles in films such as *Blue Steel*. This is significant in terms of the films' representations of the female characters. Miou-Miou's transformation does not have the same resonance for, as we have seen, there is no equivalent French tradition of 'action' heroines or 'women with guns'.

Evidently this hybridity is highly relevant in terms of the film's status as a remake. *True Lies* is not a separate artefact, entire unto itself. Rather it deliberately sets out to draw upon and rework the codes and conventions of popular Hollywood cinema. As such it will be consumed in a thoroughly intertextual fashion; depending upon their position and cultural capital, different audiences will view the film in terms of its references to other films, other artefacts: this is a built-in feature of its identity. However, unfamiliar with *La Totale*, American audiences will read *True Lies* in terms of its references to other Hollywood films rather than through a linear relationship to its French source.

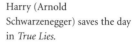
Harry (Arnold Schwarzenegger) saves the day in *True Lies*.

Many of the differences described so far are inscribed within the bodies and the personae of the films' male stars, and through their particular constructions and representations of masculinity. The cinematic star is a highly unstable signifying structure. A star image is not restricted to the body on-screen, but must also incorporate the body 'off-screen' as constructed by a huge variety of media texts (photographs, interviews, fanzines, critical pieces and so on). In his seminal work on stars, Richard Dyer groups these texts under four separate headings: promotion, publicity, films, and commentaries and criticisms. In other words, the image on screen is only one part of the total star identity.[8] The star is then a polysemic signifying system, made up of multiple texts and both visual, verbal and aural codes; Dyer describes this multiplicity as 'structured polysemy', numerous codes which come together (but are not necessarily reconciled) within the screen body of the individual star.[9] This polysemy is reinforced by the inherent paradox of the star, the fact that he or she is always both ordinary *and* special. Star publicity will invariably stress both their extraordinary qualities (beauty, talent, glamour) and their normality (they are just like us). This polysemy means that the star image can never be entirely fixed or complete. Indeed the star image offered by promotion and publicity offers us fragments of the star (a photograph, some information about his or her private life) which invite us to view the star on-screen, 'The star image is paradoxical and incomplete so that it functions as an invitation to cinema, like the narrative image. It proposes cinema as the completion of its lacks, the synthesis of its separate fragments.'[10] However this synthesis is in many ways illusory. Certainly the star's performance can simply contain and reconcile the disparate elements of the star image, yet the performance can also play upon the very impossibility of reconciling these polysemic features, perhaps making a deliberate attempt to extend, transform or transgress the received identity.

As we have seen in earlier chapters, this polysemy and instability are equally central features of cinematic constructions of gender and, more specifically, masculinity. Just as star images, based upon performance and spectacle, must subsume contradictory features, constantly open to shifts in signification, so masculinity in the cinema should be seen in terms of an unstable performativity. Drawing upon Barthes's work on photography, *Chambre claire: note sur la photographie* (1980), John Ellis describes cinema in terms of the 'photo effect'. Spectators know that films are photographed and edited together long before they are actually projected and viewed by the cinema audience, yet they offer an experience of immediacy, 'Cinema is present absence: it says "This is was".'[11] In just the same way, the star performance is defined by presence (the figure on-screen) and absence (the knowledge that this figure is always already 'not there'). This reinforces the instability of the star image, the inability of the filmic representation to fully circumscribe its multiple meanings. Cinematic constructions of masculinity can also be seen to fall into this particular double bind. The masculine is defined by presence, by what we actually see on the screen (the male body and the male star's actions) and by absence, by what it is not; in other words, by the feminine or the unsuccessful masculine.

This presence/absence binary constitutes the essential paradox of hegemonic representations of masculinity. Following Laura Mulvey's positing of the male gaze and the female object (male 'looker' and female 'to be looked at'), Steve Neale explores the extremely problematic nature of the very act of representing the masculine.[12] To construct the masculine on-screen the male body must be displayed but, if the gaze is (heterosexual) male, this body can not be the object of this gaze. Neale claims that this dilemma is overcome by representing the male body as never merely the object of the gaze; its display is both justified and masculinised (or heterosexualised) through action, or it is mediated through the looks of other on-screen characters.

Cuts from moments of bodily display to moments of action reveal the anxiety inherent to mainstream representations of masculinity, the need to displace the possibility of a homo-erotic gaze. This double bind is carried through to the male star himself who must submit his body to a process of grooming or 'beautification', subsequently becoming the object of the gaze, while at the same time resisting connotations of homosexuality or femininity.[13] This is especially true of the muscular stars of the 1980s action cinema. Stars such as Sylvester Stallone and Arnold Schwarzenegger constructed star identities around developed muscular bodies, frequently revealed in well-oiled semi-nudity. This muscularity was emphasised in the case of Schwarzenegger by his early career as a body-builder: his star image incorporated knowledge that he was a former Mr Universe. The feminine implications of this bodily presence were denied by a near hysterical heterosexual masculinity displayed in the innumerable action sequences of the films in which these stars appeared (this evidently recalls the albeit less muscular action of the three men of Nimoy's film). However, the built bodies of these stars revealed another instability in the construction of masculinity. As Richard Dyer explains, the displayed male body, exemplified by the pin-up, contains an inherent contradiction between passivity and activity. As pin-up (or object of the cinematic gaze) the male body is passive, is there to be looked at. Dyer complicates this passivity, arguing that the model 'actively' prepares him or herself to be looked at and in looking we must collaborate with this act.[14] Nevertheless, it remains the case that most mainstream displays of the male body attempt to deny suggestions of passivity, either through action (in cinematic works), or through objects which connote action and hence heterosexual masculinity such as weapons and sporting implements, or through a tightening of muscles which reveals the body's potential for action (in photographs). Moreover, the depiction of the muscular body contains a paradox in that developed muscles are both a sign of natural phallic power and hence an unproblematic patriarchal masculinity *and* evidence of the labour that has produced such a body.[15] Thus the very display of the muscular body, the excess of the built physique, reveals the performative nature of masculinity so causing the vacillation of any attempt to define a straightforward 'masculine' clearly distinguished from a posited 'feminine'. As Dyer's work demonstrates and as the films discussed in Chapters 3 and 5 reveal, masculinity, like femininity, is a multiple, shifting masquerade.

Thierry Lhermitte emerged from the *café-théâtre* of the 1970s and is essentially a comic star. As we have seen, the *café-théâtre* tended to involve comic plays that set out to mock the habits and the social mores of the French petty-bourgeoisie. The derision of social types and institutions was a key element of this type of drama. Certainly a French audience would perceive Lhermitte as part of this tradition; the very success of many of the stars of the *café-théâtre* (Coluche, Michel Blanc, Miou-Miou and Josiane Balasko for example) means that their theatrical origins have become an integral part of their star identities. This aspect of Lhermitte's persona will by reinforced by the on-screen presence of Miou-Miou and Michel Boujenah, and the involvement of script-writer Didier Kaminka, all of whom began their careers in the *café-théâtre*.

Lhermitte was specifically part of *Le Splendid*, a theatre which Pierre Merle, in his work on *café-théâtre*, describes as more '*franche-rigolade*', more comic and less political, than many of the other groups.[16] Indeed, Merle points out that although a myth of marginality grew up around the *café-théâtre* (it was often seen as a product of the events of May 1968 when in fact its roots can be traced back to turn-of-the-century cabarets and some of its leading exponents were already established by the mid-1960s), this vision was often misplaced. Indeed this may be particularly true of *Le Splendid*, many of whose participants became the *nouvelles stars* of French cinema during the 1970s, 1980s and 1990s (Lhermitte, Balasko, Blanc, Christian Clavier and Gérard Jugnot for example). Their careers flourished as they starred in *café-cinéma*, films based on the successes of the *café-théâtre*. These films were hugely popular, translating the derisive comedy of the source plays while toning down their non-conformism or political potential. They would draw upon the traditions of French popular comedy while at the same time presenting the social derision and naturalistic use of language outlined earlier in the chapter. As a result the very presence of Lhermitte in *La Totale* will suggest a comedy centred on social derision, a suggestion borne out by the film's parody of both the Secret Services and cinematic representations of the spy, and the petty-bourgeois family.

Lhermitte's physique is quite significant in terms of this trajectory. Pierre Merle claims that to have a non- or anti-heroic physique was practically a *sine qua non* of the *Splendid* (he cites Balasko as an example). However, Lhermitte was the exception to this rule (or as Merle states, the exception that *proved* this rule). Certainly Lhermitte does possess a form of matinée-idol good looks; in *La Totale* he is shown to be slim-hipped, elegantly dressed and debonair, in many ways a Bond-like figure. His handsome physique is revealed by the contrasting presence of his sidekick Albert (Eddy Mitchell) whose irregular features, overweight body and unkempt clothes serve to reinforce the charm of Lhermitte. This is also emphasised by the sequence in which Lhermitte is sent to visit a prostitute; he removes his own garments, marked as staid and unfashionable, typical of the civil servant he is pretending to be, and dons an elegant suit. He becomes an archetypal cinematic hero and completes a successful mission by planting a bug on the prostitute's television (and subsequently sleeping with her). Nevertheless, despite these markers of a conventionally attractive or heroic physique, Lhermitte's identity as a comic star, the 'handsome' member of *Le Splendid*, prevents the spectator from taking him entirely seriously. His comic trajectory reinforces the film's parodic qualities: he may be handsome but he is not a true cinematic hero.

Lhermitte's rather slight body also marks him as a non-action hero in distinct opposition to Arnold Schwarzenegger. Significantly, in *True Lies* Harry is shown to defeat the villains and rescue his family through a combination of cunning and, more important, brute strength and action. In contrast, François's victories arise almost entirely through cunning and/or chance. For example, in the first sequence to reveal François as a spy, he is chased by a group of villains. He flees into a sewer only to arrive at a sharp drop at which he hesitates. This somewhat non-heroic hesitation forms a striking contrast to Harry's unceasing pursuit of the motor-cycle riding terrorist in *True Lies,* and his immediate attempt to follow his prey on a death-defying horseback leap from one New York skyscraper to another. As François hesitates, so he turns and finds himself face to face with his pursuer. He announces his imminent death to Albert over his microphone but is saved as the villain has run out of bullets. Unlike Harry, François achieves victory through luck rather than strength or ability. He is most certainly not a conventional hero, a fact figured by Lhermitte's star persona.

We have seen that *La Totale* is essentially a domestic comedy and this is reinforced by Lhermitte's non-heroic image. This emphasis is stressed by the initial presentation of François as a family man; we see him quietly working with Albert when his wife phones to ask him at what time he will be home. At this point we have no knowledge of his true identity. Much of the film is devoted to the family narrative: François's attempts to save his marriage and rectify the behaviour of his recalcitrant son. Many scenes take place around the family meal table, revealing an archetypal bourgeois French family with mother, father, son and daughter, and mother-in-law busy in the kitchen. Moreover, a great deal of the film's comedy arises from the disparity between this narrative and the spy plot, from the incongruity of a secret agent who is entirely unaware of the events going on in his own household. This is reinforced by the deliberate cross-over between the two narratives; for example, as François enters his darkened house he shows clear anxiety, grabbing a tennis racket and entering the room slowly only to be met with a surprise birthday party. Similarly, as the family awaits his return, Julien, his son, surveys the street with a pair of binoculars in an act of looking more common to the spy genre than the domestic comedy.

This emphasis on the domestic comedy is both necessitated and extended by Lhermitte's comic star persona. *La Totale* sets out, far more vociferously than *True Lies*, to mock the family and petty-bourgeois life-styles. The film's opening scenes show François discussing his birthday with Albert; he states that he knows exactly what his wife has organised for his birthday as she has done the same thing for the past eighteen years. François's acknowledgment of the routine nature of his marriage is matched by Hélène who not only seeks excitement through her liaison with Simon (Michel Boujenah), but also tentatively suggests to her husband that he may like to give up his job in the public sector and try his chances in private enterprise. It is significant that François's assumed occupation should be as a *fonctionnaire* with *France Télécom*; as an employee of a large public company he possesses the archetypal, conventional French petty-bourgeois post. This post becomes a salesman in *True Lies*, a profession whose particular resonance in American culture is exemplified by Arthur Miller's *Death of a Salesman*. Nevertheless, the film does not seem to offer the private sector as a solution; although we are told that François's friends have achieved financial success in this domain they are also depicted as overweight and bespectacled, in sharp contrast to François's slim physique (and true identity).

François does ultimately save his family, restoring excitement into his marriage and disciplining his son. In many ways he represents a patriarchal masculinity, mobilised through both activity and paternity. However he also transgresses the codes of bourgeois family life by sleeping with a prostitute and finally mocking marriage as he and Hélène masquerade as a married couple celebrating their tenth wedding anniversary at the close of the film. This image of the conventionally married couple (both reassume the dull clothing they have discarded since Hélène has become a spy), enjoying the vicarious sexual pleasures of the *Folies Bérgères*, forms a marked contrast to the real pleasures afforded by the renewed marriage of François and Hélène. In other words, the film both derides marriage and yet at the same time underwrites it. This limited subversion is, as already stated, a common feature of many French comic films of the 1980s and 1990s. However, it is also made possible by Lhermitte's identity as both conventional romantic hero (his good looks) and potentially subversive comic.

Although both films set out to mock the monotony of suburban family life, *La Totale* is both more biting in its satire and more successful, partly due to the very bodily presence of the two male stars. Both François and Harry assume a different identity according to the particular persona they are performing at any given moment in the film. This is figured by their dress; they wear a suit at work, black overalls and masks when on a mission, and a shirt and cardigan at home with the family. However, whereas Lhermitte's physique and identity as comic star allow him to don a cardigan and become the typical suburban family man, Schwarzenegger's muscular body bulges beneath the cardigan; only too obviously he is still Schwarzenegger, the action hero, masquerading as husband and father.

This difference serves to demonstrate the fundamental distinction between Lhermitte and Schwarzenegger; the latter is a star with a well-defined persona whereas Lhermitte can perhaps be best described as an actor. In other words, despite possessing certain connotations (comedy, derision), his identity is not fixed, he is able to perform a variety of roles. The incongruity of François as either spy or dull family man ultimately depends upon Lhermitte's performance within the film rather than his wider image. Similarly Lhermitte does not carry connotations of a particular construction of masculinity. Unlike Schwarzenegger, whose identity has been defined by action films and focus on the built body, Lhermitte has played a variety of comic roles which develop no specific masculinity. This fluidity is carried through to *La Totale* where masculinity is shown to be quite multifarious; François is cinematic hero and comic star, family man and adulterer. The film seems to both offer and, through comedy and satire, question an idealised version of active masculinity *and* caring paternity. This is ultimately reconciled and reinforced as François saves his marriage through the revelation of the plurality of his identity and a display of active masculinity: despite the film's derision of the petty-bourgeois male and the action hero, it is finally a combination of the two that wins the day.

True Lies is perhaps a more interesting film in terms of its mobilisation of its male star for the simple reason that Schwarzenegger has a far more clearly defined identity than Lhermitte. Moreover, the film can be seen as an explicit attempt to renegotiate and extend this identity and the particular construction of masculinity it implies. Schwarzenegger began his career as a body-builder, subsequently performing in a series of muscular, Hollywood action films (for example *Conan the Barbarian,* John Milius, 1981, *Commando,* Mark L. Lester, 1985, and *Predator,* John McTiernan, 1987), hence his star image has been constantly defined through the body.[17] Towards the end of the 1980s, he tried to remake his image, largely through the use of humour and the revelation of a gentler side (often figured through paternity). This process can be perceived in the one-liners of his action roles, yet it became more explicit as Schwarzenegger undertook comic performances in films such as *Twins* (1988), *Kindergarten Cop* (1990) and *Junior* (1994). This transformation is played out in *True Lies*; Schwarzenegger is simultaneously action hero (and thus marks the film as part of the action/spectacle genre) and family man.

True Lies initially presents Schwarzenegger as an action hero, stressing the film's primary status as action/spectacular movie. Indeed the film opens with an extended sequence (lasting over thirteen minutes) depicting Harry's attempts to both enter, and subsequently escape from, a Swiss château inhabited by the villains. The sequence demonstrates Harry's cunning and charm (his command of various languages and his attractiveness to the opposite sex, embodied in the film's female villain, Juno Skinner, played by Tia Carrere) and his physical strength and agility (his defeat of his pursuers and eventual escape). He is marked as both tough action hero and intelligent, witty Bondesque hero.

This dual identity is continued throughout the film and is resonant of Schwarzenegger's earlier roles in films such as *Terminator,* in which displays of action were accompanied by black humour. However, there is a significant difference between the action hero depicted in *True Lies* and that revealed in Schwarzenegger's earlier 'muscular' films. Discussing the emphasis on the body in films such as *Rambo III* (Peter MacDonald, 1988), Yvonne Tasker claims that it is this emphasis that distinguishes muscular cinema from other action films.[18] In the *Conan* and *Terminator* films, Schwarzenegger's body is displayed, his muscularity affirmed. In contrast, in *True Lies* he never reveals his body, he remains dressed throughout the film. As he embraces Helen, having single-handedly defeated the terrorists and seemingly thwarted their planned nuclear attack, his biceps are revealed through a tear in his shirt. This slight revelation of his developed body recalls his identity as muscular hero, an identity which is coupled with his status as husband and family man.

Indeed the film plays constantly on Harry's identity as both action hero and family man. He is shown to have a wife and child, and part of the narrative is devoted to his efforts to save his marriage and family. His distress at his wife's apparent infidelity and his concern for his daughter are part of an attempt to humanise Schwarzenegger's star identity, to transform him from the one-dimensional muscular hero to a more complex performer. However, the film devotes less time to the family narrative than does its French source. Moreover, the performative nature of Harry's role as husband and father is stressed. As he arrives home after the opening action sequence and we learn of his identity as family man, Albert (Tom Arnold), his colleague, gives him a present for his daughter and reminds him to put on his wedding ring; in other words, he teaches him how to behave like a father and husband. Similarly, upon discovery that Dana (Harry's daughter) is stealing from her father, Albert advises Harry on how to deal with this problem. Albert is portrayed as an unsuccessful husband (his wife is having an affair and he has no children) yet even he is able to tell Harry how to be a family man. Indubitably this underlines our knowledge that Harry is not really a family man, both in narrative terms and in terms of Schwarzenegger's star persona.[19]

This knowing performativity is a constant feature of *True Lies*. Although the film explicitly sets out to extend and redefine Schwarzenegger's star identity, it makes frequent reference to his earlier image. The film contains a number of close-ups on Harry's face set in a narrow-eyed glare. This is the glare of the Terminator, of the muscular hero, and as such the audience knows it will precede or accompany a display of action on Harry's part. For example, as he chases the villain, Salim Aziz (Art Malik), each in a glass elevator, we see Aziz's point-of-view shot of this type of close-up. The scene then cuts to Aziz's look of terror: like the audience, he has realised that he is not dealing with Harry Tasker but with the Terminator. This glare is perhaps used to most effect in a domestic scene in which Helen lies to Harry about her activities in order to cover up her liaison with Simon (Bill Paxton). As she speaks the scene cuts to a close-up on Harry's face set in this familiar glare; the juxtaposition of the domestic scene and this reference to Schwarzenegger's earlier identity once again underlines the process of transformation that is at work in the film.

A similar knowingness is displayed towards the end of the sequence depicting Harry's destruction of the villain's hideout. He emerges from the battle framed by a red sky and an apocalyptic landscape highly resonant of the post-nuclear future of the *Terminator* films. Moreover, during the course of the battle, Helen, amazed by Harry's prowess, cries 'I've married Rambo.' This intertextual reference manifestly serves to underline Schwarzenegger's incorporation of his former identity in this film. Indeed, this very play upon Schwarzenegger's star persona creates a *mise en abîme* humour; the duality of Harry's narrative identity is reflected and constructed by this mobilisation of Schwarzenegger's identity as both 'new' softer hero and 'old' muscular hero. This intertextual play, absent from *La Totale* due to Lhermitte's very different persona, perhaps makes the treatment of the narrative theme of dual identities and deceit more interesting in the American production than in its French counterpart.

Schwarzenegger's star image is evidently not constructed by his cinematic performances alone. As an Austrian national and a body-builder, Schwarzenegger risked connoting suggestions of 'otherness' and fascism. As a result his identity has been built around an emphasis on his 'Americanness' (in marked contrast to the excessive 'Frenchness' of Depardieu's American persona). Magazine articles and press releases reveal that he is married to a member of the Kennedy family (and hence the American establishment), that he was appointed head of the President's Council on Fitness by George Bush in 1990, and that he appeared on stage at the Olympic Games in Atlanta. The result of these efforts is that Schwarzenegger is now widely perceived by audiences as 'American', despite his strong Austrian accent. Whereas in earlier films he would either play a foreigner or a mythical figure and his dialogue would be limited, he is now able to unproblematically represent the all-American hero. This assumed ethnicity is reinforced by *True Lies*. Although many muscular action films of the 1980s were set in non-specific locations, despite its opening sequence in a Swiss château, the narrative of *True Lies* is emphatically located within the United States. Indeed the film represents Harry's pursuit of, and ultimate triumph over, a group of terrorists intent on exploding nuclear missiles in various American cities. The terrorists are described as Arab fundamentalists engaged in jihad. Their exact nationality is not revealed (thus the film demonstrates the homogenisation of the 'other' central to attempts to reinforce the 'nation') yet it is surely crucial that they should be portrayed as Middle Eastern terrorists. By defeating these villains, Schwarzenegger defeats America's principal contemporary 'enemy' and hence underwrites his own assumed nationality. It is also significant that his initial victory takes place on the Florida Keys, whose very landscape and proximity to Cuba makes it an important symbol of invasion and liminality in the United States.[20]

The remaking of Schwarzenegger's star identity is significant in terms of representations of masculinity. Certainly it begs the question as to why there would be a need to soften his image as muscular hero at this point in his career. It is worth remarking that Schwarzenegger was not alone among the muscular heroes of the 1980s in his endeavours (consider Sylvester Stallone's spectacle-wearing and professed interest in fine art). Susan Jeffords sees this transformation of the muscular hero as the result of the particular American socio-historical conjuncture. She claims that whereas the action films of 1980s Hollywood addressed a perceived deterioration in masculine forms of power in the wake of the advances of the feminist movement, the renegotiation of these identities in the late 1980s and early 1990s demonstrated a shifting construction of masculinity which would enable men to 'discover' their 'inner selves', to become 'whole'.[21] This development of a more introspective masculinity was exemplified by the appearance of a 'men's movement' in the United States, largely instigated by the activities and texts of figures such as Robert Bly and Sam Keen, which set out to reassess traditional 'masculine' roles.[22] This renegotiation was made apparent by the displacement in Hollywood films of the muscular hero in favour of a gentler, more sensitive male. As we have seen, these nurturing qualities were frequently figured through representations of paternity (notably the 'new men' of *Three Men and a Baby*). In *Kindergarten Cop*, *Junior* and even *Terminator 2*, Schwarzenegger's identity is redefined through his relationship with a child (a relationship constructed in terms of father-hood). This process is evidently extended in *True Lies* as Harry is shown to be both a loving husband and a caring father. The action hero does not disappear (Harry does after all rescue his daughter by storming a building in a Harrier jump jet) yet he is both humanised and extended by demonstrations of affection towards his family.

This redefinition of masculinity, the displacement of the action hero in favour of the father and the husband should not necessarily be perceived as progressive in terms of mainstream gender constructions, as analysis of *Trois hommes et un couffin* and *Three Men and a Baby* revealed. In order to construct men as 'fathers', women all too often dis-appear. The masculine appropriation of typically 'feminine' activities (parenting, caring) can be considered fundamentally non-progressive, as an effacement and usurpation of women.[23] This position is interesting in terms of the representations of masculinity con-structed by *True Lies*. Harry is shown to be a parent, ultimately the more caring and effectual parent as he rescues his daughter from the terrorists. However it would be wrong to claim that 'woman' is eliminated from the film. Rather Helen is confined to a stereotypical feminine role as mother and housewife. She is shown to go out to work but significantly it is through so doing that she meets Simon and her marriage is threat-ened. Helen does eventually become Harry's accomplice, suggesting that the film creates a space for women within the 'masculine' world of action and power. However, this interpretation is problematic as Helen becomes involved entirely through Harry's agency and remains clearly marked as non-masculine as she screams hysterically, drops her gun and finally has to be rescued by her husband.

The film's rather problematic gender positions are best illustrated in the sequences depicting Helen's interrogation and her strip-tease in front of her husband. Harry and Albert hide behind a two-way mirror and question Helen as to her involvement with Simon. The sequence cuts between shots of Helen and Harry, and Harry and Albert, occasionally switching to close-ups on a featureless video image of Helen which func-tions as a lie detector. Helen is being interrogated for her attempts to penetrate the domain of the masculine, to seek action and power through her liaison with Simon. Her powerlessness is stressed as she becomes the object of this interrogation. This process is then furthered as Helen is ordered to a hotel room and forced to strip and dance 'sexy' for an invisible onlooker (her husband, although she is unaware of this fact). By per-forming this dance Helen, like Maggie and Nikita, becomes the object of the fetishised gaze and firmly gendered as feminine. This scene also perhaps seeks to displace anxi-eties about Schwarzenegger's possible identity as object of the gaze. As we have seen, the depiction of the masculine in mainstream cinema necessitates the disavowal of its status as mere object of the gaze; by fetishising Curtis, Schwarzenegger is firmly marked as powerful subject of the gaze and a non-problematic masculinity is confirmed. It is per-haps significant that although *La Totale* does depict a similar interrogation sequence, it includes neither the faceless video image nor the bedroom performance; instead Miou-Miou simply lies on the bed in a darkened room until Lhermitte enters. The film does not need to insist upon this fetishisation of the woman as it is not engaged in the same interrogation and redefinition of masculinity.

True Lies engages in both a remaking and an extension of Arnold Schwarzenegger's star identity and a concomitant renegotiation of masculinity. This locates the film within its particular context of production; the intertextuality of its representation of Schwarzenegger's image reinforces its position within the hybrid genre films outlined previously, and its construction of a new masculinity, comprising both action and affection figured through the family, situates it within other paternal/family narratives produced in Hollywood in the late 1980s and early 1990s.

Ultimately, both of these films can be seen to reveal the polysemy and the performativity of both the masculine and star identities. This is revealed by the specific mobilisations of their male stars and by the narratives themselves, which are after all centred upon a depiction of men performing dual identities. This is particularly evident in *True Lies* where the very attempts to redefine Schwarzenegger's persona display the non-immanent nature of both stardom and gender constructions. In some ways these films can then be seen to play out anxieties about the binary logic of gender, as in differing ways they depict masculinity as masquerade. However, they ultimately re-affirm traditional gender roles through the reconstruction of the nuclear family; this locus of well-defined gender roles is mocked (in *La Totale*) and threatened (in both films, albeit most seriously in *True Lies*) but it is finally saved and gender binaries are not subverted. Both Lhermitte and Schwarzenegger are defined in relation to Simon, would-be lover of Hélène/Helen. He too is engaged in performance, pretending to be a spy in order to attract women. However, unlike the films' heroes, his performance is unsuccessful and this failure, coupled with his cowardice in the face of François/Harry, serves to reinforce the masculinity of the heroes, to negate the vacillation suggested by their own performativity. This is made particularly clear in *True Lies* as Simon cowers in fright, his cringing demeanour contrasting with Harry's impressive stature. 'I'm nothing,' he cries, 'I have a small penis.' The scene cuts to a close-up on a bemused-looking Schwarzenegger; apparently he does not have the same problem. Despite the film's negotiations he remains the site of phallic authority.

Despite obvious similarities, *La Totale* and *True Lies*, through their different uses of genre, their different stars, their contrasting mobilisations of these stars, and their varying constructions of masculinity, can be seen to be entirely separate artefacts, emerging from very different cultural, economic and industrial contexts while simultaneously revealing the instability of identity central to much contemporary cinematic production. That both films are ultimately conservative perhaps says something about a tendency to reinstate the patriarch and the family in both French and American popular culture of the post-1960s, post-women's movement, 1990s. Political discourses stressing the importance of the family point to its role as a hegemonic ideological construct in contemporary American society. The crisis in legitimacy of both the traditional family (witness the decline in marriage and the birth rate in France throughout the last decade) and the French democratic model, suggest a possible need to reinvoke grand narratives and models of patriarchal stability. However, as the above analysis demonstrates, how each film arrives at this affirmation is quite different.

I will now turn to a second pair of films which extends this performance and instability of identity, *La Cage aux folles*, a Franco-Italian co-production directed by Edouard Molinaro and released in 1978, and *The Birdcage*, directed by Mike Nichols and released in 1996. Once again the material trajectories of each film do not correspond to the 'vampirisation' so often invoked to categorise the remake process. *La Cage aux folles* (a co-production and thus not a straightforwardly 'national' product) was nominated for an Academy Award and is still one of the top-grossing foreign language films in the United States. Evidently this success may appear limited when compared to the career of the domestic product, nevertheless it does suggest that this particular source text has not been, and can not be entirely assimilated by the target culture through the production of the remake. Furthermore, the film gave rise to two sequels, released in 1980 and 1985 respectively, revealing a dissemination or afterlife which extends beyond the remake and problematises the binary relationship between the two films. Moreover, the commercial career of *The Birdcage* described in Chapter 1 is particularly fascinating as it illustrates the process of exchange and interaction which typifies the remake.

Nevertheless, at first glance the two films may seem to fall easily into the original/copy binary. Their narrative structures are almost identical and they share various lines of dialogue and even a certain number of gags. Each film takes place in a drag club (the 'Birdcage' or 'Cage aux folles' of the title). Armand, the proprietor of the club (Ugo Tognazzi/Robin Williams) is preparing a surprise for his temperamental star chanteuse and life companion (Michel Serrault/Nathan Lane). The surprise is the return of Armand's son, the result of an unfortunate heterosexual encounter twenty years previously. However, the son also has a surprise and announces that he is getting married, not only to a woman but to the daughter of an arch-conservative politician (Michel Galabru/Gene Hackman). The father's initial resistance to the marriage is put aside when his party for moral order is caught up in a sex scandal. He and his wife decide to distract the media by staging a traditional white wedding. Of course they have yet to meet their prospective in-laws and the central focus of the film is the dinner party in which Armand

La Cage aux folles: Albin (Michel Serrault) disguises Charrier (Michel Galabru).

attempts to pass for straight and his partner disguises himself as the boy's mother. The film concludes with the media's discovery of the politician's presence in the apartment (situated of course above the club) and his escape through the club disguised in heavy drag. The closing sequence shows the wedding of the young couple, highly traditional but for the array of drag queens seated among the guests of the bridegroom.

As this plot summary makes clear, the film's narrative and indeed its humour, are constructed via the representation of stereotypes. Each film involves a limp-wristed and hysterical drag queen, a neo-conservative and ultimately hypocritical politician, and his supportive wife. The stereotype serves a useful narrative and comic function as it connotes certain information in an apparently straightforward manner, eschewing complexities and difference and invoking consensus, 'Stereotypes proclaim, "This is what everyone – you, me and us – thinks members of such-and-such social groups are like", as if these concepts of these social groups were spontaneously arrived at by all members of society independently and in isolation.'[24] This invocation of consensus does seem to be borne out by the mobilisation of stereotypes in this pair of films. Despite their differing temporal and spatial contexts of production, the two films employ seemingly identical stereotypes. As such they suggest that these are stereotypes which transcend national boundaries and the rigid definitions of gender and identity they construct.

At first sight these films do then appear to underwrite critique of the remake: the Franco-Italian source is reproduced in the United States, cultural specificities are ignored and a copy is produced based upon a set of consensual and normative stereotypes. However, such an account of the films is overly reductive. Without a doubt their narrative structures and comedy are based upon some rather problematic clichés yet these same clichés also enable a far more complex understanding of gender, sexuality, the family and their relations to the nation than this rather simplistic, and I think essentialist, assessment suggests.

Through its reconstruction of the stereotype of the drag queen, *The Birdcage* seems to claim that this is an identity able to transcend national boundaries. Indeed drag's ability to position itself outside rigid constructions of identity is revealed by its explicit subversion of gender. Its very excess and emphasis on performance underline the non-essential nature of gender, what Judith Butler has described as its 'performativity'. Indeed Butler invokes the cultural practices of drag as instances of the subversive power of gender parody, claiming that in imitating gender, 'drag implicitly reveals the imitative structure of gender itself – as well as its contingency.'[25] Certainly this notion of performance is at the heart of both of these films, not only through the drag acts of the club but also through Armand and Albert's attempts to 'play straight', to 'perform' a 'normal' family life. This is made particularly clear in the sequences which show the couple trying to perform what they perceive to be an unproblematic heterosexual masculinity. It is striking that in both films the model for such a notion of masculinity is John Wayne. John Wayne provides an iconic version of masculinity, a straight, white masculinity reinforced by his connotations of conservatism and a red-blooded antipathy to liberal agendas. This version of masculinity has a particular resonance in the United States where Wayne's performances in the western establish connections to a 'national' masculine embodied in the myths of the Far West and the Final Frontier. However, as a

Hollywood produced masculinity it is able to transcend national boundaries, a fact revealed by its presence in both films. Nevertheless, this version of masculinity, however far-reaching its resonance may be, is *no more* than a performance. It emerges from the cinematic, thus from performance and artifice and this is underlined in the sequences in which the characters mimic Wayne's construction of masculinity, ultimately revealing it to be no more 'natural' than their own constructions of gender.

This revelation of artifice can be seen as a key theme in each of these films and it unquestionably recalls the performative masculinities displayed in *La Totale* and *True Lies*. Moreover, just as gender is revealed to be about performance through the contrast between the characters' 'natural' gay and/or drag identities and their performed heterosexuality, so the family is here shown to be a locus of semblance and hypocrisy. In both *La Cage aux folles* and *The Birdcage* the father of the would-be bride is an important member of a party devoted to moral order and the reinstatement of 'traditional' values. The hypocrisy of this movement is soon made visible by the death of the party's leader while in bed with an under-age, black prostitute. The wedding is agreed to in an attempt to minimise the ensuing scandal and the senator's use of his daughter for his own political ends provides a striking contrast to the gay couple's selfless attempts to help their son. Both films stress the closeness and affection shared by this couple and the coldness and apparent frigidity of the straight marriage. As the dinner party ends in confusion and the revelation of each participant's true identity, so the gay home is shown to be the 'true' family as the son declares his love for his 'parents' (both of them male) and their affection is set against the continuing political posturing of the senator and his wife.

Both films seem to want to claim for themselves a liberal agenda established through their deconstruction of normative notions of gender, sexuality and family. This is particularly true of the remake which makes constant references to contemporary politics, explicitly criticising the rise in a highly reactionary conservatism in American society in the 1990s. In a notable exchange during the dinner party sequence, Senator Keeley condemns Armand as a typical European, claiming that he mistreats his 'good, old-fashioned' American wife and going on to state that all Europeans, apart from Margaret Thatcher, are involved in extra-marital affairs. This opposition between European decadence and traditional American values derides and undermines a specifically national construction of morality (the 'true' woman is constructed as a 'true' American and yet *we* know she is a man), and yet simultaneously reveals the film's 'national' construction of politics and identity. It is striking that such contemporary references are more or less absent from the Franco-Italian source. In place of the politically constructed moral code, the film suggests a bourgeois Catholic morality which is not confined to a specific national culture. Nevertheless, although these constructions and representations are not as explicitly confined to contemporary discourse as those of the remake, it would be erroneous to deny the film's evocation and interrogation of its context of production entirely. Indeed, the film's very status as a co-production and its roots, which can be seen in theatrical traditions of vaudeville and farce traceable in France and Italy, can be understood to give rise to its specific representation of gender and family.

Despite their mobilisation of seemingly identical stereotypes, it is evident that the films' construction, and more importantly mockery of notions of gender, family, morality and so on emerge from and interrogate very specific cultural and political contexts. This is particularly true of the remake. Both films do represent a drag culture which through its performativity transgresses rigid notions of gender and suggests the utopian possibility of a non-essentialist identity politics. However, somewhat paradoxically, this representation is firmly anchored in a very specific geographical and temporal space. Indeed, *The Birdcage*'s specificities are quite striking as Hollywood production usually tends to avoid such detail in its quest for global audiences. Such overt reference to contemporary American politics and society reveal the film to be a new text, something other which does not simply reproduce its French source and which also demands new forms of reception shot through with a knowledge of its particular context of production.

So once again these films can then be seen as examples of the complexity and hybridity of the remake process. Rather than merely copying a French text within Hollywood, the process has produced another text which reworks the narrative and its concerns in new ways. The films' mobilisation of stereotypes may suggest a rigidity and denial of difference in keeping with the critiques of the remake discussed in earlier chapters. However, as the preceding comments have demonstrated, both *La Cage aux folles* and *The Birdcage* can be understood as quite open texts based upon notions of alterity and performance.

Nevertheless, it would be wrong to embrace whole-heartedly the films' apparent espousal of a liberal agenda. Ultimately they do reinstate the conservative ideologies that they set out to deride. Although the films mobilise stereotypical identities in order to reveal the hypocrisy that lies at the heart of normative constructions of gender, sexuality and family, the very use of these stereotypes prevents anything more than a very limited problematisation. Stereotypes are always already defined against a norm, and as their function is to provide consensus and information which can be readily understood, so nuance and difference must be discarded. As a result the gay characters of both films remain little more than two-dimensional caricatures, constructed by and for dominant (and here read heterosexual) ideology. In a review of *The Birdcage* in the *Washington Post*, one critic remarked:

> ... the depiction of homosexual life here is romanticized: there is no sex and no AIDS, and the characters are gay in that cuddly, non-threatening, all-American way that Liberace was gay. [...] With a flash of sequins and ostrich plumes, *The Birdcage* offers an alternative definition of the nuclear unit. In shaping a homosexuality acceptable for mass consumption, though, the filmmakers have come close to turning gays into colorful cartoon creatures. That's a costly stereotype, and, ultimately, too high a price to pay for a place at the table.[26]

The films' apparent destabilising of identity is in fact confined to various forms of stereotypical excess which must of course be defined against some notion of normality. So the films' gay characters, despite their generally sympathetic roles, are unable to escape the confines of a very limited perception of what gay identity may be. The problematising of fixed identities suggested by the drag performance is curtailed by the films' narrow and negatively stereotypical representation of gay sexuality. This is problematic in the source film but is perhaps exacerbated in the remake where the very contemporary political references are matched by a vision of gay culture which ignores the present reality of gay politics and fixes its representations in a highly outmoded notion of effeminacy and hysteria.

This curtailment of the films' purportedly liberal agenda is reinforced by the ultimate reinstatement of the family as ideal social group (in line with the conclusions of *La Totale* and *True Lies*). Certainly the gay family is held up in both films as the better unit, more loving and lacking the hypocrisy of its conservative counterpart. Nevertheless, this critique of the nuclear family is confined to mockery of the politician's family and the desirability of the family unit is never called into question. This is reinforced at the end of each film as the young couple is married so reinforcing traditional moral and social values. Again, this can perhaps be seen to be most problematic in the remake. Whereas *La Cage aux folles* remains ultimately a comedy rooted in the traditions of vaudeville and farce, *The Birdcage*, through its contemporary references, sets out explicitly to critique certain ideological discourses. However by confirming the need for family and by showing the wedding, with its happy mix of Jewish and Catholic doctrine, gay and straight guests, as an idealised vision of the melting pot, the film ends by re-affirming long-standing notions of American society and national identity, the very same notions which have enabled the rise of the arch-conservatism it apparently sets out to deride.

Ultimately the films should be seen as highly ambivalent texts, each incorporating various discourses which are open to further 'translation' as they are viewed by different audiences. Indeed it is this very ambivalence which makes this particular pair of films so very interesting in terms of a discussion of the remake, and of translation and adaptation more generally. Like *La Totale* and *True Lies* the films explore constructions of identity, revealing the performative nature of gender and sexuality. In all four films this potentially progressive exploration is curtailed by conservative closure and a re-

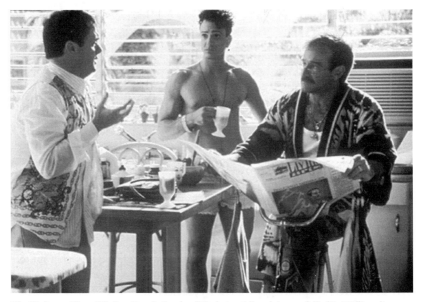

The Birdcage: Albert (Nathan Lane), Agador (Hank Azaria) and Armand (Robin Williams).

affirmation of the family unit, a curtailment which emerges from their status as mainstream, popular entertainment. Nevertheless, through the very acknowledgment of these issues the films recall their own status as remake and/or source, their own fluid identities. Indeed, as I suggested at the outset of this chapter, the films can in many ways be seen as a metaphor for the remake process. Just like the remake, the narrative concerns of each film both transcend national boundaries and fixed notions of identity while simultaneously rooting themselves within, and re-affirming, particular constructions of the nation. Just as *The Birdcage* both undermines and yet ultimately re-affirms gender and sexual stereotypes, so the remake process calls into question constructions of national cinemas, of production and reproduction, and yet finally demands the retention of both. The remake, and indeed all forms of translation, reveal the performative nature of the text, an instability which manifests itself through its very translatability. Films can be remade, texts can be translated and thus they are not fixed in immutable identities. However, through the very process of rewriting these texts are reinscribed within new contexts which assign to them new forms of identity. It is only through subsequent rewriting, or through an acknowledgment of the circles of intertextuality and hybridity which link source and target, that the non-essential nature of these identities becomes apparent once more. Which brings me back to the stereotype. In his essay 'The Other Question: The Stereotype and Colonial Discourse', Homi Bhabha argues that the racial stereotype of colonial discourse can be read as a fetish in that it serves to mask difference and affirm the wholeness of the coloniser (in other words, sameness of skin and colour) and thus offer the fantasy of a pure origin.[27] In just the same way, those discourses which maintain the binaries of original and copy, those rewritings which deny the plurality of both source and target texts, posit an unbroken, vertical trajectory of translation which re-affirms the authenticity and the uniqueness of individual works. Thus they are akin to the limited performance of gay identity and drag in the films discussed here. While their very status as remake or translation must reveal the plurality and non-essential nature of the text, their reinscription of texts within certain sets of discourse may curtail this plurality and offer the fantasy of a whole text, entire unto itself.

I would like to leave Armand, star of *The Birdcage*, to conclude this chapter. In response to his partner's anxious queries as to the authenticity of his attempts to walk like John Wayne, Armand says 'No, no, it's perfect. I just never knew that John Wayne walked like that.' Performance and reproduction make us see things in new and different ways. So let us look at the remake and its source as texts that are at once both different and the same, as texts which enable us to see that we never really knew what each one looked like anyway.

Notes

1. Yvonne Tasker, 'Dumb Movies for Dumb People: Masculinity, the Body and the Voice in Contemporary Action Cinema', in Stephen Cohan and Ina Rae Hark (eds), *Screening the Male: Exploring Masculinities in Hollywood Cinema* (London: Routledge, 1993), pp. 230–44.

2. José Arroyo, 'Cameron and the Comic', *Sight and Sound* vol. 4 no. 9, September 1994, pp. 26–8.

3. Ginette Vincendeau (ed.), *Encyclopedia of European Cinema* (London: Cassell/BFI, 1995), p. 89.

4. This also reinforces the location of *La Totale* within its particular material and industrial context as television is now central to the financing of the French film industry, both through co-productions and through the *compte de soutien.*

5. Cameron's later hit, *Titanic* (1997) continued this budget-breaking trend.

6. See Thomas Schatz, 'The New Hollywood', in Jim Collins, Ava Preacher Collins and Hilary Radner (eds), *Film Theory Goes to the Movies* (London: Routledge, 1993), pp. 8–36.

7. Yvonne Tasker, *Spectacular Bodies: Gender, Genre and the Action Cinema* (London: Routledge, 1993), p. 61.

8. Richard Dyer, *Stars* (London: BFI, 1979), p. 68.

9. Ibid., p. 72.

10. John Ellis, *Visible Fictions*, 2nd edn (London: Routledge, 1992), p. 93.

11. Ibid., pp. 58–9.

12. Steve Neale, 'Masculinity as Spectacle: Reflections on Men and Mainstream Cinema', *Screen* vol. 24 no. 6, Winter 1983, pp. 2–16.

13. Pat Kirkham and Janet Thumin (eds), *You Tarzan: Masculinity, Movies and Men* (London: Lawrence and Wishart, 1993), p. 25.

14. Richard Dyer, 'Don't Look Now: The Male Pin-up', *Screen* vol. 23 nos. 3–4, September–October 1982, pp. 61–73.

15. Ibid., p. 72.

16. Pierre Merle, *Le Café-théâtre* (Paris: Presses Universitaires de la France, 1985), p. 29.

17. Tasker, *Spectacular Bodies*, p. 82.

18. Ibid., p. 79.

19. It is surprising that the son in *La Totale* becomes a daughter in *True Lies* given the prominence of the father/daughter relationship in French cultural production described in Chapter 3. The shift may well result from the films' constructions of masculinity and Arnie's far more effective 'musculinity'. To have a recalcitrant or rebellious son would undermine his patriarchal authority. A wayward daughter simply allows him to express the caring, sharing side of his nature.

20. This representation of location is perhaps one of the key features in any definition of these films as 'national' artefacts. Just as *True Lies* is located within and around the United States, so the spatial construction of *La Totale* is built around Paris. Moreover, whereas threats to the 'nation' in *True Lies* come from outside, in *La Totale* they are both internal and external. The villains are also 'Arabs' and yet the 'Arab' country to which François and Hélène are taken turns out to be *Barbès* in the very heart of Paris. This depiction of the 'other' as at once within and without the nation (which recalls *Pépé le Moko)* articulates constructions of French identity as both coloniser and colonised, and concerns about the new plurality in French society in which the immigrant is both 'French' and 'other'.

21. Susan Jeffords, 'Can Masculinity be Terminated?', in Cohen and Hark (eds), *Screening the Male: Exploring Masculinities in Hollywood* (London: Routledge, 1993), pp. 245–62.

22. See Robert Bly, *Iron John: A Book About Men* (New York: Addison-Wesley Publishing, 1990) and Sam Keen, *Fire in the Belly: On Being a Man* (New York: Bantam,1991).

Susan Faludi's feminist perspective on masculinity published in 1999 continues these explorations.

23. See Jeffords, 'Can Masculinity be Terminated?'.

24. Richard Dyer, 'The Role of Stereotypes', in *The Matter of Images: Essays on Representations* (London: Routledge, 1993), p. 14.

25. Judith Butler, *Gender Trouble: Feminism and the Subversion of Identity* (London: Routledge, 1989), p. 137.

26. Hal Hinson, *Washington Post*, 8 March 1996.

27. Homi Bhabha, 'The Other Question: The Stereotype and Colonial Discourse', *Screen* vol. 24 no. 6, Winter 1983, pp. 18–36.

Conclusions

The attempt to draw conclusions is always a somewhat perilous enterprise. This book began by describing the reductive accounts of the remake practice of the 1980s and 1990s. It questioned the straightforward linear trajectories established by this critique, going on to posit in their place a genealogical approach which would replace the vertical routes which lead from authentic 'original' to debased 'copy' with the circles and bifurcations of intertextuality and hybridity. To end such an approach with an affirmation of conclusions may seem to negate its very identity, closing the circles and streamlining the broken pathways. Nevertheless, while eschewing attempts at completion or closure, it is possible to suggest plural conclusions which are themselves bound up with the notions of contingency, polysemy and difference so intrinsic to this work.

It is clear that the remake is not a recent phenomenon. Indeed, it has played an important role in cinematic production since the early days of film. Despite this endurance, contemporary accounts of the numerous remakes of recent years have tended to condemn the practice and to deny its own history in order to lend it increased significance as a very *real* and very *current* manifestation of American cultural imperialism. Such negativity does sometimes seem somewhat excessive. Remakes are not always particularly enjoyable, nor do they necessarily achieve great profit at the box-office, yet although they share these attributes with many other cultural artefacts, they are subjected to a uniform hostility rarely levelled at the latter.

By locating such critique within a specific socio-historical conjuncture, it becomes apparent that it is perhaps not really about *the films* at all. Indeed, as the various remarks cited in the preceding chapters demonstrate, the majority of these negative accounts tell us very little about the filmic texts, revealing instead a great deal about reactions to the changes in French society experienced throughout the 1980s. The dissemination of a discrete French identity via post-colonialism, decentralisation and shifts from citizenship to the tropes of consumerism, enabled a plurality and acknowledgment of difference previously absent from the Jacobin tradition of the French State. This in turn provoked an anxiety which led to a shoring up of a uniquely 'French' identity, principally through the discourses and products of culture. Central to these changes, and the attendant anxiety, was the apparently unstoppable spread of a globalised economy and the marginalisation of France it seemed to threaten. As a dominant player in this 'new world order', the United States epitomised this threat and the fears it caused, hence the reinvocation of the anti-American discourses so prominent in the Cold War period. By condemning the remake as *vampirisation*, the draining of the life-blood of French culture by powerful Hollywood producers, French commentators underlined their fear at

France's precarious position in the global economy. Both the condemnation of the remake and French reactions to the GATT can be seen as manifestations of these particular concerns; as they defend the French audiovisual product against American competition, so they defend long-standing constructions of the nation and of cultural identity, destabilised by the political and economic changes of recent years.

Just as the remake can be located within an enduring history of similar transposition, so these anxieties should be perceived as a contemporary articulation of persistent French antagonism towards the United States, rooted in the incommensurability of the two countries' democratic traditions. They emerge from the specific contemporary conjuncture and from a macro context of similar fears and similar defence. Moreover, the mobilisation of the audiovisual industry as a site of potential threat and a means of bolstering up the 'nation', should not be abstracted from its particular past. As the reception of the Blum–Byrnes agreements in France shows only too clearly, audiovisual production has long been seen as an exceptionally powerful tool in the construction of a 'national' identity (or indeed a 'transnational' identity, as European audiovisual policy demonstrates). However, as Hollywood became established as the dominant cinematic producer, so the audiovisual industry also became a site for struggle *against* an American imposed hegemony (and subsequently, a globalised non-differentiation), and *for* the maintenance of individual cinemas and identities.

This mobilisation of the audiovisual demonstrates the location of this dialectic within wider discourses about cultural reproduction and the effects of mass culture. The United States' *cultural* (as opposed to political or economic) threat to France went hand in hand with the emergence of the culture industries and their perceived attack upon 'authentic' artistic creation. Hollywood menaced French cultural identity not merely through its economic might but because it epitomised the mass production which was anathema to the defenders of a French tradition of 'great' art. The result of this has been an enduring attempt to differentiate French cultural identity via the tropes of 'high' culture and authenticity, and an ensuing denial of the mass/popular production so central to the French cinema industry. Condemnation of the remake emerges from, and reinforces, these critical discourses, establishing as it does a distinct opposition between the authentic French 'original' and the 'debased' American 'copy'.

The endurance of these Manichean discourses belies their problematic nature. As the preceding chapters have demonstrated, any attempt to define a cinematic work as uniquely French or American, as a product of 'high' or 'popular' culture, must always acknowledge the mutability of such definitions. These identities are constructed (and disseminated) by the film's contexts of production and reception. Whether or not a film is perceived as 'French', or as part of 'high' culture, will depend on where and when it is produced and where and when it is consumed. As films shift across space and time so they become something other, their identities can never be fixed. This is perhaps one of the great paradoxes of the binary oppositions constructed around the remake. This very process of spatial and temporal transformation reveals the polysemy and instability of the filmic text (its plural identities and potential meanings) and yet it is appropriated by the French critical establishment and inscribed within a linear trajectory of immanence and fixity.

Ultimately, the sterility of these accounts of the remake is revealed by the very identity of the practice as a form of *cinematic* production. The repetition and reproduction which transpire as a film is remade in Hollywood, and which provoke such outrage among so many French critics, are an intrinsic part of the cinematic text and the cinematic apparatus. This is particularly true of contemporary production. The bricolage and intertextuality of postmodernism have become a built-in feature of numerous cultural artefacts, as manifested by their knowing references to previous texts, both cinematic and other. This process is extended by the synergy of Hollywood production, the deliberate marketing of individual films across a wide range of products which necessitates open-ended, plural texts able to generate a variety of images. This plurality in production is matched by a similar diffusion in terms of consumption. Any attempt to describe the act of cinema viewing as a unified, unbroken process was always already extremely problematic. Spectatorship could never be defined as a single gesture as it altered according to the moment and space of consumption, and the age, gender, race, sexuality and class of the individual viewer. Nevertheless, the notion of an audience 'community' was enabled by the location of cinematic spectatorship within a movie theatre; the collective nature of this viewing process was called upon to support descriptions of an undifferentiated 'mass' or 'national' audience. However, even this tenuous attempt at establishing a totalised concept of spectatorship must surely be discarded as the movie theatre gives way to the fragmentation of videocassettes, satellite and digital television, and the internet.

However, this identity, constructed through repetition and fragmentation, is not confined to contemporary cinematic production alone. The filmic text, and the industry from which it emerges, has always been inextricably bound up with these very terms. The centrality of fragmentation is evidenced by the filming process itself, as scenes are shot in a non-linear fashion and edited together to form an 'entire' artefact at a later date. The distribution and exhibition of films are also based upon repetition and reproduction as films are made to be copied, to be viewed and reviewed across space and time. Indeed, the notion of seeking difference through the 'same' is a key concept in this description of cinematic practices. The establishment of genre conventions in 1930s Hollywood underlines the early mobilisation of this search for novelty through repetition as well-defined generic traits were constantly re-articulated via differing narratives, stars and *mise en scène*. The numerous action films of 1980s Hollywood, and the various negotiations of paternity in France and the United States, reveal that this is an enduring feature of cinema. It should also be stressed that this is not true of Hollywood production alone. The generic conventions of French cinema, and its repeated re-articulation of similar themes, demonstrate the centrality of this search for difference through the same in non-Hollywood production. Furthermore, the very attempt to define a 'national' cinema via the tropes of 'high culture' and 'Frenchness' can be seen as part of this same process as a distinct identity is only enabled through relationship to Hollywood cinema. In other words, a film is defined as 'French' because it is *not* an American production, as a 'high' cultural artefact because it is *not* identical to the 'mass' production of Hollywood. Distinction is enabled by forming a space within the dominant production context; French cinema and Hollywood cinema are both different *and* the same.

To posit the inherent repetition and intertextuality of cinematic production ultimately reveals the sterility of condemnation of the remake practice. How can it be possible to criticise the remake as non-original, as a copy, when all films can in some way be seen as copies? Moreover, why condemn the remake, which may well be consumed as an 'original' film, and accept other productions which set out to underline their relationships to other texts and elicit thoroughly intertextual readings? The remake is one aspect of a much wider process of cinematic reproduction and to condemn it is, in many ways, to condemn cinema itself. Indeed, the very term 'remake' is perhaps redundant. If all films can be seen as diffuse, hybrid, signifying systems then surely all films can be seen as 'remakes', or as equally 'original'. Moreover, to describe a film as a remake is to establish a binary relationship between a French film and a subsequent American production. However, as films become increasingly intertextual and production increasingly globalised, such pairings appear highly problematic, leading us to wonder if the 'true' remake of *Le Salaire de la peur* is indeed *The Sorcerer* or *Speed* (Jan De Bont, 1994)? Is the 'true' adaptation of Jane Austen's *Emma* the film of the same title or the 1995 production *Clueless* (Amy Heckerling)? Why should *The Assassin* be perceived as a more serious 'threat' to the identity of *Nikita* than Luc Besson's later film, *Léon* or any other action thriller?

Rather than express outrage at this particular form of cinematic production, let us then see the remake as an addition, an extension of an always already plural and openended signifying system. The remake both creates material profit for the French cinematic industry (through the sale of rights) and establishes the afterlife of the French text through its rewriting in another context. Indubitably this is part of a cinematic industry in which the production of Hollywood plays a dominant role and so the negative implications of the process should not be ignored. The remake is symptomatic of a cinematic culture in which the international distribution and exhibition of non-Hollywood products is extremely limited. As such it can be seen as a 'fluent' rewriting which effaces the presence of other cinemas and other cultures. Yet it must be stressed that this is only one aspect of a highly complex process of adaptation, dissemination and extension. The remake creates new texts which are at once the same and other. In so doing it establishes new audiences both for the remake itself and for the source film. Finally it is a process which reveals much about the particular contexts of production and reception of individual films and about the nature of 'cinema' itself. As I hope this book has demonstrated, an analysis of all forms of adaptation in terms of their relations to specific socio-historical conjunctures, and the ways in which they quote, incorporate, and yet differ from other texts, can tell us much about cross-cultural transposition and transformation and the various circumstances from which these texts emerge. Rather than ask which is the 'better' text, the source film or the remake, let us examine the ways in which these films construct and articulate their shared identities and their difference. Let us see them as both separate artefacts and as the hybrid exemplars of an endlessly repeating, and endlessly repeatable, signifying system.

List of Remakes, 1930–99

The Road to Glory (1936, Howard Hawks, 20th Century-Fox).
Les Croix de bois (1931, Raymond Bernard, Pathé-Natan).

One Rainy Afternoon (1936, Rowland V. Lee, Pickford-Lasky/United Artists).
Monsieur Sans-Gêne (1935, Karl Anton, Amora Films).

The Woman I Love (1937, Anatole Litvak, RKO).
L'Équipage (1935, Anatole Litvak, Pathé-Natan).

The Soldier and the Lady (1937, George Nicholls, RKO).
Michel Strogoff (1935, Richard Eichberg, Ermolieff).

Algiers (1938, John Cromwell, United Artists/Walter Wanger).
Pépé le Moko (1937, Julien Duvivier, Paris Film Productions).

Port of Seven Seas (1938, James Whale, MGM).
Marius, Fanny, César (1931–6, Alexander Korda, Marc Allégret, Marcel Pagnol, Auteurs
    Associés/Paramount).

Prisons Without Bars (1938, Brian Desmond Hurst, Columbia/London Film Productions).
Prisons sans barreaux (1936, Arnold Pressburger, Cipra).

The Lady in Question (1940, Charles Vidor, Columbia).
Gribouille (1939, Marc Allégret, Lauer et Compagnie).

Lucky Partners (1940, Lewis Milestone, RKO).
Bonne Chance (1935, Sacha Guitry, Distributeurs français).

Forty Little Mothers (1940, Busby Berkely, MGM).
Le Mioche (1936, Léonide Moguy, Gray Film).

I Was an Adventuress (1940, Gregory Ratoff, 20th Century-Fox).
J'étais une aventurière (1938, Raymond Bernard, Ciné Alliance).

Lydia (1941, Julien Duvivier, Korda/London Film Productions).
Un Carnet de bal (1937, Julien Duvivier, Productions Sigma/Lévy/Strauss).

Scarlet Street (1945, Fritz Lang, Universal/Diana Productions).
La Chienne (1931, Jean Renoir, Braunberger–Richebé).

The Postman Always Rings Twice (1946, Tay Garnett, Loews/MGM).
Le Dernier Tournant (1939, Pierre Chenal, Lux).

Heartbeat (1946, Sam Wood, RKO).
Battement de coeur (1940, Henri Decoin, Ciné Alliance).

Lured (1947, Douglas Sirk, United Artists/Oakmount).
Pièges (1939, Robert Siodmak, Speva Films).

The Long Night (1947, Anatole Litvak, RKO).
Le Jour se lève (1939, Marcel Carné, Sigma).

Casbah (1948, John Berry, Universal).
Pépé le Moko (1937, Julien Duvivier, Paris Film Productions).

The Man on the Eiffel Tower (1949, Burgess Meredith, A&T Films/Gray Films, USA/France).
La Tête d'un homme (1932, Julien Duvivier, Les Films Marcel Vandal and Charles Delac).

The Thirteenth Letter (1951, Otto Preminger, 20th Century-Fox).
Le Corbeau (1943, Henri-Georges Clouzot, Atelier français/Continental Films).

The Blue Veil (1951, Curtis Bernhardt, Wald-Krasna/RKO).
Le Voile bleu (1942, Jean Stelli, Compagnie Générale Cinématographie).

Taxi (1953, Gregory Ratoff, 20th Century-Fox).
Sans Laisser d'Adresse (1951, Jean-Paul Le Chanois, Films Raoul Ploquin).

Human Desire (1954, Fritz Lang, Columbia).
La Bête humaine (1938, Jean Renoir, R&R Hakim/Paris Film).

Fanny (1960, Joshua Logan, Mansfield Productions).
Marius, Fanny, César (1931–6, Korda, Allégret, Pagnol, Auteurs Associés/Paramount).

Paris When it Sizzles (1964, Richard Quine, Paramount).
La Fête à Henriette (1952, Julien Duvivier, Régina/Filmsonor).

The Sorcerer (*Wages of Fear*) (1977, William Friedkin, Universal/Film Properties International).
Le Salaire de la peur (1953, Henri-Georges Clouzot, CICC/Véra Films/Filmsonor/Fonorama, France/Italy).

Willie and Phil (1980, Paul Mazursky and Tony Ray, 20th Century-Fox).
Jules et Jim (1962, François Truffaut, Films du Carrosse/SEDIF).

Buddy Buddy (1981, Billy Wilder, MGM).
L'Emmerdeur (1973, Edouard Molinaro, Films Ariane/Mondex/OPIC, France/Italy).

The Postman Always Rings Twice (1981, Bob Rafelson, Lorimar Productions/Northstar).
Le Dernier Tournant (1939, Pierre Chenal, Lux).

The Toy (1982, Richard Donner, Rastar Productions/Columbia).
Le Jouet (1976, Francis Veber, Renn Productions/Fideline/EFVE).

Breathless (1983, Jim McBride, Breathless Associates/Greenberg Brothers).
A bout de souffle (1960, Jean-Luc Godard, Georges de Beauregard/Société nouvelle de
    cinéma).

The Man who Loved Women (1983, Blake Edwards, Columbia/Delphi/Edwards).
L'Homme qui aimait les femmes (1977, François Truffaut, Films du Carrosse/AA).

The Woman in Red (1984, Gene Wilder, Orion).
Un Éléphant ça trompe énormément (1976, Yves Robert, Gaumont/Guéville).

Blame it on Rio (1983, Stanley Donen, Sherwood Productions).
Un Moment d'égarement (1977, Claude Berri, Gala/Renn Productions).

The Man with One Red Shoe (1985, Stan Dragoti, Victor Drai Productions).
Le Grand Blond avec une chaussure noire (1972, Yves Robert,
    Gaumont/Guéville/Madeleine).

Down and Out in Beverly Hills (1986, Paul Mazursky, Touchstone/Silver Screen II).
Boudu sauvé des eaux (1932, Jean Renoir, Films Michel Simon).

Happy New Year (1987, John G. Avildsen, Columbia/Weintraub/Delphi IV).
La Bonne Année (1973, Claude Lelouch, Films 13/Rizzoli, France/Italy).

And God Created Women (1987, Roger Vadim, Vestran Pictures/Crow).
Et Dieu créa la femme (1956, Roger Vadim, Iéna/UCIL/Corinor).

Three Men and a Baby (1987, Leonard Nimoy, Touchstone/Silver Screen III).
Trois Hommes et un couffin (1985, Coline Serreau, Flach Film/Soprofilms/TFI Films).

Cousins (1989, Joel Schumacher, Paramount).
Cousin, Cousine (1975, Jean-Charles Tacchella, Pomereau/Gaumont).

Three Fugitives (1989, Francis Veber, Touchstone/Warner Bros./Silver Screen IV).
Les Fugitifs (1986, Francis Veber, Fideline/EFVE/Orly/DD Films).

Men Don't Leave (1990, Paul Brickman, Warner Bros.).
La Vie continue (1981, Moshe Mizrahi, Cinéproduction).

Quick Change (1990, Bill Murray and Howard Franklin, Devoted Productions/Warner Bros.).
Hold-up (1985, Alexandre Arcady, Cerito/Ariane/Cinévideo, France/Canada).

Paradise (1991, Mary Agnes Donoghue, Touchstone/Buena Vista/Interscope/Lepetit).
Le Grand Chemin (1987, Jean-Loup Hubert, Flach Film/Séléna/TF1).

Oscar (1991, John Landis, Touchstone/Silver Screen IV/Ponti Vecchio/Landis Belzberg).
Oscar (1967, Edouard Molinaro, Gaumont).

Pure Luck (1991, Nadia Tass, Silver Lion Films/Sean Daniel Company).
La Chèvre (1981, Francis Veber, Gaumont/Fideline/Conacine).

Sommersby (1993, Jon Amiel, Regency Enterprises/Alcor Films/Le Studio Canal Plus).
Le Retour de Martin Guerre (1982, Daniel Vigne, Société française de cinéma/FR3).

The Assassin (*Point of No Return*) (1993, John Badham, Warner Bros.).
Nikita (1990, Luc Besson, Gaumont/Cecchi Gori/Tiger, France/Italy).

Intersection (1994, Mark Rydell, Paramount).
Les Choses de la vie (1969, Claude Sautet, Fida Cinematografica, France/Italy).

My Father the Hero (1994, Steve Miner, Touchstone/Film par film/Cité Films).
Mon Père ce héros (1991, Gérard Lauzier, Film par film/Orly/TF1).

True Lies (1994, James Cameron, Lightstorm Entertainment).
La Totale (1991, Claude Zidi, Films 7/Film par film/MDG Productions/TF1).

Mixed Nuts (1994, Nora Ephron, TriStar).
Le Père Noël est une ordure (1982, Jean-Marie Poiré, Trinacra Films).

Nine Months (1995, Chris Columbus, 20th Century-Fox/1492 Productions).
Neuf Mois (1994, Patrick Braoudé, AFCI Productions/France 2 Cinéma/UGC Images).

The Birdcage (1996, Mike Nichols, United Artists).
La Cage aux folles (1978, Edouard Molinaro, United Artists/PAA/Da Ma, France/Italy).

Diabolique (1996, Jeremiah Chechik, Morgan Creek Productions/James G.
Robinson/Marvin Worth Productions/ABC Productions).
Les Diaboliques (1954, Henri-Georges Clouzot, Filmsonor).

The Associate (1996, Donald Petrie, Buena Vista/Hollywood Pictures/Interscope
Communications/Polygram Filmed Entertainment).
L'Associé (1979, René Gainville, France 3/Magyar/Maran).

The Mirror Has Two Faces (1996, Barbra Streisand, TriStar Pictures Inc./Barwood Films).
Le Miroir a deux faces (1959, André Cayette, Franco-London Films/CEI-Incom/Paris Union
Films/SNEG).

Jungle 2 Jungle (1997, J. Pasquin, Disney/TF1).
Un Indien dans la ville (1994, Hervé Palud, ICE Films/TF1).

Fathers' Day (1997, Ivan Reitman, Northern Lights/Silver Pictures/Warner Bros.).
Les Compères (1983, Francis Veber, DD Productions/EFVE/Fideline Films).

Return to Paradise (1998, Joseph Ruben, Tetragram/Polygram Filmed Entertainment).
Force Majeure (1989, Pierre Jolivet, CAPAC/Fildebroc).

Bibliography

Anderson, Benedict, *Imagined Communities: Reflections on the Origin and Spread of Nationalism* (London: Verso, 1991); 2nd edn.

Ang, Ien, *Living Room Wars: Rethinking Media Audiences for a Postmodern World* (London: Routledge, 1996).

Babington, Bruce and Peter William Evans, *Affairs to Remember: The Hollywood Comedy of the Sexes* (Manchester: Manchester University Press, 1989).

Bach, Stephen, *Final Cut: Dreams and Disaster in the Making of* Heaven's Gate (London: Faber and Faber, 1986). '

Balio, Tino, *The American Film Industry* (Wisconsin: University of Wisconsin Press, 1976).

Barthes, Roland, *Chambre claire: note sur la photographie* (Paris: Gallimard, 1980).

Baudrillard, Jean, *Simulacres et Simulation* (Paris: Galilée, 1981).

Benjamin, Walter, 'The Work of Art in the Age of Mechanical Reproduction', in Hannah Arendt (ed.), *Illuminations* (London: Harcourt Brace, 1968), pp. 219–53; trans. by H. Zohn.

Benson, Edward, 'Martin Guerre, the Historian and the Filmmakers: An Interview with Natalie Zemon Davis', *Film and History* vol. 13 no. 3, September 1983, pp. 49–65.

Benson, Edward, 'Decor and Decorum. From *La Chienne* to *Scarlet Street*: Franco–US Trade in Film During the Thirties', *Film and History* vol. 12 no. 3, September 1982, pp. 57–65.

Bergala, Alain (ed.), *Jean-Luc Godard par Jean-Luc Godard* (Paris: Cahiers du cinéma-Éditions de l'étoile, 1985).

Besson, Luc, *L'Histoire de Nikita* (Paris: Éditions Bordas, 1992).

Bertrand, C. J. and F. Bordat (eds), *Les Médias américains en France, influence et pénétration* (Paris: Belin, 1989).

Bhabha, Homi, 'The Other Question: The Stereotype and Colonial Discourse', *Screen* vol. 24 no. 6, Winter 1983, pp. 18–36.

Bloom, Harold, *The Anxiety of Influence* (Oxford: Oxford University Press, 1973).

Bourdieu, Pierre, *La Distinction: critique sociale du jugement* (Paris: Les Éditions de Minuit, 1979).

Boujut, Michel and Jules Chancel (eds), 'Europe–Hollywood et retour', *Autrement* no. 79, April 1989.

Brown, Gene and Harry M. Geduld, *The New York Times Encyclopedia of Film 1941–46* (New York: Times Books, 1984).

Bruzzi, Stella, *Undressing Cinema: Clothing and Identity in the Movies* (London: Routledge, 1997).

Butler, Judith, *Gender Trouble: Feminism and the Subversion of Identity* (London: Routledge, 1989).

Carroll, Raymonde, *Cultural Misunderstanding: The French–American Experience* (Chicago: Chicago University Press, 1990).

Carroll, Raymonde, 'Film et analyse culturelle: le remake', *Contemporary French Civilisation* vol. 13 no. 2, Summer/Fall 1989, pp. 346–59.

Clarens, C., 'Ten Great Originals', *American Film* vol. 9 no. 3, December 1983, pp. 82–6.

Cohan, Steve and Ina Rae Hark (eds), *Screening the Male: Exploring Masculinities in Hollywood Cinema* (London: Routledge, 1993).

Collins, Jim, Hilary Radner and Ava Preacher-Collins (eds), *Film Theory Goes to the Movies* (London: Routledge, 1993).

Costigliola, Frank, *France and the United States: The Cold Alliance Since World War Two* (New York: Twayne, 1992).

De Grazia, Victoria, 'Mass Culture and Sovereignty: The American Challenge to European Cinemas, 1920–1960', *Journal of Modern History* vol. 61 no. 1, March 1989, pp. 53–87.

Derrida, Jacques, 'Living On: Border Lines', in Peggy Kamuf (ed.), *A Derrida Reader: Between the Blinds* (Hemel Hempstead: Harvester Wheatsheaf, 1991), pp. 256–68.

Doane, Mary Ann, 'Film and the Masquerade', *Screen* vol. 23 nos. 3–4, September–October 1982, pp. 74–87.

Durham, Carolyn A., 'Taking the Baby Out of the Basket and/or Robbing the Cradle: "Remaking Gender and Culture in Franco–American Film"', *The French Review* vol. 65 no. 5, April 1992, pp. 774–84.

Durham, Carolyn A., *Double Takes: Culture and Gender in French Films and Their American Remakes* (Hanover: University of New England Press, 1998).

Dyer, Richard, *Stars* (London: BFI, 1979).

Dyer, Richard, 'Don't Look Now: The Male Pin-up', *Screen* vol. 23 nos. 3–4, September–October 1982, pp. 61–73.

Dyer, Richard, *The Matter of Images: Essays on Representations* (London: Routledge, 1993).

Dyer, Richard and Ginette Vincendeau (eds), *Popular European Cinema* (London: Routledge, 1992).

Ellis, John, *Visible Fictions: Cinema, Television, Video* (London: Routledge, 1992); 2nd edn.

Falkenberg, Pamela, 'Hollywood and the Art Cinema as a Bipolar Modeling System: *A bout de souffle* and *Breathless*', *Wide Angle* vol. 7 no. 3, 1985, pp. 44–53.

Ferro, Marc, *Cinéma et histoire* (Paris: Gallimard, 1993); 2nd edn.

Fischer, Lucy, 'Sometimes I Feel Like a Motherless Child: Comedy and Matricide', in Andrew S. Horton (ed.), *Comedy/Cinema/Theory* (Berkeley: University of California Press, 1991), pp. 60–78.

Friedberg, Anne, *Window Shopping: Cinema and the Postmodern* (Berkeley: University of California Press, 1993).

Gauteur, Claude and Ginette Vincendeau, *Anatomie d'un mythe: Jean Gabin* (Paris: Éditions Nathan Université, 1993).

Genette, Gérard, *Palimpsestes: la littérature au second degré* (Paris: Seuil, 1982).

Gevinson, Alan and Patricia King Hanson, *American Film Institute Catalog: Feature Films 1931–1940* (Berkeley: University of California Press, 1993).

Gripsrud, Jostein, 'French–American Connection: *A bout de souffle*, *Breathless* and the Melancholy Macho', in Kim Christian Schroder and Michael Skovmand (eds), *Media Cultures: Reappraising Transnational Media* (London: Routledge, 1992), pp. 104–23.

Harlé, P. A., 'Attention aux remakes', *La Cinématographie française* no. 1038, 23 September 1938, p.11.

Hayward, Susan, *French National Cinema* (London: Routledge, 1993).

Hayward, Susan, *Luc Besson* (Manchester: Manchester University Press, 1998).

Hayward, Susan, 'Besson's "Mission Elastoplast": *Le Cinquième Élément*', in Phil Powrie (ed.), *French Cinema of the 1990s: Continuity and Difference* (Oxford: Oxford University Press, 1999).

Higson, Andrew, 'The Concept of National Cinema', *Screen* vol. 30 no. 4, Autumn 1989, pp. 36–47.

Higson, Andrew, 'Representing the National Past: Nostalgia and Pastiche in the Heritage Film', in Lester Friedman (ed.), *British Cinema and Thatcherism* (London: UCL Press, 1993), pp. 109–29.

Horton, Andrew and Stuart McDougal (eds), *Play it Again Sam: Retakes on Remakes* (California: University of California Press, 1998).

Hubert-Lacombe, Patricia, 'L'Accueil des films américains en France pendant la guerre froide, 1946–1953', *Revue d'histoire moderne et contemporaine* vol. 33, April–June 1986, pp. 301–13.

Jameson, Fredric, *Signatures of the Visible* (London: Routledge, 1992).

Jeffords, Susan, *The Remasculinization of America: Gender and the Vietnam War* (Bloomington and Indianapolis: Indiana University Press, 1989).

Kaplan, E. Ann, 'Ideology and Cinematic Practice in Lang's *Scarlet Street* and Renoir's *La Chienne*', *Wide Angle* vol. 5 no. 3, 1982, pp. 32–43.

Kirkham, Pat and Janet Thumin (eds), *You Tarzan: Masculinity, Movies and Men* (London: Lawrence and Wishart, 1993).

Krutnik, Frank and Steve Neale, *Popular Film and Television Comedy* (London: Routledge, 1990).

Kuisel, Richard, *Seducing the French: The Dilemma of Americanization* (Berkeley: University of California Press, 1993).

Lacorne, Denis, Jacques Rupnik and Marie-France Toinet (eds), *The Rise and Fall of Anti-Americanism: A Century of French Perception* (London: Macmillan, 1990); trans. by Gerald Turner.

Lefebure du Bus, O, 'Les remakes américains de films français', *Séquences* no. 170, March 1994, pp. 52–3.

Leitch, Thomas, 'Twice-told Tales: The Rhetoric of the Remake', *Literature and Film Quarterly* vol. 18 no. 3, (1990), pp. 138–49.

Limbacher, James L. (ed.), *Haven't I Seen You Somewhere Before? Remakes, Sequels and Series in Motion Pictures, Video and Television, 1896–1990* (New York: Pierian Press, 1991).

Loosely, David, *The Politics of Fun: Cultural Policy and Debate in Contemporary France* (Oxford: Berg, 1995).

Mancini, Marc, 'French Film Remakes', *Contemporary French Civilisation* vol. 13 no. 1, Spring 1989, pp. 32–46.

Mathy, Jean-Philippe, *Extrême–Occident: French Intellectuals and America* (Chicago: University of Chicago Press, 1993).

Mazdon, Lucy, 'Rewriting and Remakes: Questions of Originality and Authenticity', in G. T. Harris (ed.), *On Translating French Literature and Film* (Amsterdam: Rodopi, 1996), pp. 47–63.

Mazdon, Lucy, 'Remaking Paternity: *Mon Père ce héros* and *My Father the Hero*', in Phil Powrie (ed.), *French Cinema of the 1990s* (Oxford: Oxford University Press, 1999).

Merle, Pierre, *Le Café-théâtre* (Paris: Presses Universitaires de France, 1985).

Milberg, Doris, *Repeat Performances: A Guide to Hollywood Movie Remakes* (New York: Broadway Press, 1990).

Modeleski, Tania, 'Three Men and Baby M', *Camera Obscura* no. 17, May 1988, pp. 69–81.

Morgan, Janice, 'In the Labyrinth: Masculine Subjectivity, Expatriation and Colonialism in *Pépé le Moko*', in Matthew Bernstein and Gaylyn Studlar (eds), *Vision of the East, Orientalism in Film* (London: I. B. Tauris Publishers, 1997), pp. 253–68.

Mulvey, Laura, 'Visual Pleasure and Narrative Cinema', *Screen* vol. 16 no. 3, Autumn 1975, pp. 6–18.

Neale, Stephen, *Genre* (London: BFI, 1980).

Neale, Stephen, 'Art Cinema as Institution', *Screen* vol. 22 no. 1, 1981, pp. 11–39.

Neale, Steve, 'Masculinity as Spectacle: Reflections on Men and Mainstream Cinema', *Screen* vol. 24 no. 6, Winter 1983, pp. 2–16.

Nowlan, Robert A. and Gwendolyn Wright Nowlan, *Cinema Sequels and Remakes, 1903–1987* (Jefferson, NC: McFarland and Company Inc., 1989).

Ory, Pascal, *L'Aventure culturelle française* (Paris: Flammarion, 1989).

Picard, Anne-Marie, 'Travestissement et paternité: la masculinité remade in the USA', *Cinémas* nos. 1–2, Autumn 1990, pp. 114–31.

Portes, Jacques, 'Les Origines de la légende noire des accords Blum–Byrnes sur le cinéma', *Revue d'histoire moderne et contemporaine* vol. 33, April-June 1986, pp. 314–29.

Powrie, Phil, *French Cinema in the 1980s: Nostalgia and the Crisis of Masculinity* (Oxford: Oxford University Press, 1997).

Powrie, Phil, *French Cinema in the 1990s: Continuity and Difference* (Oxford: Oxford University Press, 1999).

Protopopoff, Daniel and Michel Serceau (eds), 'Le Remake et l'adaptation', *Cinémaction* no. 53, October 1989.

Reid, John H., *A Feast of Films* (Sydney: Rastar Press, 1990).

Saada, Nicholas, 'Psycho 1998 de Gus Van Sant: L'originale copie', *Synopsis* no. 2, Spring 1999, pp. 74–5.

Sorlin, Pierre, *The Film in History: Restaging the Past* (Oxford: Blackwell, 1980).

Sorlin, Pierre, 'War and Cinema: Interpreting the Relationship', *Historical Journal of Film, Radio and Television* vol. 14 no. 4, 1994, pp. 357–66.

Smith, Steve, 'Godard and Film Noir: A Reading of *A bout de souffle*', *Nottingham French Studies* vol. 32 no. 1, Spring 1993, pp. 65–74.

Tasker, Yvonne, *Spectacular Bodies: Gender, Genre and the Action Cinema* (London: Routledge, 1993).

Venuti, Lawrence, *The Translator's Invisibility* (London: Routledge, 1995).

Vincendeau, Ginette, 'France, 1945–65 and Hollywood: The Policier as International Text', *Screen* vol. 33 no. 1, Spring 1992, pp. 50–80.

Vincendeau, Ginette, 'Family Plots: The Fathers and Daughters of French Cinema', *Sight and Sound* vol. 1 no. 11, March 1992, pp.14–17.

Vincendeau, Ginette, 'Hijacked', *Sight and Sound* vol. 3 no. 7, July 1993, pp. 22–5.

Vincendeau, Ginette (ed.), *Encyclopedia of European Cinema* (London: Cassell /BFI, 1995).

Vincendeau, Ginette, *Pépé le Moko* (London: BFI, 1998).

Zemon Davis, Natalie, ' "Any Resemblance to Persons Living or Dead": Film and the Challenge of Authenticity', *Historical Journal of Film, Radio and Television* vol. 8 no. 3, 1988, pp. 269–83.

Index

Page references in **bold** type refer to detailed analyses of the film in question; those in *italics* refer to illustrations. References to footnotes (given only where these contain separate information of interest, not to simple citations) are indicated by 'n.' following the page number.